CHARLES MIRANDA has been a journalist for more than 20 years, working in both newspaper and radio. In 2004, he co-wrote *My Brother's Keeper*, a bestseller about the notorious Bra Boys surfing family. Currently managing editor of the *Daily Telegraph* and the *Sunday Telegraph*, he was formerly the crime and foreign affairs correspondent, and the London-based European Bureau Chief for News Ltd newspapers. He broke the Mark Standen story.

DECEPTION

The true story of the international
drug plot that brought down Australia's
top law enforcer Mark Standen

CHARLES MIRANDA

ALLEN&UNWIN
SYDNEY•MELBOURNE•AUCKLAND•LONDON

First published in 2012

Allen & Unwin
Sydney, Melbourne, Auckland, London

83 Alexander Street
Crows Nest NSW 2065
Australia
Phone: (61 2) 8425 0100
Fax: (61 2) 9906 2218
Email: info@allenandunwin.com
Web: www.allenandunwin.com

Cataloguing-in-Publication details are available
from the National Library of Australia
www.trove.nla.gov.au

ISBN 978 1 74175 964 8

Set in 11/15 pt Utopia by Post Pre-press Group, Australia
Printed and bound in Australia by the SOS Print + Media Group.

10 9 8 7 6 5 4 3 2

The paper in this book is FSC® certified.
FSC® promotes environmentally responsible,
socially beneficial and economically viable
management of the world's forests.

Contents

Cast of Characters

	European players
Louis Aurik	Dutch police officer
Jan Boersma	Dutch investigator/commissioner
Rene Asbeek Brusse	Dutch builder (codenamed Bob the Builder)
Eric the Fatman	Belgian drug man
'Fat Ron' and **Foxtrot** (codenames)	Hogan associate and codename for the leader of the Dutch drug syndicate
'Hogan' (alias)	British-born criminal; registered informant of the NSW Crime Commission. Aliases include Seamus Kinch, Derek Woevenden and James McCarthy; also known as Jimmy Knuckles, Jimmy Short Legs and Jim
Jan (aka 'Mr Cloutier'; codenamed Charlie)	Dutch drug associate
Loek (aka 'Rashid')	Dutch drug associate
'Reservoir Dogs'	Dutch drug syndicate
Cees van Spierenburg	Dutch national prosecutor

Australian players

Peter Bodel	Australian Federal Police agent, based in The Hague
Phillip Bradley	head of the NSW Crime Commission
Bakhos 'Bill' Jalalaty	Australian Lebanese-born food importer; Mark Standen's drug co-conspirator
Mick Keelty	AFP Commissioner
Glen McEwen	senior AFP investigator
Tim Morris	AFP Assistant Commissioner
Mark William Standen	the NSW Crime Commission's top investigator
Brett Thompson	AFP investigator
Terry Venchiarutti	senior AFP agent
Paul Watt	AFP agent
Frank Wheeler	Texan debt collector, based in Australia

List of Operations and Organisations

Operations

Lacerta — AFP drug investigation, commenced in 2006, based in Sydney after information about Dutch drug runners

Mayer — Dutch drug investigation, Dutch version of Octans, into the Breda Group cartel

Merlin — Dutch drug investigation, called Operation Tahoe in Australia

Mocha — AFP drug investigation in 2005 looking at import of cocaine

Octans — top-secret undercover probe into Mark Standen's dealings, combining Operations Statice and Lacerta

Skysail — AFP drug investigation into synthetic drugs from the Netherlands

Statice — AFP investigation into Mark Standen, based in Canberra created at end of 2006

Tahoe — AFP investigation under the NSW Crime Commission's Gymea brief commenced in 2002; linked to Operation Merlin in the Netherlands

Windmill multi law enforcement agency probe led by British National Criminal Intelligence Service into Dutch synthetic drugs

Organisations

Australian Federal Police (AFP) Australian

Europol the European law enforcement agency designed to combat international crime and terrorism, with a specific focus on terrorism, large-scale criminal networks, international drug-trafficking and money laundering, organised fraud, currency counterfeiting and people smuggling

National Crime Authority (NCA) Australian

National Crime Squad Dutch

National Criminal Intelligence Service (NCIS) British

NSW Crime Commission law enforcement body entrusted with finding criminals and seizing their assets

Operation Gymea/ Gymea Reference created by NSW Police and the NSW Crime Commission in 1997 to look at organised crime groups, the importation, manufacture or distribution of drugs, and corruption by current or former police

Synthetic Drugs Unit (SDU)	set up in 1997 and consisting of Dutch police, customs, the Fiscal Information and Investigation Service and the Criminal Investigation and Information Service. The unit is controlled by a public prosecutor and coordinates information flows, international legal assistance, expands international networks and assists in criminal investigations
Serious Crime Agency	Netherlands
Serious Organised Crime Agency (SOCA)	British; answers directly to the Home Office
Team 5	Louis Aurik's Dutch anti-drugs team

1

Out of Africa

31 May 2006

The new-model Mercedes-Benz races along the motorway in the Netherlands towards the Belgian border. Looking in the rear-view mirror, François thinks about his future. Only a few years ago he and his family were forced to flee their home in the Democratic Republic of the Congo in Central Africa and seek asylum in Europe.

Now the former Congolese senior government official is about to enjoy untold riches, courtesy of his war-torn former homeland. In the boot of his car are three large canvas bags that once carried flour, but now conceal 92 kilograms of the chemical ephedrine—enough to make about $20 million worth of the deadly party drug methamphetamine, also known as 'ice'.

It's only a sample.

François sees himself simply as a salesman, showing buyers in Antwerp a sample of what he and his contacts in the Congolese capital Kinshasa can produce on demand. If all goes well there will be many showings, he thinks.

Suddenly a two-way radio on the front passenger seat crackles to life. 'All is clear,' a voice announces. François smiles and unconsciously steps on the accelerator as he races a little closer to his dream.

The voice on the radio is that of Jan, a well-built Dutch sports trainer driving a second leased Mercedes on the motorway. The 62-year-old Dutchman is shadowing François and his haul as part of a counter-surveillance operation to ensure François is not being followed by police. It is just a precaution and no trouble is expected.

Jan too appreciates how much is at stake. His criminal syndicate has a lot of stock sitting in a warehouse in the Congo, and the 92 kilograms in the boot of François's car is just a small part of a much larger worldwide operation.

No, his black courier friend will not be trailed today, Jan thinks as he follows the tail lights of François's Mercedes.

But Jan has no idea his car is being bugged, and that police are not only recording his every conversation on the two-way radio, but also tracking his car via satellite technology—leading them directly to François, the drugs, and a shadowy Belgian figure known only as Eric the Fatman.

Half an hour later, in the half-light of early evening, Jan arrives in Antwerp, about the same time as his associate parks his car. From a safe distance he watches as François steps out of his Mercedes, smiles broadly and shakes the hand of a large man. All seems to be going to plan. The men have a short conversation before moving to the back of the vehicle.

But Jan's smile quickly turns to a grimace as the area is suddenly bathed in the blue strobe lights of several screeching Belgian police cars.

To the surprise of the men standing at the back of the Mercedes, heavily armed police race in from all sides of the street, directly to the open boot of the car, knowing exactly what they are looking for and finding it: sacks of flour, containing another substance within. Police expect to find weapons in the car, but there are none. On the back seat, however, officers find a folder of paperwork, including shipping manifests, names, addresses and postal orders.

In the Fatman's car, officers find a sports bag containing €55,000 in several bundles. But for the Dutch police, neither the cash nor the drugs are important: it's the paperwork that is a treasure trove of evidence. They ignore Jan parked in the dark a short distance away; only a small handful of officers even note he is there.

Senior police coordinating the raid knew Jan would head back to Amsterdam and unwittingly lead them directly to his masters, whom they had spent months trying to identify. It's the paperwork that will lead them to the drugs and provide the evidence to shut this criminal syndicate down.

Jan discreetly watches the drama for a moment, puts his indicator on and slowly pulls away from the kerb; in his rear-vision mirror he sees François and the other large man being held against the car and handcuffed by some of the now numerous police officers poring over both men's cars. He curses quietly to himself.

He doesn't look back until he reaches Amsterdam, where waiting for him is a return airline ticket to Sydney, Australia, a stash of cash, and a 15 kilogram 'sample' of ephedrine. It's over for his Congolese friend and it's now his turn to be the salesman.

Jan's curses are picked up on the police microphone hidden in his car, bringing smiles to the faces of the police listening in.

Dismantling drug operations is never easy, but the pace at which they are closing in on this one has police confident they will have these men and their drugs in court by Christmas.

'These things that are happening are not right,' the old Dutchman tells the men crowding around the table at a small, smoky snack-bar cafe in northern Amsterdam.

It has been two months since courier François and his fat friend dealer were arrested—and then unexpectedly released, with all charges dropped. In a bizarre twist of fate and legal technicality, Belgian police 'accidentally' tainted the flour bags' contents during forensic testing of its purity, rendering the evidence invalid.

It was a worrying episode, but the release of the pair is inconsequential. What concerns the six middle-aged businessmen gathered at the cafe is two subsequent police busts.

The Dutch National Crime Squad south division and its Belgian counterpart had intercepted almost 100 kilograms of Mexican-produced cocaine in an airfreight consignment sent to Belgium. The haul was to have funded expansion of the six men's criminal cartel, each run being an investment for further growth in the competitive illegal market.

Then, a month ago, another 300 kilograms of the drug-making chemical ephedrine, this time from the Congo, was seized, again in transit to Belgium.

'We need to change everything—our suppliers, our routes, our distributors, *everything*,' the older man growls angrily, to nods of agreement from the others at the table. 'There is just too much at stake here and the police seem to know every time we move.'

Everybody knows exactly what is at stake—a 3000-plus kilogram stockpile of ephedrine hidden in the Congo—the biggest

4

stockpile of its kind in the world, worth hundreds of millions of dollars on the underground market, ready for international distribution. In Australia, once synthesised into drugs, such a haul would be worth more than $700 million.

The men are chatting about the operation when one of the mobile phones on the table rings. For a moment, no one is sure whose phone is whose, until one of the businessmen grabs his Nokia and steps away from the table. The call is from an associate of the group known only as Loek, or Rashid as he likes to be referred to during telephone conversations. He is a cautious man who doesn't like his real name broadcast.

On the other side of the world, in a warehouse in the Congo, Dutchman Loek is aware of the three seizures and the recent arrests, but is told it's business as usual and to prepare the 'Australian package'.

It *is* a worry, but the leak that led to the police raids in Belgium did not come from here, Loek thinks, glancing around at the heavily armed local militia-men patrolling the warehouse. There is too much money to make here for anyone to be acting as an informant for the Dutch or Belgian police, or anyone else. The local authorities are also corrupt—and many are on the drug payroll anyway.

Surrounding Loek are hundreds of crates, some carrying coconut milk, others branded with the stamps of foreign aid agencies. Some are aid crates carrying pseudoephedrine stocks to help local medical groups and charities combat the rising number of cold and flu cases that in places like the Congo can turn deadly. To medical aid groups such as Médecins Sans Frontières and the local United Nations Office for the Coordination of Humanitarian Affairs that distribute the medicines, they are valuable in combating debilitating eye disease and preventable and treatable nose and throat infections—but to corrupt port officials, backed by Congolese tribal rebels, the stock is liquid gold that Westerners will pay a lot of money for.

The rebels have been siphoning off the crates for months, from larger consignments coming mostly from India and China, but also the United States and Japan, driving them off the ports and import warehouses in small tarpaulin-roofed trucks. Some of the cargo is pure ephedrine produced in China and disguised as medical supplies, with China's lax border controls allowing the cargo to be easily transported across the world.

Loek walks over to a section of the warehouse where men are furiously packing and repacking. The pseudoephedrine is being repacked with cans of coconut milk to be smuggled into Australia. It is a big haul—about 210 kilograms—and Loek knows another loss cannot be afforded.

Suddenly there is yelling, then a burst of gunfire outside. Loek tells his Dutch friends he will call them back and rushes to the window. He can't see anything, but is told government soldiers are in a fire-fight with heavily armed Mai Mai rebels.

Since November 2005, some 200,000 people had already been displaced by faction fighting that was threatening to lead to a full-scale civil war similar to that of the late 1990s, when three million people died in the Congo, as much from disease as gunshot or machete wounds.

Loek had seen things deteriorate in the country, and knows the minuscule United Nations presence is unlikely to guarantee his personal safety—let alone the continued distribution of drug chemicals. In the distance he can see smoke billowing from burning buildings as people scurry indoors to shelter from the sudden violence.

*

Back in Amsterdam, the men are finishing their coffees when Loek rings back on his mobile and tells them of the day's gun battles on public streets and the worsening situation in the former Belgian colony. The panic and fear in his voice is clear. He may be part of a ruthless criminal milieu, but witnessing such random murders is nevertheless shocking. Loek deals in drugs, not violence.

He is told to stay put and they will call him back.

After a brief conversation, the businessmen around the cafe table agree it's time to move operations. They discuss shifting the stockpile to another country, such as nearby Kenya, or the former Dutch colony of Suriname in South America. Already distrustful of their supply chain, this outbreak of civil unrest in the Central African nation is a convenient excuse to change arrangements.

The men also agree to postpone the Australian shipment, unwilling to risk losing a fourth haul in as many months.

The leader of the syndicate, an older man (codenamed Foxtrot by Dutch police), is sure the Australian shipment is secure, and that Jan (who calls himself Mr Cloutier on the telephone) is a good operative—a senior figure in the group who has been involved in high-level drug running for a while and knows how to get about undetected.

Foxtrot is wrong on both counts.

Unbeknown to the crooks gathered around the table, more than a month earlier a Dutch police officer, Louis Aurik, called the Australian Embassy in The Hague warning them that Jan (codenamed Charlie by the Dutch) had taken a trip to Sydney—and probably not for a sun-tanning stint on Bondi Beach.

Aurik told the Hague-based Australian Federal Police (AFP) agent Peter Bodel, who had taken up the post only two months earlier, they had been monitoring the phones of some of the businessmen, and for the past few days had noticed Jan calling in on a +61 telephone prefix—which meant Jan was already in Australia.

Bodel immediately called the AFP's Canberra headquarters, which in turn contacted the Sydney office, with agents there confirming with the Department of Immigration and Citizenship that Jan had indeed entered the country via Kingsford Smith International Airport. He was not wanted for any offence, and there was no red alert against his name on the computers used by Customs and Border Protection officials. He was simply one of the 82,000 passengers that pass through the air hub every day.

Telephone calls intercepted by Dutch police after Jan's arrival in Sydney confirmed he was carrying a sample that they suspected was drugs, ahead of a larger smuggling operation from the Congo.

'He is a major target for us, and now maybe you too will soon have a problem in your country,' Aurik had told Bodel, before bringing him up to speed on Jan's background, the career-criminal businessmen and their suspected operations based in the Congo, Mexico and Pakistan.

Back in Sydney, the AFP agreed a major new drug cartel was preparing to enter Australia's underbelly, and immediately set up a team of agents—codenamed Operation Lacerta—to track Jan and see who he was meeting, what shipments he was arranging, and when the mother load was expected.

As 3000 kilograms of ephedrine and pseudoephedrine hidden in wooden crates marked as tinned goods are about to be moved to Kenya, the worst floods in living memory hit the nation, cutting off major roads from the port of Mombasa to the capital Nairobi, and even across the border to Tanzania. More than 700,000 Kenyans are affected and international aid agencies prepare for airlift rescues.

No one particularly notices the convoy of ageing dusty trucks, driven by heavily armed militia, carrying a haul of wooden food crates, forced to turn around at the border and return to their warehouse home.

Another location for the biggest haul of its kind in the world will have to be found. Attention turns to Suriname, a no-questions-asked country where one of the businessmen is originally from.

But back in Amsterdam, the small group of men know Suriname can only be a short-term staging post. It is time to break the haul up and flood the world with their product. Their first target: Australia.

2

Rat in the Ranks

September 2006

Assistant Commissioner Tim Morris looks about the room at the fresh faces of the overseas liaison officers. The veteran crime fighter had left the Australian Federal Police (AFP) for only two years—to join MasterCard as a senior investigator—but these new guys, some of whom he has not seen before, have a certain look he hasn't noticed before: a mixture of street-smart and intelligence. They are young too, he realises.

The men and women in the room have been handpicked by AFP executive management to operate from twenty-five of Australia's embassies and missions around the world, to receive and distribute intelligence, coordinate operations strategic to Australia's interests, and generally be the 'eyes and ears' of police before crime reaches Australian shores.

The program has operated for many years, but under Police Commissioner Mick Keelty, a more recent focus has been to confront crime and criminals offshore. Capacity building—a barrier to trans-national crime—is what he would say each time he opened a multi-agency police program, particularly in the Asia–Pacific region. A new era of terrorism, funded by multinational criminal enterprises—particularly in drugs and money laundering—had brought with it new challenges, not just for the overseas intelligence services agents, but for AFP personnel as well.

Morris attends the meeting with the force's international division, held in a conference room at the Rydges Hotel in southern Canberra, ostensibly as a catch-up, to show them who he is and what he is about now that he's back in the AFP as its acting national manager, and to outline the plan for foreign postings. Many in the room already know him, but have never worked directly with him.

It is a set agenda, discussing the federal government's yearly budget for the national police force, and sharing intelligence of emerging trends and challenges in crime and experiences from other posts. The mood is light despite the heavy agenda, with many of the AFP agents more accustomed to swapping war stories with overseas counterparts over the phone, rather than at a fully catered conference in leafy Canberra.

During a break from the main forum, Assistant Commissioner Morris speaks to the liaison officers from The Hague and London—two of the most important AFP posts in Europe.

One of the agents, Reece Kershaw, from The Hague, looks worried and tells his boss he wants to sound him out on something. He explains how he and the London liaison officer, Paul Morris, had both just returned from a discreet meeting in a hotel in Frankfurt with a notorious British-born criminal of Irish descent, codenamed 'Hogan'.

Hogan served time for armed robberies before turning his hand to coordinating high-level drug distribution across Europe and, it is believed, the United States. He is also a registered informant of the NSW Crime Commission, a law enforcement body essentially entrusted with finding criminals and seizing their assets. Hogan had been arrested in Australia for drug trafficking and money laundering but rolled over, became an informant and promptly left the country.

The hastily arranged Frankfurt meeting occurred after British police intelligence suspected Hogan had recently resumed his illicit drugs trade in Europe.

'We've got a real bad feeling about this bloke—he may be an informant or whatever, but we reckon he's back in the game big time,' Kershaw now tells Morris. This is Kershaw's final investigation in the post, having recently handed over the top posting to another agent, Peter Bodel.

The British Serious Organised Crime Agency (SOCA), a high-profile but secretive body overseeing intelligence-led criminal investigations and answering directly to the Home Office, suspected Hogan had rejoined the European underworld. Worse still, he was telling anyone who would listen—including their undercover officers—that he was an informant of 'Australian police' and was untouchable. This came as a shock to the British, who knew him as a career criminal, but had been told less than four years ago he was in jail in Sydney, serving at least seven years behind bars.

SOCA had contacted the AFP liaison office at The Hague after its field agents came across evidence Hogan was actively working for a criminal enterprise in Portugal, where he lived and owned a nightclub, even though he was supposedly in jail in Australia.

The AFP then contacted the NSW Crime Commission and told the commission it should not be running informants overseas, as it was not under its charter. Relations between the

AFP and the NSW Crime Commission had always been cordial but tense, but if the commission had ops running overseas, the AFP should have been told about it.

The NSW Crime Commission promptly got in touch with Hogan's contact within its ranks—the investigator who had brought Hogan over from the 'dark side' of crime. Yes, the investigator told his bosses, Hogan was an informant—but no, Hogan wasn't now working on anything specific for the commission. The commission nevertheless asked its investigator to organise a meeting between Hogan and the AFP liaison officers in Europe to bring them into the loop of any potential criminal intelligence Hogan may (or may not) have and wish to pass on. After all, the taxpayers of NSW were subsidising Hogan's new-found lifestyle.

Kershaw met Hogan and now reveals to Morris that everything about him was 'wrong'. His demeanour, his twitching, and even the eight mobile phones Hogan carried suggested he was back in the drugs game—probably with his old masters the Dutch, with whom he had a lengthy criminal association. It was mostly the synthetic drugs Hogan had been interested in, and that almost always meant some form of Dutch involvement.

In Canberra, Morris takes the new information onboard and agrees to relay it to the AFP's intelligence branch, but there is little that can be done except to monitor Hogan's movements through the British. Hogan had, for whatever reason, been given immunity from prosecution by the NSW Crime Commission in 2003, and unless there was evidence to the contrary, that could not change. The NSW Crime Commission was created by an Act of Parliament two decades earlier in 1986 to ensure the state's taxpayers could reap some of the proceeds of crime identified from criminals operating within its borders. Its investigators would often identify the criminals in drug trafficking and organised crime then seek AFP assistance to bring them to justice, with assets seized and split between the two crime-fighting bodies. The two worked closely together and shared all intelligence on the criminal milieu but there always existed animosity in their professional rivalry, particularly when their covert operations crossed.

Kershaw writes up a short report of his meeting and suspicions, for some anonymous colleague to attach to Hogan's file in the AFP's headquarters in Bunda Street, Canberra.

Another year will pass before Morris—or any other AFP agent—realises the true significance of Hogan's new life in Europe.

Dutch criminal syndicates have been targeting Australia for high-volume shipments of illicit synthetic drugs since the late 1990s. While the value of drugs such as ecstasy and ice was dropping in other countries, Australia was still a high-value booming market.

The exports and seizures are relentless—in the mail, in shipping containers, even on yachts coming into ports along the eastern seaboard, including Sydney Harbour, from across the South Pacific. In nearly all instances of synthetic drugs entering the country there has been one commonality: the guiding hand of the Dutch.

An intelligence report by Europol—a central agency created in 1999 to assist predominantly northern hemisphere member states to fight organised crime in Europe—found synthetic drug production generally passed through four criminal groups before hitting the streets anywhere else in the world, including Australia.

Production on any large scale has been concentrated almost exclusively in the Netherlands and Belgium, particularly in sheds and farmhouses about the green carpeted hills of the Noord-Brabant and Limburg districts on the border of the two nations.

Since the formation of the European Union, the lack of national borders has allowed the trade to flourish, and today semi-trailers move with ease about Europe, laden with illicit cargoes.

Some have begun mobile pill-press operations, moving production around the area, never stopping in one place too long. The trucks' engines hide the noise from the generators used to drive the presses, and the mobile unit can easily dump the large amount of by-product in any number of streams and rivers in the low-lying border region.

At the behest of the European Union, in 1997 the Dutch created a specialised 230-person Synthetic Drugs Unit to tackle the issue. It immediately became apparent that while the US market for drugs was large, Australia's was larger in terms of the dollar worth of each ecstasy pill or chemical batch used as a drug precursor.

By 2001, of all the busts made by the Dutch Synthetic Drugs Unit, an average of fifteen a year involved drug labs producing ecstasy specifically for Australia's dance party scene. Some pills even carried Australian brandings such as a kangaroo or the word 'G'day', to personalise the haul. In Holland, a pill sells for about $4, but in Australia it can sell for more than ten times that. And so the risks associated with sending a shipment further afield were always far outweighed by the potential money to be made.

At the end of 2004, a highly classified Dutch–Australian intelligence brief sent from the Australian High Commission in London noted that a Dutch syndicate had, since the January 2003 arrival in Sydney of a known Dutch criminal, stored

1 million ecstasy pills and a large quantity of cash to flood the drugs market. The whereabouts of the storage was 'unknown'.

By 2006, Europol reported a dramatic increase in the shipment of chemicals used in the production of methamphetamines, or 'ice'. In what it described as a 'relatively new phenomena', intelligence had found ephedrine and pseudoephedrine was being shipped globally for drug production, either directly from, or passing through, Europe.

Pseudoephedrine, derived from the ephedra plant, is a medicine used as a decongestant to relieve the symptoms of colds, flus and asthma, but it is also a precursor compound of choice for making ice. Pseudoephedrine hydrochloride is the salt form of pseudoephedrine, and is the most common form of pseudoephedrine. Ephedrine and pseudoephedrine are mirror images of each other, but ephedrine is a naturally occurring farmed substance, while pseudoephedrine is effectively its synthetic sibling, produced in a laboratory.

For some criminal groups, it was easier to send chemicals to the other side of Europe—or indeed the world—than it was to send a drug, as it was easier to argue against any alleged criminality in exporting simply a chemical compound, rather than a known narcotic. Also, many countries en route to markets, such as the United Arab Emirates, did not even recognise the shipment of drug precursors as a potential criminal act. For this reason, in 2006 the Australian Federal Government announced plans to evaluate possible controls on the production and movement of drug precursors contained in non-prescription medication.

An intelligence report prepared by the NSW Crime Commission, dated February 2006, concluded Australia had the world's second-highest rate of methylamphetamine ('speed') usage, and the highest rate of MDMA (ecstasy) usage. It was agreed that the estimated figure of 73,000 dependent ecstasy users in Australia was probably conservative.

In the same year, Tim Morris wrote a classified internal memo warning that the use of ice in Australia was being underestimated, following a covert AFP operation and subsequent raid of a converted shampoo factory in Malaysia, where precursors and the drug itself were being made. At the time, it was the largest drug lab ever found, anywhere in the world.

'It is reasonable to conclude that some of the product would have found its way into the Australian market,' Morris concluded.

After the bust, Justice Minister Chris Ellison declared that synthetic drugs posed the biggest organised criminal threat to Australia.

Since returning to the AFP at the start of 2006, Morris, as head of the AFP's international division, has been concerned about the increased imports of the chemicals—and equally concerned about the failure of his men and women to catch the criminal masterminds behind the hauls being detected.

Sometimes the drug chemicals were found, other times evidence that the drugs had been imported or were on their way. It is not uncommon, of course, to find drugs and no owners— but not usually with such large-scale operations.

The AFP's Operation Lacerta springs to Morris' mind. After that initial tip-off from Dutch police, a team of AFP investigators, working under the randomly selected codename Lacerta, had for months been investigating the arrival into Australia of a Dutch man named Jan, and the suspected import of pseudoephedrine from the Congo—and possibly also cocaine from Suriname, as a later intelligence report would reveal.

From intercepted faxes sent from a cafe in Amsterdam, the AFP knew the hauls were on their way to Australia, with a sample already in the country, but it seemed the criminals could not get themselves organised enough to make a shipment, and that there were issues with supply from the war-torn African state.

The criminal group, which used a number of sports trainers both in the Netherlands and Australia to move the drugs and compounds, used the cover name 'MDL Food and Services' to send the faxes to and from each other and arrange orders and shipments.

To anyone else, MDL Food and Services was a consumables importer and exporter, but to the AFP and its counterpart, the National Crime Squad in the Netherlands, it was a front company—one that had been used for a while, but not exposed by authorities, with investigators keen to see where the 'orders' for drugs were coming from and going to, and where deliveries ended up. It seemed to be a slick operation, but one not worth exposing until the big orders were made.

An internet cafe known as Tara's in the north of Amsterdam— little more than a hole-in-the-wall postal and internet provider, built into a sprawling grim-looking public housing block—was under constant watch. A legitimate business, it was being used by criminals as a surrogate office. Critically, the criminals used this portal because all faxes sent from the cafe did not carry a time or place-of-origin strap on the top of sent faxes—handy if you want to pretend the fax is coming from somewhere else, such as another country.

As the Lacerta investigation progressed, it appeared at least 210 kilograms of the ice-making drug was to be imported into Australia, with two principals from Sydney's northern beaches identified as having links to Jan and being key to the drug's distribution around Sydney. But while the drug conspirators had been identified, the drug's location had not. It was not even clear to police how Jan managed to bring in his sample, let alone where in the world the main haul was. And Jan and his contacts had also been proving elusive.

About the same time, another covert AFP operation—codenamed Operation Skysail—had agents sitting off a consignment of liquid paraffin from the Netherlands, which was being stored in the middle of a Port Botany warehouse in Sydney.

Weeks earlier, Australian Customs officers did a 'cold hit' and decided to search the large consignment of paraffin, used to make coloured candle wax, for anything suspicious. After more than a week of searching and taking random test samples, Customs decided it was clear.

But out of the blue they received a telephone call from a senior investigator from the NSW Crime Commission, who told them simply to test the brown batch in the middle of the paraffin consignment. Sure enough, it tested positive for liquid MDMA—methylene-dioxy-methamphetamine: 360 litres of the stuff. Sufficient to make enough ice to fetch a high six-figure price. It was the biggest discovery of its type in Australia.

The NSW Crime Commission had many paid and unpaid informants, and no one questioned where the tip came from—tips came in all the time. It was a huge bust though, and the AFP had been just content to be in on it.

But like Operation Lacerta, it seemed the AFP's Skysail investigation would not be a complete success, with no one coming to collect the paraffin, and its original senders remaining unidentified.

Perhaps the masterminds had become suspicious of the length of time Customs took to clear the consignment for collection, or received a tip-off police were onto them.

Either way, a lot of drugs worth a lot of money had apparently been abandoned. The AFP patiently waited for the haul to be collected, but then discovered two principal suspects had just slipped through Sydney Airport and boarded a flight home to the Netherlands. They had escaped. They had been spooked.

It was a demoralising and financially costly blow to the AFP. No one liked a 'no owner seizure', and much time and effort had gone into the operation. Still, shit happened, the agents involved thought, and there was nothing particularly suspicious about the case's collapse. Privately, however, some AFP agents blamed Customs. If Customs officers had been quicker in their searching and testing, then maybe suspicion wouldn't have been aroused—and maybe, just maybe, the drug traffickers would have cheerfully come along with a truck to collect their drug-soaked haul. There were lots of leaks in Customs too: quite easily someone accidentally spoke to the wrong person, and details of the find got out. In the end it was all immaterial, and agents could not afford the time to sit and ponder what could have been.

The NSW Crime Commission was also involved in another case—a father-and-son cocaine-importing team. The two were locked up and it was a success of sorts, although the AFP was always curious why the pair never seemed very committed to collecting their cargo after it arrived; perhaps others were supposed to do that.

Too many cases with open ends, Morris thinks. The two central failed operations, Lacerta and Skysail, play on his mind. There's no apparent link between them—other than the drugs being sent from the Netherlands. Still, it was a great coincidence about the drugs arriving in Australia at about the same time . . .

The files would for now remain open, but be shelved until there was a new development.

20 December 2006

Shortly before Christmas 2006, AFP senior managers receive a call. It is urgent, it is serious, and suddenly it all makes sense.

'You've gort a beeg problem,' is how the heavily accented senior Dutch agent begins the brief conversation with an AFP agent in The Hague.

The call is eventually passed to Morris and he is stunned. In policing terms, the news is about as serious as it gets. It makes his blood run cold. A mole? A high-level mole in Australian law enforcement? It surely couldn't be.

Morris immediately calls a counterpart in Holland. His Dutch contact is more blunt than usual, and says they have come across intelligence, from extensive wire taps, that one of the largest criminal syndicates in Holland is being helped by a corrupt cop in Australia. A 'crooked hat', is how he labels the suspected bent copper.

Specifically, Morris is told, the crooked hat is helping 'fix the problems' of a syndicate, dubbed Reservoir Dogs, led by a Dutch businessman and international poker player, and a small consortium of his friends, including a former world-champion martial arts fighter and sports trainer.

The leader (codenamed Foxtrot) is well known in Dutch criminal circles; the man is a big player, and not just in the ace-and-spades scene. Critically, Dutch police have information from a Dutch national informant, formerly from Australia, whose vital intelligence led them to suspect a corrupt official.

Morris urgently rings another senior manager of the Dutch National Crime Squad, and the response he receives is cool. It is made clear—if not perhaps as a final ultimatum, then as a not-so-gentle warning: fix the problem, or the Dutch will no longer feel comfortable passing on intelligence to Australian law enforcement.

The implications are huge, on many levels.

Australia is only the second nation in the southern hemisphere to be offered a seat at Europol's crime-fighting table. It is a big deal to the AFP to be selected to apply. Getting cut off by the Dutch will mean being frozen out of the elite crime-fighting group. The potential union between Europol and the AFP has been seven years in the negotiation; Australia is to be the first signatory in the Asia–Pacific. It can't be that this is all now at stake.

The Dutch also work in with the powerful and well-funded US Drug Enforcement Agency, and if the Dutch say so, then US intelligence about the European—and ultimately Australian—drug trade route can also dry up.

The Dutch Synthetic Drugs Unit has already cemented its position as Europe's premier anti-drugs team, with its encyclopedic knowledge of drugs crime. Morris knows the AFP's liaison with this unit—a relationship of mutual assistance fostered out of necessity, which has been steadily growing stronger over the past few years—will also be damaged. Bad enough there is apparently a double agent potentially in his ranks, worse still the ripple effect it could have.

Morris meets with his commissioner, Mick Keelty, and explains the situation.

'This will catch your attention,' the cop begins in an offhand but serious way to his boss. The key thing is no one knows who the mole is, let alone who he works for, Morris tells Keelty.

Despite the work of the Wood Royal Commission in the 1990s, the NSW police force still has a corruption problem, and the Victorian force isn't much better: one of the common threads running through the testimony of underworld figures being hauled before the Victorian courts for the past two years is the help of corrupt serving or former senior police officers. Just because imports are coming into Sydney does not mean they aren't being coordinated out of Melbourne, or Adelaide, or any other capital city.

The mole can be anywhere. And anyone.

The two men conclude it is more likely to be a state police officer than an AFP officer, but risks cannot be taken. They decide to put together a small team of three agents from the intelligence branch, to review past and existing investigations in search of potential compromises.

There are not many hints in what the Dutch have told them, other than the police officer was somehow passing information to criminals to facilitate major international drug imports.

No cities, no time frames, no real clues.

In late December, three agents are assigned to the case and told to look for anything unusual in the most recent collapsed cases or arrests nationally, then work back through the years.

In less than a day, the failed Operation Skysail tops the list of jobs that did not go as planned and was potentially corrupted from within.

This is when the name Mark William Standen first emerges. He was the NSW Crime Commission's top investigator who provided the tip-off about the brown batch of paraffin in the huge Port Botany consignment.

In a mole hunt, every rock is potentially hiding a suspect, and Morris decides to turn this one over first.

Curiously he and Standen, a former senior AFP colleague, once did a one-week covert operation together in Perth. Morris struggles to remember what the job was, but he does have a flashback of spending most of his free time during the trip playing tennis at the hotel they were staying at, after Standen somehow managed to run out of expenses on the first night. Tennis was free and it was all they could afford to do, he recalls. They both became very good players by the end of that trip.

It was Standen's tip to Customs that led to the drugs being found in the paraffin, but it was just that, a tip—nothing more or less than that. This bloke is one of the most senior law enforcement figures in the country, Morris muses, and has never been seen as anything less; certainly not a double agent. It is most likely just a coincidence.

A quick cross-check of reference files shows, however, that one of Standen's long-time informants is a man called Hogan, whose name six months earlier had been brought to the attention of the AFP by undercover British law enforcers.

Hogan is allegedly back working with the Dutch drug-smuggling operations—and federal police investigations into these drug-smuggling operations collapse.

Just a coincidence? Morris asks himself.

It seems inconceivable though. Standen is one of the most senior and experienced law enforcers in the country, he keeps telling himself.

Mark Standen had served the AFP with distinction, and since working with the NSW Crime Commission has been a highly respected member of the crime-fighting fraternity—entrusted with unearthing international criminals and tracking their syndicates and drug runs, not *joining* them.

Morris orders his three intelligence agents to keep searching the records and either prove or disprove any suspicions.

*

By late January 2007, Morris knows relations with the Dutch are in danger. He has to show them their Australian counterparts are taking their tip-off seriously and working on every conceivable angle. He decides to fly to the Netherlands to personally assure the Dutch police that everything humanly possible is being done to expose the suspected rat in their ranks.

In the back of his mind he plays with the name Standen. Morris can't get over the fact he knew him personally. Hell, he thinks, they worked together for several years in the same AFP office in Sydney. In those days officers were rotated through just the three divisions within the force: fraud, intelligence and drugs.

'Fuck me,' Morris says to himself. If it *is* Standen, this would be the biggest security breach in law enforcement history. What a scandal that would be. The media would go insane, and the publicity would cause everlasting damage.

No one of his calibre or access has ever been fingered as a double agent working with the Dutch—a top cop playing double Dutch.

Morris chuckles at the term 'double Dutch': how ironic this was all happening in the Netherlands. He wonders whether the term actually ever involved the Dutch, like 'Dutch courage' for having a drink, or 'going Dutch' and splitting a restaurant bill. Probably started as a British slight against the Dutch hundreds of years ago—many foreign tags began that way by the British, from their then understandable sense of superiority as an empire. There was also that Malcolm McLaren hit song called 'Double Dutch', and something about a kids' skipping-rope game. Must Google that term later and find out, he thinks.

Morris is far from convinced the leak can be as close to home as Standen, but he nonetheless devises a cover story for his sudden mercy-mission flight to The Hague, in case someone within his ranks innocently mentions it to the wrong person.

If anyone asks, the final brush strokes are being drawn on the treaty between Australia and Europol, and he is going over to ensure everything is in place. Nothing suspicious about a deputy of police ensuring the t's have been crossed and the i's dotted, with everyone in the law enforcement field appreciating the importance of the Europol seat.

The *real* secret meeting with the Dutch is unprecedented, but such is its importance to the overall crime-fighting operations that members of the British Serious Organised Crime Agency (SOCA) are also invited to attend.

If there *is* a mole, and if it *is* of the calibre of someone like Standen, then other agencies will need to be warned, since he has the keys to the crime-fighting kingdom, as it were. Standen has knowledge of almost every major international drugs operation involving Australia, and many of these involve cooperation with the Dutch and English police, as well as the Americans and a raft of other nations. Standen doesn't just know the *who*, but the *where*, *what* and *when* of criminal syndicates and police operations. In fact, his crime-fighting stamp was all over two of the biggest drugs cases in Australian crime-fighting history: Operation Tahoe and Operation Mocha.

Inviting SOCA is also a tactical move by the AFP, for if Standen really is the 'crooked hat', the British have a lot of intelligence about Hogan before and after his arrest almost five years earlier. With the right motive, they would be more keen to hand over all the details they have about their convicted criminal. Besides, Australian law enforcement had been remiss in never bothering to tell the British that Hogan had not only been released from jail in Sydney, but had been put on the NSW Crime Commission payroll as an informer—and then promptly left the country and returned to Europe.

The two-day meeting is held behind closed doors in the ground-floor conference room of the Australian Embassy in The Hague. Not even embassy staff know anything about the meeting, other than that there's a large number of police and that trays of catered sandwiches are being ferried in. Most wrongly assume that at the forefront of discussions is the Europol treaty the AFP is trying to secure. That treaty barely rates a mention by the assembled stern-faced cops.

At the meeting are top Dutch investigators Hennie Kusters, who heads the National Crime Squad's counter-drugs unit in the south, and Jan Boersma, considered an emerging-star national crime fighter, from the north unit.

Morris is joined by Peter Bodel, who is relishing being back in the thick of things after a stint as the AFP's assigned personal bodyguard for Queensland politician Pauline Hanson at the height of her spectacular One Nation rise and fall. The men are joined by Russell Smith, who had been one of the top AFP agents from the Brisbane office, and had also spent two years as the liaison officer in London before being posted to The Hague. Morris also brings along Christian Thomas, a young intelligence analyst from Canberra.

The British police have sent two senior officers from London.

Before the meeting, Morris pulls aside his agents Bodel and Smith and makes it clear the position they are in. There is a lot to lose, apart from the drugs and the mole.

'Face to face is the only way we can deal with this issue and ensure the Dutch remain onside,' he tells his subordinates.

'We've got to go in there,' he says, pointing to the conference room, 'with all the cards on the table, including our suspicions. If we do a "full and frank" of what we think is going on, they'll put all their cards on the table as well. This has got to be warts-and-all, nothing will be left out—I think we will find the Dutch have a few things they want to impart.'

The Dutch are already impressed that a man of Assistant Commissioner level has chosen to become personally involved in the mole hunt.

They have done their homework and know Morris is not just a police veteran of more than twenty years' standing. His résumé is impressive and includes every aspect of international crime fighting, from drug operations and money laundering through to secondments with the National Crime Authority and the Australian government's financial intelligence agency, AUSTRAC.

They also know Morris had been an overseas liaison officer and in 2003 was appointed the AFP's first director of counter-terrorism. As part of that brief, he headed the investigation into the 2002 Bali bombings and oversaw the creation of the Joint Counter-Terrorism Teams. After his stint with MasterCard, he was quickly promoted to Assistant Commissioner and became Member of the Order of Australia for his leadership in Bali.

Before he even speaks, it is clear to the others in the room that the right man is heading the mole hunt, and they now look to Morris for answers. He doesn't waste time with a preamble and quickly shows his hand and reveals his suspicions.

The Dutch do likewise, and as expected know more than they initially let on. But the extent of their intelligence in identifying the leak at such an early stage staggers the AFP agents in the room.

The Dutch suspect their criminals had paid a 'crooked hat'

in Australia $200,000 to find out if a shipment—the one the AFP had the Operation Skysail team looking into—had been corrupted; namely, whether authorities were onto it.

It is also revealed that there have been eleven successful imports of drugs into Australia by the Dutch in recent months. Most, if not all, had been undetected, and their existence only revealed through telephone intercepts made some time after the hauls had entered the country. This was perhaps not so surprising, since the ratio of randomly searched sea containers, compared to the daily bulk arriving, was low. Drug detection was always going to be intelligence-driven, with random searches rarely finding anything significant.

Crucially, though, the Dutch have evidence that Hogan is involved as an intermediary, and that the planned shipments to Australia are big—in fact, bigger than big. Who got the $200,000 is not clear to them. It might have been one corrupt official, it may have been more.

But to Morris it now becomes clear that Standen, who remained unnamed at the meeting, is somehow involved in the overall picture—either as good cop or bad cop. There are just too many coincidences for there not to be some kind of link: at best an irresponsible officer with loose lips, at worst, a criminal operator within.

Hearing Hogan's name again reminds him of what his agents had told him months earlier at the meeting in the Canberra hotel: Hogan is back in the game 'big time' all right. It all fits, Morris thinks.

That conclusion is drawn before lunch. The next day and a half is dedicated to what to do about it—how to jointly probe the Australian police mole and his associates, and how to keep the internal probe covert.

The British and Dutch do not understand what the NSW Crime Commission is or how it works, and insist the corrupt officer works on international crime for the AFP. Morris leads them through a basic but thorough explanation of the organisation, and how it operates in concert with other agencies in Australia, including the AFP.

'This is an AFP problem, but it is not an AFP integrity issue,' Morris explains to the gathered. 'He is not going to be *our* guy, but he is very close to our operations and of course yours too.'

All agree that the information discussed in the room— including any names of key informants or suspects—will not be passed to agents from their respective forces working on the case in the field. It was better to let them work from a blank canvas and come up with their own conclusions.

By the end of the two-day crisis meeting the Dutch seem partially satisfied. Back in Canberra, AFP boss Mick Keelty is particularly satisfied and relieved. A few months later it becomes clear why.

25 February 2007
'In the global crime environment we now police in, no one can afford to operate as a single agency or as a single country,' AFP Commissioner Keelty tells his receptive audience at The Hague moments after the historic signing of the treaty between Europol and the AFP.

'Collaborative partnerships need to be entered into to combat the challenges of modern-day crime. This is a significant achievement in the AFP's contemporary strategy in tackling international organised crime. 'This agreement will allow the AFP unprecedented access to an extensive intelligence information database. This has come about after seven years of negotiation.'

Keelty looks about the room; it is almost as if the deal was never in doubt. With the exception of the Dutch, no one would have known what had been at stake just a few months earlier. As he begins a round of hand-shaking with representatives from some of the twenty-seven European nation members he sighs with relief, but he knows the real challenge lies ahead. The operational difficulties are still to come.

Back in Canberra, Morris and the young analyst he had taken with him to The Hague a few weeks earlier put together a plan to deal with the Dutch syndicate and their apparent Aussie mole.

Working on the reasonably firm assumption that Standen is crooked, no ordinary operation will do. Standen knows their methodology, understands counter-surveillance methods, and he knows most of the people the AFP would task with any such surveillance anyway. And what if Standen isn't working alone, or someone given the job to probe him is a mate?

It will be a waste of time to run a normal operation, Morris realises. Instead he decides on a strategy to prove or disprove Standen's guilt covertly, by simply going over the circumstances, times and places when Hogan and the law enforcer met, and how that relationship may have blossomed.

Hogan is crucial in all of this. It is almost too obvious he is the conduit between it all, Morris thinks. He starts compiling a list of names for his hand-selected team to examine the Standen–Hogan relationship. He wants to keep it small, so he limits the team to seven. He then custom-fits a room for them to work in, in the most nondescript place he can think of: a far corner of Level 3, in the AFP's austere Bunda Street, Canberra, headquarters—next door to the AFP's Performance and Monitoring Team, dubbed the 'propeller heads', as they essentially collate and measure statistics.

Morris phones one of the AFP's most respected senior investigators, Glen McEwen, and in a 'Blues Brothers' moment tells him he is putting a band together.

Morris had worked closely with McEwen during the 2002 Bali bombings, when McEwen happened to be staying a few streets away from the Sari Club on an unrelated job and was first on the scene to begin the Australian response. McEwen, a versatile agent nicknamed 'Astro' to friends in the force, is currently coordinating the AFP's investigations into people-smuggling. He is having a few beers with his girlfriend on his day off when he answers his mobile and hears Morris' voice.

'It's a very important job—organisational priority that needs to be addressed; I can't say what it is,' is all McEwen hears, before being ordered into the office on his day off for a private meeting. Thankfully he is only on his second beer and basically around the corner from police headquarters in Braddon.

Morris then chooses Craig Palmer, a young investigator formerly from the ACT Police, to act as second in command to McEwen. Palmer is the son of former police commissioner Mick Palmer, but is well out from the popular former commissioner's shadow, and is well respected as a cop and specifically a drug investigator. They are joined by top intelligence analyst Bill Lee and Christian Thomas, who had made the trip to The Hague weeks earlier. Agent Paul Watt, known for his meticulous paperwork, is also brought in. McEwen also gets on board Brett Thompson, nicknamed 'Chips'. Thompson has been working in the counter-terrorism division and is an experienced investigator, particularly in surveillance. He had been asked three years before to trail Hogan and knows well how Hogan operates.

For the rest of the team, Morris tells McEwen, expecting it will later need expanding, he doesn't need Sherlock Holmes—just young, enthusiastic and discreet officers who have nothing to do with law enforcement in Sydney, or have ever known or come across Mark William Standen.

Since Standen has worked in law enforcement for almost thirty years, it is decided the young men and women to investigate him will be plucked straight from the AFP training college in Barton, inner Canberra. They cannot afford to be halfway through an investigation before declaring a conflict of interest. McEwen himself had worked with Standen directly on numerous cases within the AFP and the National Crime Authority as far back as the 1980s.

'We didn't tell them why they had been selected—only that this is the job they've got to do, and it is easily the most confidential job the AFP has done in many, many years,' Morris later tells Keelty when the names for the new team—codenamed Operation Statice—had been pulled together.

'Don't worry, I made it clear that the only way this operation is going to be successful is if it is 100 per cent confidential. Standen means nothing to them. Some are surprised they've been chosen, but are just getting on with it. They won't talk about this outside the team.'

Like Lacerta and Skysail, Statice is a randomly selected codename. Agents are given a cover story to tell family, friends and colleagues should any ask what they are working on. Statice is, they are told to say, essentially a maritime inquiry report for, among others, the federal government, looking at trans-national crime and security on the extensive national ports network. They are to say the Waterfront Inquiry is dull and boring and they can't wait to be assigned something in the field, rather than driving a desk-bound probe for bureaucrats.

On day one, as the young agents stride into the nondescript room that they are yet to know will be their home for the next year, Morris makes it clear what he wants.

'We need to go right back to when Hogan was arrested in Sydney—who arrested him, how, what were the circumstances, what were the charges, and what happened,' he says.

'I can't stress enough the need to keep everything we discuss confidential. This doesn't work if anyone outside this group finds out.

'If we assume Standen is corrupt, remember we don't know how wide his circle is. It could include Customs officers; it could include our own people.

'We have to go over everything—and I mean *everything*—as if we are doing the whole prosecution of Hogan again.

'Check databases, Customs records, telephone records, talk to the guys who did the surveillance ops. Don't make any assumptions without fact. Come up with a fresh brief and we'll see where we go from there. I want to know everything about this couple.'

Morris gives them a deadline of October 2007 to finish the investigation and the fresh brief of evidence, which he says should be based on Commonwealth offences as opposed to any NSW ones. This is crucial: Hogan had already been charged and exonerated on state criminal charges, so the new brief has to be based on Commonwealth offences. It will be the only way to mount a new case against him should they need to.

It is a long slog, looking over a lot of material, dating back many years. Boxes of files clutter the desks and small floor space. Before long, McEwen is planning a trip to the Netherlands to talk to someone in the Dutch underworld who he thinks can fill in a few blanks. It will be the first of many overseas trips related to his complex brief.

Hogan is obsessive about chess playing. He likes the tactics and the need to stay three or four steps ahead of the opponent. He plays the game like life.

Hogan, who often uses aliases including Seamus Kinch, Derek Woevenden and James McCarthy, is mostly known as Jimmy Knuckles, Jimmy Short Legs or just Jim to his mates. He has travelled in and out of Australia for some time, but never came to Australian police attention until his last trip in 2002.

British police files first record his name in 1969, when as a ten-year-old he was caught stealing. He seemed to always be in trouble and being picked up by police. By the age of fifteen, the Briton had a string of convictions, particularly for burglary and theft. His crimes culminated in a thirteen-year sentence for a violent armed robbery in Manchester in 1987, but he was let out after seven years for good behaviour. By that stage he had amassed thirty convictions for fraud and theft, as well as a firearms offence.

He hung about the streets of Birmingham and East London with a group akin to the motley crew in the movie *Lock, Stock & Two Smoking Barrels*; his mates had colourful nicknames like Nick the Greek, One Eye and The Shoe. Jimmy would hold court in his local pubs. He was a clever crim and liked everyone to know about his exploits. He once detailed how, after one robbery, when he was running away from the scene, he came across a twelve-year-old boy. He stuck his fist down the boy's throat, rattled it around and came up with saliva; he then wiped the boy's saliva onto his balaclava and threw it on the front seat of a second decoy getaway car, while he fled in another vehicle. If police later tested the DNA in the balaclava that was found in what they would assume was the getaway car, they would not match it to Hogan; and if they ever did find a match, they'd be hauling in a twelve-year-old boy and accusing him of armed robberies.

'It's all about creating the doubt, it is,' Hogan would tell his partners in crime, much to their delight. 'You got to be clever—cleverer than them bastards,' he would say. It was never clear how many of his tales were true, but they loved his stories just the same.

After his last prison stretch, Hogan learnt there were easier ways to make money than being a front man armed with a weapon, and began liaising with the Dutch criminal underworld to import synthetic drugs. Like the Dutch, he realised there was more money in the illicit drugs game in Australia, and in 2002 moved to Sydney to act as an intermediary—a facilitator—between the Dutch and Australian criminals, for what was to become the biggest ecstasy haul seized to that date.

Hogan's moves were known to British police, with a September 2002 confidential report noting 'the suspect is a well-documented drugs trafficker, historically based in Birmingham area and Portugal. He has for some time been a target for Her Majesty's Customs and Excise and the National Crime Squad but is currently believed to be in Australia.' Indeed, British Customs Service had created a large detailed link diagram—a 'family tree' of sorts—of Hogan's extensive links and associates globally.

The report goes on to say that Hogan had graduated from multiple fraud and theft offences, and had since 1995 moved to large-scale drug trafficking, predominantly to the UK from Holland. It noted that in 2001 he was suspected of having access to 200 kilograms of cocaine in Panama. Another report concluded he 'may be making preparations for settling in Australia as he is sick and tired of law enforcement attention in the UK'. To that end, it was suspected he had bought a multi-million-dollar waterfront property in Sydney's northern beaches.

In late 2002, three imports of at least 1.5 tonnes of ecstasy reached Australia—enough to feed dance clubs across the eastern seaboard and South Australia for months. One shipment made it through to the market, but the other two were detected by the AFP, who assigned a team of detectives—codenamed Operation Tahoe—to uncover the source.

It was an ingenious plot. Together with a Dutch criminal, who had previously been facilitating large-scale ecstasy hauls to the United States, Hogan and his associates set up a company in Australia to import horticultural products.

They then used an unrelated but legitimate company in the horticultural business to piggyback their ecstasy shipments, thereby avoiding raising suspicions about any imports of equipment. They told the legitimate company it could cut costs and help them both if they merged their import operations.

Initially, four pallets of pot-plant holders arrived; these were stored at a depot in South Dowling Street in the inner Sydney suburb of Alexandria, before being moved across Sydney to more discreet locations. Police surveillance uncovered a customer network of well-known Sydney underworld figures, but not before a number of deliveries had already been made. The NSW Crime Commission was the lead agency on the job, backed up by the AFP and NSW Police.

Heavily armed Operation Tahoe police moved in on several properties on Christmas Eve that year. A delivery van carrying PVC piping stuffed full of 254 kilograms of ecstasy was found in an apartment garage in Sylvania. While the haul, worth $45 million, was a record, it was only a fraction of what had come into the country from the Hogan-related Dutch group.

There were several arrests immediately, but Hogan, who had based himself in Bondi, was not picked up until the following March. Within days he had rolled over.

Those who could have given evidence against Hogan changed their minds. One was Hogan's New Zealand-born housekeeper-turned-girlfriend, who, on his orders, threw a small quantity of drugs hidden in a McDonald's packet out the window the moment police came through his door. Unfortunately for Hogan, the packet landed near a security guard below, who found the 150 grams of ecstasy inside and called police. That was when Hogan was first arrested. However, Hogan's girlfriend fled the country after his arrest, having received a number of anonymous threatening phone calls. Hogan's Australian-based Dutch colleague also fled after hearing about the seizure and the arrests on the radio news that morning. His local criminal contact, a cafe owner in Bondi, went to ground.

The main drugs haul that had yet to be shifted was left abandoned in a warehouse. At that point, the NSW Crime Commission conceded there was insufficient evidence to successfully convict Hogan with anything significant, and Standen personally appealed to the NSW Director of Public Prosecutions to let Hogan off all charges, as a trade-off for providing information about the operation. Drugs and money-laundering charges were withdrawn in June, and by July Hogan was given bail. Three months after the Standen appeal, the remaining drugs charges against Hogan were dropped.

For reasons that always baffled the commission and the AFP, despite the small McDonald's bag of pills they could hope to convict him on, Hogan, in a meeting with Standen and others in the NSW Crime Commission building in March 2003, gave up everything related to the plot—including the location of the drugs and cash, as well as details about the syndicate, how it worked, and how members would often come to Australia.

Crucially, Hogan revealed where a large stockpile of drugs was hidden in Sydney, as well as $1 million in cash—proceeds of drug sales—hidden in a storage unit garage.

But he didn't stop there. He detailed not only his Dutch cohorts—known in some circles as the 'Breda Group' on account of their concentration in that area of the southern Netherlands— but also members and operations of a rival cartel known as the Maastricht Group, and an all-female ecstasy gang known as Octopussy. He had it all: names, details of past, present and future large-scale drug shipments—and, of particular interest to the NSW Crime Commission, details of up to $60 million being laundered out of Sydney and Melbourne and elsewhere in the region, including Singapore.

Hogan's courting was hailed as possibly the most valuable ever achieved. An AFP intelligence report concluded: 'This is a unique opportunity for the AFP, in a strategic sense, to combat the emerging threat of MDMA importation into Australia from the Netherlands.'

Hogan's relationship with Australian law enforcers and the flow of information would continue for years—mostly through Standen, who in turn would pass some information to Dutch crime fighters. The Dutch of course wanted Hogan to speak with them directly, but he refused, saying he would only deal through Standen. He didn't trust the Dutch police. Hogan's intelligence was always rich and accurate, and sometimes even detailed, with descriptions of suspects with beards, short or tall, or big teeth.

Hogan had details of 'clogs' (as he called Dutch suspects) involved in importing to Australia 165 kilograms of MDMA concealed in industrial drills from Germany; British criminals from Liverpool exporting drugs with wine from Spain; narcotic shipments from Brazil and Panama; secret cartel meetings on the island of Aruba in the Caribbean; significant money laundering from Dutch people travelling to Australia, but sending money to Barcelona in bundles of €500 notes; and details of associated big-time criminals from Germany, Belgium, Hong Kong, China, Manchester, Bangkok, Melbourne, Darwin and finally Sydney—where some of them spent lazy, sunny days, remotely moving drugs and money using their mobile phones, from cafes overlooking Bondi Beach.

Hogan would read in the newspaper about a big US Drug Enforcement Agency bust in Dubai, and would then provide Standen with the context to its relationship to Australian players. He would also talk of criminals he was in contact with in 'hospital', code for jail.

It all tied in with intelligence gathered by the AFP in London, which had reported back to Canberra, months earlier, details of the Dutch moving drug-precursor chemicals from Africa and China, via Greece, into the Netherlands, to then ship to Australia. Such was the flow of intelligence that two Dutch police agents travelled to Sydney to personally meet with Standen and take copies of his intelligence notes.

In the Netherlands, Tahoe was codenamed Operation Merlin, and was one of their biggest police operations ever. But like Tahoe, the case fell over in the courts, with insufficient evidence to prosecute any Dutch nationals.

Cees van Spierenburg, the national prosecutor who ran the case in the Netherlands, told colleagues it was always going to be difficult to secure a court victory against all five men Merlin identified as being behind the plot, even with their rich intelligence and evidence.

'The problem with Merlin is we did not see by way of telephone taps or surveillance these people involved; if we had, it would have been easier to prosecute,' he told Australian law enforcers visiting the police headquarters in Breda. They did have one witness, but as the Dutch legal saying states, 'one witness is no witness'.

The case did give police on both sides of the equator crucial insight into the 'compartmentalisation' of criminal enterprise. If one person from one aspect of the operation, such as transport, was caught, they could not be linked to or spill information about others in the operation, as most times the people in each compartment did not know who was working in the others.

Shortly after he left Australia in 2003, Hogan again became of interest to British police within the National Criminal Intelligence Service, for suspicious associations with Dutch criminals. A covert operation they were running—under the umbrella Operation Windmill—had been investigating Dutch drugs coming across the English Channel, and had tracked Hogan on a flight to Aruba near Venezuela, where he reconnected with his Dutch masters and discussed what went wrong in the Australian deal—and just as importantly, the Australian law enforcers he had dealt with.

By this stage Hogan was firm friends with Standen, and he made that association known. He would often ring Standen out of the blue for a chat, not about the criminal world, but personal issues such as his family, including a sick daughter, his own misspent youth and his desire to be a legitimate businessman. He also often lamented his personal safety fears: his list of enemies would be long if they ever found out he was talking.

To Morris, the strategy to nail Hogan is simple enough: work back through the files, find fresh evidence, then convert the original Tahoe NSW drugs and money-laundering offences into Commonwealth charges. To change the charges from state to Commonwealth offences, the team must reinvestigate every aspect of the case, and—courtesy of McEwen's Dutch contacts— dig up some new evidence.

The team members know if they can secure a successful prosecution and lock Hogan up, then they can perhaps get him to roll over—for real this time—with a deal for less jail time, in exchange for giving up his crooked cop mate. Hogan would have to do some jail, that was a given, but just how long would effectively be up to him.

Within about two months, the Statice team has a lucky break. After much negotiation, the office of the NSW Director of Public Prosecutions reluctantly hands over its copy of a brief of evidence that had been initially collated in 2005 to prosecute Hogan.

The facts are already known, and elements contained within the brief are based on police reports anyway—but attached to the brief are later letters written by Standen, urging the state Director of Public Prosecutions to drop charges against Hogan. One letter claims a chief witness is now unreliable and has left the country, and is no longer willing to give evidence.

With a single signature, the charges against Hogan were dropped. That was the moment Hogan became an informant of the NSW Crime Commission.

These letters confirm a direct link between Standen and

Hogan. It was known of course that Hogan was his informant, but the extent to which Standen manoeuvred to get Hogan out of jail and have charges against him dropped is only now realised.

Hogan had provided information to the commission, and specifically Standen—including names of criminals, the address of a warehouse containing a couple of hundred kilograms of ecstasy left over from the Tahoe plot, and the whereabouts of almost $1 million in cash. He says there was another $1 million, which had been moved to Melbourne by an associate. But Hogan was just treading water, waiting for his lucky break—which came a few months after his initial arrest.

According to police records, Standen came to the AFP office in Sydney and proposed a money-laundering sting. Standen said he could send someone to deliver money to a bureau de change in inner-city Sydney, which would remit it, and the AFP could then identify the accounts the money was going into.

It was a big job that could expose the money-changer as a money launderer, and possibly uncover criminal links between those sending the money and those receiving it.

Of the seized $1 million, about $300,000 was handed to the two money agents—who then spirited it away. While the remittance agents were charged and locked up in the first such case to be brought before Australian courts, Hogan never revealed which accounts the money ended up in, and instead promptly fled overseas.

Some in the AFP believed there was something amiss in the association between Standen and Hogan. Standen had heard the rumours himself, but simply dismissed it as jealous rivalry, believing himself a better investigator than his former AFP colleagues.

Digging deeper, Operation Statice now establishes that Hogan is suspected of shifting $60 million out of Australia, to Holland,

via London, sometime around his stay in 2003 and 2004, with
the help of the Australian relative of a Dutch man, via money-
changers and a diamond trade.

3

Enter the Grocer

Working long hours and in cramped conditions, the Statice team beavers away on its brief, with McEwen giving his boss Morris almost daily updates. It is all going pretty well. New witnesses have been found, including one key figure in jail in the Netherlands, ready to do a deal.

Such is the intricacy of the case that, when they learn that a phone call was made to Hogan from a particular phone box years earlier, the call list is found and matched. Information is always coming in, and surprisingly, agents are able to match the few records that still exist with certain telephone calls—which are in turn traceable to mobiles, their registered users, and even Commonwealth Bank safety deposit boxes.

The Statice team's work is meticulous and unique in breadth and detail. Within months the team confirms there were three Tahoe shipments, rather than just the one police knew about in 2002, and they now have new evidence and witnesses to prove it.

The Hogan aspect of the brief is in the bag. Then something happens that dramatically changes the course of the investigation—and the life of Mark Standen.

Statice is right on target with its strategy to arrest Hogan on the old Tahoe matter, and get him to turn informant for the AFP, when in May 2007, a single-page fax from the Netherlands is sent from MDL Food and Services to someone in Australia.

It is a shock to Morris, particularly. AFP Intelligence hasn't picked up anything from the bogus food exporters from Holland for a while—and now here is a fax sent to a new person: a Bakhos 'Bill' Jalalaty, at BJ's Fine Foods Pty Ltd, on Chicago Avenue in Blacktown, western Sydney.

Whoever receives that fax from the bogus company is in the market for drugs: it is that simple. These MDL faxes, sent from the hole-in-the-wall Tara internet cafe, have only one purpose, and it is criminal activity.

The introductory fax states:

We would like to introduce our company MDL Food In Delhi India who is the manufacturer and supplier of vegetables, food and beverages to government and local groceries all over India and Middle East.

We have wide range of varieties and private labelling in all kinds of food products and are able to provide the needed services and support for marketing and promotional activities. Since our market expansion, it also concerns Arab countries such as Kuwait, Saudi Arabia, Iran, Iraq, Lebanon, Syria and UAE. We also supply approved halal products.

After months of silence from MDL Food and Services, the AFP's Operation Lacerta team—still actively tracking the movements of the mysterious Dutch sports trainer, Jan, and his links to a big Dutch drug syndicate, many months after the trail ran cold—is excited by this development.

It puts them back in business with a new local target—although at this stage they have no idea of their discovery's far wider implications. Resources are suddenly directed towards finding out everything possible about the Lebanese-born Bill Jalalaty.

Lacerta determines the 47-year-old Jalalaty (or BJ as the team prefers to call him—easier than using his surname), is a clean-skin food providore. Born in Lebanon, he migrated to Australia with his family when he was eight years old. He married in 1987 and has one son, now nineteen years old. He has no prior police record and has never been mentioned on any intelligence reports.

It seems odd that a simple grocer operating from a desolate industrial park in Blacktown suddenly wants to buy drugs.

The family man's finances seem normal enough, including the usual mortgages, and while not overly successful, the food business and another enterprise specialising in game and poultry have a legitimate solid financial footing and have been supplying quality produce to a range of restaurants and upmarket delis across Sydney. His wife is listed as a director and secretary for the family businesses. They live in a modest home in Maroota, near Wiseman's Ferry, north-east of Sydney.

BJ had apparently been a body-builder at some stage, although some police armed with a recent photograph of him joke it was presumably when he was a lot younger.

Lacerta entertain the idea that the fax was sent by accident, or was intended for another Lebanese man named Jalalaty and the wires got crossed. But as they look deeper into his background they uncover a vital connection.

Jalalaty became divorced in 1990, then married a woman named Dianne. She is initially of little interest to the AFP agents, until they discover her maiden name—and surprisingly, that she is a former senior AFP agent.

A quick check of records shows Dianne was stationed in the same bureaus and on many of the same operations as Mark Standen—a relationship that is later confirmed, with communication intercepts placed on Jalalaty's telephones and computers showing a strong connection to Standen.

Just for good measure, the same fax sent to his Blacktown warehouse is also sent to Jalalaty's home. That is all the confirmation investigators need.

For Morris, the stakes suddenly go through the roof.

The Lacerta team has made an accidental connection between a Dutch-based criminal syndicate and Australian suspects—one of whom is talking to one of the most senior law enforcers in the country.

To Morris, taking the scenario to its logical final point, Standen is suddenly not only involved with questionable characters, and not possibly just giving a few odd tip-offs as had been suspected, but is potentially directly involved in a drug operation.

Lacerta's brief is to expose a potentially still active drug operation—and apparently here is Standen now communicating with someone who, in turn, is linked by fax to a Dutch drug group.

Morris knows he will eventually have to merge Operation Statice from Canberra, with its covert historical brief on Hogan and Standen, and Operation Lacerta from Sydney, with its contemporary probe on MDL Food and Services, and its apparent drug plot in Australia.

But he won't do it yet. Instead, he decides to oversee parallel secret investigations. Neither side will know of the other's existence.

In Australia, besides Morris and Commissioner Keelty, only McEwen is aware of the full extent of both covert operations. It is like putting together a giant jigsaw puzzle, with two teams working on the same picture and not realising it. There are different targets now—the two guys Lacerta had been chasing are long gone—but a new one has been identified, Jalalaty, and he is connected to Standen. And of course the ultra-covert Statice team is chasing its two key men.

The Lacerta crew is reminded of how important its brief really is, although not yet fully informed why. A jigsaw puzzle is how he will describe it to the Statice team, Morris decides. 'A jigsaw puzzle that only works if all the pieces come together and we get the full picture,' he tells them later.

Standen first met Bill Jalalaty around 1995, shortly after Dianne left the AFP and hosted a dinner party for her former work colleagues. Standen and Dianne had worked together for many years after she joined the AFP in 1980, and moved to Sydney five years later as a Drugs Unit plain-clothes officer. They were great friends, but he didn't necessarily consider her husband— whom she met two years earlier and left the force to join his meat and poultry business—a mate, despite sharing many meals at the Jalalaty home.

Then, in about 2005, at one particular feast of osso bucco that Dianne had prepared, Bill Jalalaty gave a detailed account of his meat business, and in particular dissected the cost of every food item on their plate. He bragged about the high prices in the supermarket, and how he could get the product for cheaper and on-sell and still make a profit.

'Why don't you expand and deal with all these other products, if you can do better?' Standen asked Jalalaty—to which Jalalaty replied that he would, and offered to take Standen along for the ride.

Standen made a fuss of the generous offer, but this was his aim all along: to get the simple grocer to expand his import business for quite another reason.

Standen started regularly visiting the Jalalaty family home, more often not to see Dianne now, but her husband. Bill liked golf, but once lamented he didn't know how to buy off the internet, so Standen bought him the clubs he wanted off eBay.

Jalalaty would deliver foods to NSW State Parliament and the David Jones deli in Elizabeth Street, and would then lunch with Standen in his nearby Kent Street NSW Crime Commission office. They would catch up for hot chocolates pretty much every time Jalalaty had a delivery in the city.

In that same year, 2005, during those cafe breaks, Standen told his friend about his acquaintance Hogan, and how he started out as a criminal suspect, but then became a valuable informant, blowing the whistle on drug and money cartels around the world, before becoming what Standen considered a solid friend.

Standen suggested the two should meet: they might be able to help each other. He told Jalalaty that he'd told Hogan he wanted to have a laser eye operation—and Hogan offered to send him the money as a Christmas present.

Standen then telephoned Dianne, who kept the accounts for the family business, and told her the story as well.

'I have a friend in Europe who wants to send me some money,' he told her. 'It's going to help get my eyes lasered. I don't want the money to be sent to me directly—I don't want work to know . . . could I get it sent to you?'

'Yeah, you could get it sent to Bill's account, but I'll have to ask him,' she replied.

'Will he care?'

'I can't see why he would. Do you know how much?'

'No.'

'Do you have a ballpark?'

'Maybe $5000, could be $10,000. Don't really know.'

Jalalaty, however, later told his wife it would be closer to $50,000.

Jalalaty's bank details were passed on.

What Standen did not tell Dianne was that Hogan was a crook-turned-informer, and that he, Standen, could not afford the money to go into his own bank account, since he was not planning on informing his employer, the NSW Crime Commission, of the generous gift.

Within days, just before Christmas that year, Hogan—through a British businessman and long-time associate—had deposited £20,000 ($47,500) in the account, to be passed on to Standen.

The following month, Bill Jalalaty travelled to Bangkok for four days to meet the generous Hogan in person, and a conspiracy began.

It was perfect: Jalalaty had an established import/export business and no criminal record. Jalalaty said he could get United Arab Emirates citizenship, and from an already criminal warehouse base there, move goods and money back and forth as if they were the operations of a legitimate business.

Jalalaty immediately felt his small meat business would have to expand to meet the potential new work—and Hogan agreed to help.

Some weeks after the Bangkok meeting, Hogan arranges for another Australian-based associate to deliver $1 million in cash in a sports bag to Jalalaty.

Initially Jalalaty is taken aback by the 'loan', as he has never seen so much money in his life. It is to fund new infrastructure, such as a lease for a bigger warehouse, a forklift, shelving to store goods, and eventually to pay for any shipments to arrive.

But Standen, who since 2003 suspected Hogan had a large stash of cash somewhere still in Australia, considers the cash as a potential private slush fund.

He and Jalalaty discuss how they can invest the cash and live off the interest until Hogan wants the money back or it needs to be spent on actuals related to 'the business'. Jalalaty says he has a friend who knows about such things.

Hogan doesn't even need to know. Jalalaty immediately rings a property developer friend, who in turn introduces him to Sydney clairvoyant and part-time investor Bruce Way.

Way then contacts an American commodities broker, who recommends him to a Bahamas-based businessman who is promising 15 per cent returns on any money invested in a $500 million money pool, to deal in the high-risk trading of unsecured bank debts.

Jalalaty sees only the promise of 15 per cent returns and sends Way $580,000 from the sports bag, hiding the rest in the back of a cupboard in his Maroota home. But this money soon vanishes, somewhere in the Caribbean.

Jalalaty breaks the news to Standen in a cafe near his work.

'There is something I need to run by you, bit of a problem,' he begins. 'You know the investment I made? Well, I am having some difficulty getting the dividend or getting my return on the investment.'

'What sort of difficulty?'

'Well, it was due in December, but I still haven't got it.'

'Well, are you expecting it?'

'Well, I'm not sure, I think the people are . . . it's such a good deal that the people don't want to give me the return, because they want to reinvest the money to increase their overall profit.'

'Well, maybe you should write them a letter of demand.'

'Yeah, that's a good idea.'

Standen offers to help draft the letter, but he is privately furious. No one has even met the Bahamas businessman. He can't believe his business partner has been so stupid, and regrets leaving him in charge of the money.

He tells Jalalaty he will find the money. Bizarrely, Jalalaty then wants to wheedle Way's home address from the Roads and Traffic Authority so he can front him direct.

Standen tells him there are easier, more legal, ways to find Way's address, such as looking up the publicly available electoral roll. He says he also has other ways—and immediately phones the notorious debt collector Frank Wheeler.

'When should I go to police?' Jalalaty asks Standen.

'The police don't get money out of a bloke overseas in Switzerland or the Bahamas. They just say it is impossible. The only way to do it is with Frank. Frank has to go and ask this bloke, he has to.'

Frank Wheeler is a broad Texan with an imposing personality and a reputation for getting the job done. In recent years he had been a regular face around the NSW Crime Commission, so much so he even asked for a job there. Standen recommended against it—too much baggage from a life as a standover debt collector, working for the likes of Tim Bristow and Michael 'No Thumbs' Pestano. NSW Police also held an intelligence file on him that was less than flattering.

Standen liked Wheeler, however. He was a real character and they shared a passion for inventions, often talking about some things they hoped to one day develop.

'I have a friend who has come to me and he's lost $1 million and there's nothing I can do to help him,' Standen tells Wheeler, who simply nods, smiles broadly and says he'll get onto it. He's heard a similar line a few times before.

Meanwhile, Standen asks a NSW Crime Commission junior analyst to contact the Australian Transaction Reports and Analysis Centre (AUSTRAC)—the law enforcement body entrusted with tracking unusual or large money movements in and out of Australia—to see what Way and the supposed American commodities contact have been up to.

Wheeler calls Jalalaty and the pair meet at the Doncaster Hotel in Sydney's east to discuss Bruce Way, the lost money and the man in the Bahamas. They suspect there is in fact no American commodities broker, and that Way has been tricked into sending the money to a dummy account set up by fraudsters.

Wheeler likes to hand out his two-sided business cards to show he means business. The front states his position as 'private investigation; finance; investment; recovery of money's'; the back offers 10 per cent discounts for funerals and medical emergencies. He also has a third card, which states he never gives out a third card—making the point that he always gets results, one way or another. Wheeler promises to do all he can to get the money back.

Wheeler then meets Standen at the NSW Crime Commission office in Kent Street to further discuss the issue. Some time later he turns up at Bruce Way's home and later the workplace of Way's wife. Way becomes fearful, particularly when handed the Wheeler business calling card.

A few weeks later, the AFP listening into hours of telephone intercepts can't believe what Standen and Jalalaty have got themselves into. The plot is still the primary focus, but the sideshow with Wheeler is just downright bizarre.

Just when they think the investigation can't stray any further left field, they hear evidence Wheeler is now calling none other than Roger Rogerson—the former decorated NSW Police detective sergeant, whose spectacular fall from grace saw him accused and acquitted of murder and fraud, and finally jailed on a string of convictions, including lying to the Police Integrity Commission, which had been looking into corruption in the NSW ranks.

Wheeler speaks to his associate Rogerson and says he believes he has now traced the whereabouts of the money, but Jalalaty doesn't want to spend $50,000 to take 'the boys' over to the Bahamas to collect the cash.

Rogerson meets Jalalaty for himself—firstly in The Rocks, where the grocer turns up with his son, then later at a meeting in Parramatta, where Rogerson is given some papers of the loans affair. He gets $200 as a payment for his time and tells Jalalaty he has 'connections' who can help in these sorts of matters. They talk fees and passports, but this is the last contact Rogerson has with the group. He too thinks the whole thing is ridiculous, and if anyone is stupid enough to make such an investment then too bad. These people are hopeless and it is more trouble than it is worth for him to get involved.

On 15 June, Standen gets Wheeler to meet with Way and order him to his Kent Street office to discuss the lost monies. Way has no idea what Standen's involvement is, and presumes he is under general investigation by the all-powerful NSW Crime Commission for transferring monies offshore. He meets Standen, together with Wheeler, and says he too has been a victim of the Bahamas businessman. He has lost money himself and can therefore not pay anyone back. A paper trail confirms Way's story.

After the meeting, Standen, Wheeler and Jalalaty agree that Way did lose money of his own and is just a hapless victim himself, and that the American commodities broker does exist. He is tracked down to a US address in West Palm Beach.

Out of frustration, Jalalaty even calls the American broker's home phone number and speaks to his wife, who says he has gone to Switzerland. With his money no doubt, Jalalaty thinks.

Standen rings Jalalaty. He wants the money, but this is a sideshow to the real deal and he doesn't want to think about it anymore.

'Well I have done my bit,' he tells his grocer friend. 'I mean I have told him [Wheeler] I can't use my position to do anything— you know you just can't do that. But at this stage I just ask the right questions, you know; now it's up to him to do his job.'

'Frank's good at that sort of stuff, very dark you know, I mean Frank met him [Way]. Let him sort it out I reckon, let him sort it.'

But the 'boys' will never go over to the Bahamas, the money will never be recovered, and the extent of the scam never truly unravelled. The money spirited away to America is found to have been done via a company in Harrow, Middlesex in the United Kingdom, but it's never coming back—and everyone, including Way, who has lost his own fortune, knows it.

For police, it is a startling yet entertaining sideshow to their primary investigation, and again reinforces the amateur status of the people they are dealing with.

Officers joke that Standen may be a street-smart cop, but his lust for cash has clearly blinded his judgement about whom he chooses as associates.

In The Hague, AFP agent Peter Bodel receives almost daily telephone calls from detectives back in Australia who are still working on Operation Skysail. They can't understand how one of the biggest MDMA seizures in Australian history doesn't seem to be getting the backing from AFP chiefs and the dedicated resources it deserves. The Netherlands appears to be the nexus of the plot they are investigating, but according to Skysail, the AFP liaison officers there don't want to know about it.

If only they knew, Bodel thinks as he fobs them off yet again.

Many of the Skysail agents are his friends—not just colleagues—and lying to them is not easy. He tells them yes, it is a big job, and he will help investigate it at the Dutch end and enact the necessary search warrants, and so on. In essence, every time they ring he thinks of another excuse why it can't be done right away.

No one can know of the existence of Operation Statice, or potential links to any other operation including Skysail, which appears to fall right into the middle of their more important top-secret brief. AFP chiefs could have killed Skysail off altogether, to stop it stumbling onto their other now more serious briefs— but to do that could ring alarm bells with others, in particular Standen.

As Bodel puts the phone down on yet another request for help from a Skysail mate, he turns to office colleague Russell Smith. 'They can't understand why it is they have apparently got a world-record seizure job and nobody wants to know about it,' Bodel says.

'I tell them "it seems like it's not getting our full attention, but we're on it, and as soon as we get anything we'll let you know."'

'They buying it?' Smith asks.

'Don't know. They probably think we're just sitting on our hands over here enjoying the European weather,' he replies, looking out the window at the bleak cold blowing into The Hague from the North Sea.

'It's getting hard lying to them, but we can't let them in on our suspicions and what we're really trying to do here. Nothing worse than an "off" copper—I can't stomach them.'

'I tell you, it's a shock for me. I worked with that bloke Standen for years,' Smith says.

'I know. That's why we have to be on guard all the time. We don't know who is ringing for what. I'm asking myself every time someone from Sydney or Canberra rings, "Was there a reason for them ringing? Why were they asking me that? Was that a genuine call, or were they fishing for something else?"'

'Oh well, this is a lock-down situation, and until someone busts someone, we can't trust anyone outside of Statice.'

It is an unprecedented situation, with one AFP team actively stymieing another, but the implications are too huge and both men know it. And they are both about to 'up the ante' in the probe.

Bodel lifts the telephone receiver and calls his Dutch counterpart, Louis Aurik. 'I think we need to chat . . . in person,' is all he says, before agreeing to drive to the anonymous Dutch National Crime Squad headquarters, south of Amsterdam.

Aurik, a burly, affable thirty-year crime fighter, knows the matter must be serious, since the two speak all the time and neither usually feels the need to travel from one city to another to speak in person; in peak hour it can take more than an hour each way.

Located a few kilometres south of Amsterdam, the nondescript National Crime Squad building is nestled behind a roadside petrol station and a KFC outlet, and looks like any other building in a satellite industrial park off a busy highway. The only thing distinguishing it from any other building on the site is its lack of signs, and the fact there are always at least a dozen cars parked out front, even on a weekend; the undercover police headquarters is staffed around the clock. For some reason its street address does not appear on satellite navigation devices either, although this could be due to a mapping glitch, the Dutch police think, rather than a clandestine effort by the state.

Bodel and Aurik decide to meet outside the office and grab a coffee nearby. The 54-year-old Aurik is stunned when finally told all the detail of the suspected 'crooked hat'. Suddenly his investigation into a few sports trainers potentially plotting to send drugs to Australia—codenamed Operation Mayer—takes on new importance. He doesn't need to be told the implications for all law enforcement.

The Dutch officer had no idea an alleged corrupt law enforcer was potentially involved in his case, but was always curious as to why so many resources were apparently being dedicated to it—both here in the Netherlands, and with the Australians on the other side of the world.

The AFP know that for the case to successfully run its course and to gather enough evidence to prosecute Standen, they need someone like Aurik on side. He is well respected in his field and not afraid to tell his immediate supervisors where to go. They are already putting pressure on him to wind up the Dutch end of the probe, since there is already enough evidence to prosecute for a conspiracy to export drugs to Australia.

'So that's why you were so keen to keep the job going,' he tells Bodel after he is briefed. He isn't told any names, but says he doesn't need to know.

'All I need to know is that this man is important to you and has implications for both of us,' he says.

Like his bosses, Aurik is confused by the existence of the NSW Crime Commission and doesn't understand how it operates. Bodel laughs and says neither do the Australian public and half the law enforcement community.

After Bodel's meeting with Aurik, Bodel and Smith return within the week to the National Crime Squad headquarters, where they put on a PowerPoint presentation to explain where the investigation is at, and to detail the NSW Crime Commission's position in relation to national Australian crime-fighting activities.

The big chiefs may have shown each other their hands at the earlier meeting at the Australian Embassy in The Hague, but it is time now for a select few men and women on the ground in Amsterdam to get up to speed on the drug probe and to take the case forward.

For this meeting, Jan Boersma, who was already privy to the existence of the 'crooked hat' since his meeting with Morris months earlier, comes along. It is initially tense as Bodel and Smith detail the multi-level plot and the suspected involvement of the unnamed law enforcer. They do not, however, give any real hint as to his identity. When they put up a giant head-shot photo of the partially bald Jalalaty, smiling broadly with a pencil-thin moustache, some in the audience spontaneously burst into laughter. It is hardly the mug shot of a dead-stare angry criminal they have been expecting.

'This is your big crook in Australia?' someone in the audience yells out.

Bodel laughs along and says how crooks come in all shapes and sizes, before going on to explain how Operation Lacerta is locked down and completely confidential. In a roundabout way he impresses upon all the need to maintain secrecy, no matter how kooky they think Australian crooks look.

After the meeting Boersma chats to Aurik about the presentation. 'What do you make of all that?' Boersma asks.

'This is why we need to keep our operation going—it is now more important for the Australians, but for us too. I don't really understand how this commission works, but it looks like the crooked officer knows and has been involved in a lot of international crime fighting. Who knows how much he knows about what we have been doing?'

Like his counterpart Morris, Boersma is at the top of his field. The 43-year-old father of four, church-going devout Protestant has had a stellar career since joining the Dutch police in uniform as a beat cop in 1989.

He did his stint looking at robberies and burglaries, before being given the job of looking into the integrity of a few men within his own force, so he knows what it is like to have a crooked hat.

He made headlines in the 1990s when, armed with a crowbar, he busted into all the lockers in his police station and found weapons, drugs and stolen goods—most of which had been confiscated from criminals, but never registered or surrendered by his men. He was promoted as a team leader in the Serious Crime Agency and there learnt the art of catching top criminals, not so much focusing on the targets, but looking at the periphery first, patiently building a case before striking.

As Commissioner, he will make the final decision on when to strike. He is frustrated by the 'Australian case', since he has enough evidence to arrest the Dutch criminals and charge them with a drug conspiracy. But now that the mole has been identified, he appreciates the need for further investigation. The Australians, he thinks, will not let him down, and will let him know when there's a good time for them both to strike.

The covert Dutch Operation Mayer brief—now running in conjunction with the AFP's Operation Lacerta—is enlarged to take into account the added gravitas of the Australian leak. More resources are dedicated to Aurik's already busy team, working on what had begun as a standard drugs probe.

Aurik and his Mayer detectives had initially been tracking Jan the Dutch sports trainer when they uncovered the fact he had travelled to Australia, and surveillance pointed to him wanting to move a quantity of ecstasy or drug precursors. At that stage, when Aurik contacted Bodel to alert him to the suspect's trip Down Under, it was deemed a standard case of a known drug distributor making a run.

But then Aurik's team makes a vital breakthrough.

One night his surveillance team is sitting off a restaurant in Amsterdam, where their target suspect, Loek, is expected, when a fleet of dark luxury cars pulls up. The windows are heavily tinted and the occupants cannot be seen. In the darkness, their quick scurry into the restaurant also offers little clue as to their identities. It is clearly a meeting between one of Jan's men and three other unknown males, who police suspect are accomplices. Photographs of the suspect figures are taken, but the listening devices fail and nothing more is gleaned.

For several days, officers work from the licence plate numbers of the cars. The cars have been leased to bogus companies linked to shelf companies worth only a few Euros—a sure sign of something a little sinister. Eventually police uncover the names of those behind the cars and type them into a police national database. This points them to something bigger—their original 2002 Operation Merlin, codenamed Operation Tahoe in Australia. It is a startling breakthrough: some of those apparently involved in the criminal enterprise being probed by Operations Mayer and Lacerta have some link to the original Merlin/Tahoe case.

This revelation opens up a wealth of new leads. It is conceivable that all the suspects being probed by the earlier Merlin police team are now also involved in the Mayer case. Not only have the criminals apparently not been scared off by their arrest and failed court prosecution, but they are actively still in the game and have more drugs ready for shipment to Australia.

Boersma looks at the list of names. Many are well-known, leading figures in legitimate business; some are on the national sporting circuit and the world-class poker-playing scene. Suspect Loek is a director of an international investment company; another businessman lives in a castle of sorts in Germany, and Spain.

Having names helps. On another surveillance running sheet, Aurik, who is also an assistant prosecutor and knows the importance of keeping good notes, is able to attach names to events:

I observed a BMW with German registration [S------9] used by [Loek], parked in the parking area of the Brasserie Quality Centre located at Transistorstraat 60 in Almere. About 4.25pm, I observed vehicle drive off with [Loek] and an unidentified male inside. About 4.30pm, I observed three males talking with each other in the parking area. I recognised these as [Fat Ron], [Peter] and [Hogan]. About 4.32pm, I observed [Peter] and [Hogan] step into an AudiA6 with registration [6----N].

'They are just businessmen, legitimate businessmen, not criminals—how come they go into this sort of business?' Boersma asks Aurik. 'It is interesting to know why normal legal businessmen—how come they go into this business? How do they come into contact with these drugs and other people? How come?'

'If we know these things then our job would be easier,' Aurik replies.

'Well that wouldn't be any fun now, would it? muses Boersma. 'I think it's because, being in a circle of people internationally and travelling, they come into contact with other people and come across information. Maybe they feel it's less criminal because it is ephedrine, not cocaine?'

'I don't know, but it is more *potent* than cocaine. Crystal meth is three and a half times more "verslavend" [addictive] than cocaine.'

National prosecutor Cees van Spierenburg, who is now in regular contact with Boersma and Aurik, offers his experienced view during one of their many regular meetings.

'I'm not surprised Merlin suspects are now suspects in this one. These people are only doing these things for the money. Organised crime is trying to earn as much money in the easiest way possible, in the shortest amount of time—so if you are able to sell a tablet for $25 and you are making it for 25 cents and you can send large shipments, you can make a lot of money.

'Whether these businessmen are importers or exporters, they work together for one criminal cause to make money. And everyone in between can make a lot of money—they can make 100 per cent or more on their responsibility in the chain from production to consumption.'

Van Spierenburg reminds them that most criminals can continue to operate from behind bars, so if all their assets are not seized, they will generally continue to operate their racket after serving their time or being found not guilty in court.

Within weeks, back in Sydney, the Lacerta team is intercepting more and more communications between Jalalaty and Standen, and a definite conspiracy is emerging.

Lacerta agents, who have not yet been told about Statice or its brief, cannot believe it when they independently uncover the connection between a senior law enforcer and their target.

It is clear this is not a normal informant–officer relationship. One early theory had it that Jalalaty was spying on criminals and passing information to Standen, but the exchanges of coded emails had more sinister overtones. Police also establish that Standen has in the past formally asked his superiors at the NSW Crime Commission whether he could go into business with Jalalaty, as a legitimate importer of goods, but was knocked back, with bosses frowning on secondary employment as a distraction from his primary professional role.

It is becoming clear Standen is not just acting as a technical adviser or as a 'cockatoo', warning a criminal group of drug detections. It appears he is actively engaged in an importation of drugs.

Morris knows the stakes are high and he can no longer keep the two covert operations separate. Lacerta agents have to be brought into the wider picture. They have to be brought into the 'joke', he thinks.

Morris calls Keelty on his mobile.

'I need to brief you on something ASAP. It's got to be tonight, and not over the phone but face-to-face,' he tells Keelty.

The pair meet at a cafe in the suburb of Campbell in Canberra's inner north, some time after 8pm. Keelty knows the Statice brief has been completed, but the latest Lacerta revelation is staggering: one of the NSW Crime Commission's most senior figures is, potentially, actively engaging in drug trafficking. It is unbelievable.

Critical to the Keelty–Morris conversation is how to move forward, and more importantly, how to inform the NSW Crime Commission. There are competing imperatives. On the one hand the AFP has to maintain strict operational security, but needs the commission's help in the investigation. On the other hand, with so many connections to the AFP of both Standen and Jalalaty, what will happen if the commission discovers one of their own is being investigated by a counterpart law enforcement agency and they have not been told?

Keelty already has a very frosty relationship with the NSW Crime Commission, but that relationship will be irreparable if the commission finds out on its own what is going on.

'It's a dilemma. On the one hand we have to maintain operational secrecy, but on the other, what if we get caught investigating Standen before the job comes to fruition?' Morris asks. 'The stakes are enormously high and we still don't know how many—if any—others are involved.'

'What if the crime commission comes to us and says we've ascertained you're investigating our chief investigator?' Keelty asks rhetorically.

'That's a meeting I wouldn't want to be at,' Morris says, wincing.

'That's a meeting no one would welcome,' Keelty agrees.

It is decided to risk the latter.

'We keep them out at this early stage,' Keelty says finally.

Operational secrecy is paramount, since it must still be assumed that other law enforcers could be involved in the plot. It is Keelty's call, and Morris knows it will be Keelty who will have to break the news to the NSW Crime Commission, one way or another, when the right time comes. Thank God for the chain of command, he thinks.

They know the chances of the police probe being able to run for more than a few weeks is impossible. It is now too big, too many people are involved, including round-the-clock surveillance teams. Here they are investigating a man who is legitimately ringing up AFP personnel almost on a daily basis as part of his work; it is bound to leak that he is himself being investigated.

And there are still legitimate fears that other law enforcers from other agencies may be involved in the conspiracy. If Standen, on a salary package of $247,000 a year, is willing to turn to the dark side, what would a law enforcer on the average $65,000 a year wage be willing to do?

Standen will also be on the lookout for anything unusual in the manner of those he deals with. That is what he is trained to do: be suspicious, find out what people are trying to hide. And with his high-level access to computer files and daily surveillance reports, it is likely he will catch wind of most—if not all—ongoing covert operations.

By July 2007 it is finally decided to merge the two AFP operations—Statice and Lacerta—and create a new super undercover probe, dubbed Operation Octans. It is the largest police team of its kind ever assembled, for what Morris and Keelty believe will be the most sensitive and ambitious covert internal–external investigation mounted in AFP history.

Agents are initially shocked by the existence of the two parallel investigations, but then appreciate why they had each existed in isolation.

The Octans operatives are told the timer has started, and to work fast on stacking up the evidence. They expect Standen or the NSW Crime Commission will find out about the dual probe within months, if not weeks. Some privately believe there has always been something rotten about the commission, that it just can't be trusted. Every intercept, every clue, might be their last before the operation is exposed, and should be treated as such. Everything Standen did should be treated as potentially incriminating. His involvement is now not an issue, and it is no longer a question of *if* but a matter of *why*.

'I've got some news. I've got some extra pieces for our jigsaw puzzle. It's all coming together,' is how Morris announces the merger to his shocked troops. Everyone speculates on how it was the relationship between master, Standen, and servant, Hogan, has flipped. A look at Standen's recent financial transactions gives them a clue.

The head of the NSW Crime Commission, Phillip Bradley, is shocked to say the least at the briefing he receives. Since March 2007, the commission had established a new unit and procedures to centralise the handling of registered informers being dealt with by its staff. The unit, known as G3, was set up on Level 3 of the commission building, and access was extremely limited. Its purpose was to ensure staff integrity and that staff were adhering to regulations surrounding informers. Specifically, it took away the overseeing of informers from individuals such as Standen and instead gave responsibility to a management team.

Some AFP operatives are unhappy with the timing of the G3 unit's creation, complicating their investigation into the commission's top investigator and his association with a criminal informant. Any previous evidence gathered alleging a conspiracy between Standen and Hogan might be ruled invalid if Standen suddenly registers his informant meetings with G3. However, Standen has no intention to register such meetings, as Bradley confirms that Standen has no notification in place. And although Standen is known to be sloppy with record-keeping and paperwork, no one could be that sloppy. Just to be sure, at Bradley's direction, a colleague rings Standen and specifically asks whether Hogan is an active or inactive informer. After some prevarication, Standen confirms Hogan is 'inactive'.

Some weeks later, Bradley advises staff in an email of the need to maintain integrity in the handling of informers. Again this advisory could not have come at a worse time for the AFP staff, who fervently hope the warning will not deter Standen, who is already being carefully watched.

Indeed, the AFP know that Standen has a personal Yahoo account that he accesses at work and home, but he also has access to the Hotmail account all the other conspirators use at random from anywhere. It is this account they need to gain access to—and the only way is through Standen's own computers. Within weeks, federal police covertly install camera devices in Standen's home and work computers that take snapshots of his computer screen every ten seconds. Investigators view these remotely to see what accounts Standen is accessing.

They find five Hotmail email accounts accessed from his work computer at the commission's Kent Street headquarters as well as his home computer, including the email accounts called jojoswitzerland, tuckedupinbed, rentaspace and dnalreztiws ('Switzerland' spelt backwards).

In June 2007, a Dutch builder named Rene Asbeek Brusse (codenamed Bob the Builder) travels firstly to the Congo, then Dubai and later Pakistan, for what he believes is an international negotiation for a cement contract. Brusse happens to be a friend of Jan, who introduced him to Loek, who he said was looking to employ a reliable sales manager of sorts.

Brusse initially thought there never seemed to be much going on and that he got paid for doing nothing, but then he began to travel overseas and meet people.

In an Islamabad hotel, he meets up with countryman Jan and an elderly half-blind man named Abdul who, he jokes later with friends, 'wears a dress', referring to the long Pakistani traditional shirt gown worn by men. On Abdul's bed he sees a document with Dutch telephone numbers, and on which he reads 'pseudoephedrine hydrochloride quality control laboratory certificate of analysis'. As if the around-the-world trip ostensibly for a 'cement' deal isn't unusual enough, Bob the simple builder is now even more suspicious. Then there were those instructions to constantly change his mobile phone SIM card.

He decides to steal the document. When he is back home in Holland, he looks up the chemical compound on Google and realises that what he inadvertently has been trying to ship in a container of cement and rice is in fact a drug precursor.

He telephones, then meets, Loek and has a furious argument.

'See,' Loek patiently explains. 'If you purchased something for 50 cents and then sent it to the other side of the world, it has to be making one Euro, otherwise don't do it. If you take a product from Albert Heijn [a supermarket chain] and the product costs 50 cents, then you couldn't have purchased it at Albert for 50 cents from the other side of the world—then people would say that is not right. Do you see that?'

Brusse simply responds 'thanks but no thanks'. He is told to get rid of the analysis report, but he doesn't: he is already in too deep, and it is his insurance should the cartel turn on him.

Despite his apparent reluctance, Brusse will go on to make three trips to the Congo, five to Pakistan, two to the United Arab Emirates and one to Kenya at the behest of the Dutch cartel. During one trip to Pakistan, he opens a bank account under the name Global Biz, which is to be the central international money transfer point for operations.

As warrants are issued to have listening devices put in place on suspects in Australia, one of the early calls recorded is Jalalaty speaking to an associate: 'When they import the drug, right, it comes in a form and then they pour the acid over it and the product cleans it, crystallises it and it uses hundreds of litres of it . . .'

Further investigation shows Jalalaty has stockpiled forty 25-litre drums of acetone in his warehouse, alongside pallets of B-52 energy drinks. He also purchases a large bladder and tap to use for pouring acetone—the acid for crystallising the drug.

If there were still any police doubts about Jalalaty's involvement, they are dissolved by the acid.

4

Reservoir Dogs

Mark William Standen was born on 1 March 1957 as one of six boys in the inner-western Sydney suburb of Burwood. He hoped to join the RAAF by the time he left St Patrick's College in Strathfield in 1974. One brother was a commercial pilot and another an airline steward, and young Standen loved the thought of flight and the way fighter pilots in particular were held in such high regard.

But instead, in June the following year, he joined the Federal Bureau of Narcotics, then an arm of the Australian Customs Service, as an investigator tracking drugs being smuggled through Sydney's busy wharfs.

He was young, brash and confident and superiors recognised his skill and determination to weed out corruption. He would go far in the service, he was told.

Three years later, in February 1978, a bomb exploded outside the Sydney Hilton Hotel, the venue for that year's Commonwealth Heads of Government regional meeting, killing three people and injuring eight others.

A later review of the attack and Australia's law enforcement capabilities, by former head of Scotland Yard, Sir Robert Mark, identified Australia's then woeful ability to meet the challenges of terrorism and international cross-border crime.

There was talk of a new 'super force' of law enforcers that would be entrusted with overseeing Commonwealth crime fighting. It was an exciting prospect for officers such as Standen.

But in May 1979, as the federal government announced the planned formation of the Australian Federal Police, an act of complacency by the young officer threatened his dream.

That month, he and two other narcotics officers had raided the house of a well-known drug dealer in Bondi. There they found eighteen foils of hashish, but little else. It was a disappointing result and the dealer was not charged.

Two weeks later, however, Standen realised he still had the drugs in a drawer. It was a major slip. He told a supervising officer, who knew the breach would effectively end his subordinate's career. It was a stupid mistake, but young Standen was a professional, clever and tenacious officer who had a bright future in law enforcement.

The pair decided to flush the evidence down a toilet in their Old Customs House offices, then falsify entries in the bureau's log book about the evidence seized, and destroy a signed statement by the suspect about what was found in his apartment. They decided the bust never happened; it wasn't a large amount anyway, and too small to fall under any federal drugs laws. And the dealer was never charged, so it was all dead in the water.

But then NSW Police arrested the same suspect on an unrelated matter—and he happened to mention in passing that he had already been raided by another law enforcement agency, and had surrendered his drugs to those narcotics agents just months earlier. An internal investigation ensued.

Standen and his supervisor were charged under the Public Service Act for destruction of evidence and failing to report the bust. Recommendations were made that the pair not be allowed to join the proposed AFP force when it was formalised in October that year. The ban was signed by the federal narcotics bureau's commissioner, Sir Colin Woods.

Standen was furious and appealed against the move that would have effectively ended his career. By October 1979, Standen was told he would, after all, be given his new AFP badge, after the charge and ban were dropped due to 'indecision' by the Department of Administrative Services on whether to uphold the action.

The director of operations at the narcotics bureau, Brian Bates, was surprised by the decision, but in all the amalgamation upheavals the issue was not pursued. At least, not that year.

Standen then moved to the Sydney offices of the AFP's 35-person drug investigation unit in Redfern's landmark TNT twin towers complex.

They were heady days. The AFP was powerful—more powerful than its NSW counterparts—and ran high-profile international drugs crime investigations that blurred the distinction between criminal and police. They had many informers, and often called on state counterparts to turn a blind eye to some offences in the hope of exposing others.

'It was like living inside a grubby episode of *Miami Vice*,' was how one officer would later describe the unit's ways.

Only a young NSW Police detective by the name of Roger Rogerson had a higher policing profile in the community—and even the AFP was in awe of the 'Dodger's' ability to make big busts and, on the face of it, weed out organised drugs trafficking and money laundering.

In 1982, the Stewart Royal Commission into corruption and drug trafficking raised Standen's name as a minor example of something 'unquestionably dishonest', but by then Standen was recognised as an exceptional officer with an uncanny knack of cracking cases and criminals. His forensic analysis of a criminal's modus operandi was second to none. The Royal Commission had bigger fish to fry, and the episode was filed away again, despite Standen's name and the 'drugs in the toilet' issue being raised in federal parliament during question time by the Opposition Labor Senator Nick Bolkus.

In the early 1990s, Standen married and he and his wife had the first of their four children. He had by then been seconded to the National Crime Authority for two years, where he again impressed superiors as a chief investigator. He was able to attract quality informants and pass on good intelligence on the burgeoning illicit drugs scene.

The only issue of concern was his gambling. He was becoming a heavy gambler, losing tens of thousands of dollars on the horses—but then others in the force were living hard-drinking, hard-gambling lives, so his vice was just accepted by his colleagues. Standen racked up debts, but continued to live the fast life.

Once when he was still at the AFP, he had attended a training course at the police college in the Canberra suburb of Barton. Each officer was given a *per diem* allowance, on top of accommodation, to spend on food, drink and essentials while away from their home base. On the weekend ahead of the training program, Standen went to the TAB in nearby Manuka and blew his entire week's allowance on a number of horse and dog races.

He laughed off the loss on the Monday when he began the course; colleagues felt sorry for him and passed the hat around to collect some money for him to live on. He was, after all, a mentor to many—or as one friend put it, almost a 'godfather figure' for many detectives.

'He was just so charismatic and full of life—it was the sort of thing people were happy to do,' one colleague recalled.

On his return to Sydney he continued to take a punt and was often seen watching the racing screens at hotels in the southern end of the city, near police headquarters.

During the early 1990s his star continued to shine and he could do no wrong—or at least no wrong in his own eyes. He developed a cavalier approach to work and thought little of stretching the law in pursuit of a criminal. He was hyperactive, eager. He would go out and retrieve listening devices before warrants expired, or move on criminals before logistics were fully in place.

He did have one bitter disappointment, when he missed out on a major promotion. He was a sergeant heading the drugs unit and had an opportunity to rise to superintendent in the professional standards area, but missed out. It was his first perceived professional setback and he didn't like it. Colleagues recall his mood changed, and it was weeks, if not months, before he was himself again.

But Standen's stellar career moved on. He worked largely within the drugs unit, but spent eighteen months in Canberra assisting the investigation into the driveway-execution murder of AFP Assistant Commissioner Colin Winchester, and prior to that almost two years on secondment to the public prosecutor's office, investigating the infamous Bottom of the Harbour tax scheme fraud. He eventually made it into internal affairs, where he stayed about two years.

Two years after his 1993 move to the National Crime Authority, the federal government decided to merge the organisation with the AFP, and Standen had to be re-sworn as an AFP officer. He remained there another eighteen months and rose to the rank of detective superintendent. His debts were already big, and he stunned colleagues when he took a voluntary redundancy package offered by the AFP to thin out the ranks of its upper echelons—then joined the NSW Crime Commission, which had been formed a decade earlier. His new six-figure salary package was almost double what he had earned in the AFP. It was a decent wage generally, but particularly for a crime fighter who normally came under the public service awards.

The NSW Crime Commission was looking for good investigators, particularly in the wake of the Wood Royal Commission, which had gutted the NSW Police ranks by exposing corruption among some of its most senior officers. Standen's new position as a permanent investigator was flexible, and differed from traditional investigators who were usually on secondment from other law enforcement agencies.

The NSW Crime Commission was born from the ground-breaking 1980–1984 Costigan Royal Commission into law enforcement corruption. After its report was handed down, the federal government created the National Crime Authority, but the NSW government wanted its own body with similar sweeping powers to look into corruption.

The NSW Crime Commission was set up on 20 January 1986 as a secretive statutory body, dubbed by some in law enforcement as a 'star chamber', with sweeping royal commission–style powers and no direct oversight.

While other law enforcement agencies such as the AFP, National Crime Authority, Australian Crime Commission, Australian Security Intelligence Organisation and even the

Australian Secret Intelligence Service were being forced to be more transparent and answerable to internal and external bodies and committees—and ultimately, the public—the NSW Crime Commission had no such impediment.

Under the NSW Crime Commission Act, no one has a right to call a lawyer, hearings can be heard in secret, and it is even an offence to reveal you have even been called to the NSW Crime Commission to give evidence.

The NSW Crime Commission can compel people to give statements, even if they are not suspected of a crime, can tap phones or use other forms of listening devices, and can offer criminals extraordinary concessions—from large cash rewards for help, or even pay their expenses and household bills. It can give criminals protection, new identities and even a new start overseas.

The NSW government has always been pleased with the crime commission's creation as it brings in a large amount of money from its massive assets seizures. In one year alone it raked in more than $20 million for the state coffers. Most of the seized monies were brokered between the commission and the criminals, who surrender half their ill-gotten gains in exchange for being left alone. The commission's seizures have always been high, but its arrests measurably low in comparison; it's just how it worked. Most of the criminals either live on as informants, effectively halving their proceeds of crime—legally laundered by the state through the crime commission's sanction—or just go quietly, grateful to get away with some earnings. The booty they bestow to the commission in exchange for freedom includes items such as luxury boats, cars, mansions, gold bars, cellar racks of fine wine, and even sacks full of casino chips.

For five years the NSW Crime Commission had three

commissioners, but two resigned and were not replaced; legislation was changed to leave just one commissioner: Phillip Bradley, a former federal prosecutor. Bradley joined the commission in 1989, as a 37-year-old, having also worked at the National Crime Authority and the Stewart Royal Commission, and became its chief by mid-1993, enjoying unprecedented power and influence.

In 2004 the state government secretly planned to fold the commission, and the newly created state police oversight body the Police Integrity Commission, into the overarching Australian Crime Commission, as a cost-saving exercise and to alleviate jurisdictional clashes. Bradley was to then be made the new Australian Crime Commission chief, but both moves never happened, although he would briefly act in the dual role of chief of both commissions simultaneously.

But rather than the NSW Crime Commission folding, it was given even greater powers—including immunity from Freedom of Information laws, and the ability to issue warrants within minutes.

The NSW Crime Commission's extraordinary power and operation as a state intelligence agency suited Standen's cocky and cavalier approach to crime fighting. He ensured his informants were well looked after, and many of those he kept on his books could help him further progress his career within the commission.

He was given his own team of analysts, lawyers and financial investigators, and also free rein to make confiscations, which at the time of his hiring amounted to $5 million a year. His specific brief was to confiscate even more criminal assets—and he did, being largely credited with reaching the $20 million milestone within a few years.

Standen was put in charge of the commission's Gymea Reference, which among other things was a specific brief to tackle organised crime and drug trafficking and manufacturing, and to identify current or former police or government officials suspected of protecting criminals or their unlawful behaviour. The busts from the high-profile brief were big.

Within a short space of time it was evident Standen was not just an investigator, but a leader with a wide circle of contacts—both criminal and lawful—and access to the highest echelons of law enforcement. Indeed, he knew AFP Police Commissioner Mick Keelty personally, from their days as investigators at the inception of the AFP, as well as top Customs staff.

As an assistant director of investigations, there was very little Standen did not know about crime in NSW, or even the national and international drug operations being run by counterpart agencies. Through his work, he even came to expose, in his words, 'corrupt relations' between known criminals, waterfront workers, police and government officials. He knew police—particularly those working undercover—often had to tread a fine line in their relations with criminals, but corrupt officers deserved to be exposed. However, his failure to keep an accurate record of contact reports with suspects and informers was a continuing issue. He knew it and so did his managers.

Nevertheless, Standen was infuriated when an increase to his already substantial remuneration was deferred for a year, or until he reached a satisfactory level of note-taking performance. It was a blot in his career, but again it didn't deter him. Nor did it affect his potential. An internal staff performance report by Phillip Bradley dated 24 April 1998 concluded: 'Mark has potential because he has a high level of intelligence, a great depth of experience and obvious ability in a number of areas in which the commission is involved. These include criminal investigations, financial investigations, and the use of coercive powers. Mark falls down in his organisational skills. This is evidenced by the state of his office, his inability to meet deadlines, and the lack of compliance with requirements for documents to be produced including reports to the Ombudsman, effectiveness reports and like matters.' That said, Bradley told Standen in writing that he and another investigator, Tim O'Connor, were in line for the chairmanship, to take over the running of the commission.

By 2003, ten years after joining the commission, Standen was known as a fearsome investigator.

Sydney hotelier Brad Evans discovered just how fearsome when he ran across him that year. Evans ran the Three Wise Monkeys bar in George Street, a popular after-work hangout for AFP and NSW Police officers, when he was arrested and taken to the commission's offices.

There he was spoken to by the NSW Crime Commission's solicitor, before Standen entered the room and urged him to turn informer against two other men conspiring to import up to 30 kilograms of cocaine through Sydney Airport.

'You help us and you'll only do about eighteen months in a nice work farm,' Evans claimed Standen told him.

'You won't have any costs, you won't get any fines from the crime commission, you will get your life back. But if you don't play ball I will fucking destroy you. I will destroy you financially and I will destroy your life.'

Standen told the publican he had sixty seconds to decide; Evans said he was not interested.

'The fucking gloves are off,' was all Standen apparently said before walking out of the room.

In 2003, a handwritten appraisal of Standen by his immediate boss, John Giorgiutti, noted: 'Doing a great job holding a big team together. Especially with NSWP + AFP. A team likely to be a failure without him. Value for tax payer dollar. Still some room for improvement in organisational skills but forgiven because of volume and complexity of work.' It was about this time, or not much later, that Standen was investigating a drugs case that promised to be the biggest of his career, and the biggest ever busted by the NSW Crime Commission.

Since 2004, an informant he had groomed, codenamed Tom, had been allowed to continue working as a major cocaine supplier in exchange for supplying Standen and the crime commission with intelligence on the major underworld figures in the drug trade.

In the six months before he rolled over, he told the commission he had sold more than 200 kilograms of cocaine as the right-hand man for senior career criminals, including Mr Big, Michael Hurley, and former rugby league star Les Mara. Standen had been after Hurley and Mara for almost ten years.

In February 2005, Standen gave Tom the green light to sell up to 7 kilograms of cocaine, worth more than $1 million. It was an extraordinary concession.

Agents accompanied the dealer as he went to bushland in Wahroonga and dug up his stash, before returning to Standen's office and repackaging the haul for street sale.

The AFP had been initially involved in the covert operation, but disapproved of allowing the cocaine to be sold and withdrew from direct involvement in that aspect of the case. An AFP diary note at the time simply recorded that the 'AFP cannot support further sale or condone the previous sale'.

So it was up to Standen and his colleagues to watch as Tom sold the drugs across Sydney, including to dealers and junkies in Newtown, Kings Cross, Maroubra, Rushcutters Bay and Five Dock. Only 1 kilogram was ever recovered—by Victorian police months later. In the ensuing months, however, high-profile crims Mick Hurley and Les Mara and nine other men were arrested for conspiracy to import cocaine from South America, under what became known as Operation Mocha.

Some law enforcers were staggered by Standen's 'above the law' approach, and particularly his attitude in arguing that the benefits of allowing the drugs to be sold outweighed the negatives.

One week earlier the NSW Police Commissioner at the time, Ken Moroney, had sanctioned the sale, as did the NSW Crime Commission chief, former lawyer Phillip Bradley. Andrew Scipione, the current NSW Police Commissioner, was also involved in those discussions.

Under law enforcement rules, a controlled operation cannot take place where life is in danger. 'But no one has ever died from taking cocaine,' Standen argued with law enforcers who questioned the sale.

A year later, he would repeat the claim in court during the committal hearing for one of the men arrested. 'We did some research into the health information relating to cocaine use,' he told magistrate David Heilpern. 'There are some health issues in relation to its continued use. There are no recorded deaths from cocaine use, which is one of the things we researched.'

Magistrate Heilpern found the claim staggering. 'I felt my jaw dropping at that evidence,' he told the court in April 2006.

'One conclusion that can be reached is that these reasons are not cogent or genuine. It is difficult to accept that someone who has been involved in drug law enforcement for all his working life could genuinely conclude that cocaine is such a benign substance.'

Bradley, the NSW Crime Commission head, was also indirectly criticised. 'On the face of it this is most troubling. How, one might ask, can these senior crime investigators come to the conclusion that the supply of 7 kilograms of cocaine in circumstances where it is likely that the cocaine will end up in the hands of users on the street does not seriously endanger the health of those users?'

A month later, the case against the eleven men arrested for conspiring to import the cocaine from South America was on the verge of collapse, with the drug sale deemed potentially 'illegal and improper'. Separately, lawyers for the accused lodged papers in the NSW Supreme Court to sue Bradley, as the NSW Crime Commission's chief, for allowing the apparent breach.

The finger was also pointed at Standen for creating the controversy. On the one hand he had been praised for bringing down a massive drugs conspiracy—including two of Australia's biggest traffickers, Hurley and Mara—but on the other hand, his total disregard for the law to reach that end made him a figure of scorn. At this point, internal commission staff appraisals were not compulsory and Standen elected not to have one. Since his last one in 2003, he had considered himself beyond such internal reviews and he was getting annual pay rises anyway. He didn't think his work needed extra scrutiny. It is perhaps no coincidence that 2003 marked the beginning of his improper relationship with Hogan and a shift to the dark side of crime.

For his efforts, Tom ended up with money, protection and

indemnity against a range of offences, including supplying drugs, firearms, bribing police and kidnapping.

Meanwhile, relations between the NSW Crime Commission and the AFP all but collapsed. The management committee for the NSW Crime Commission is led by three or four people, including the commission chief, the head of the AFP, the NSW Police Commissioner and the chair of the Australian Crime Commission—but AFP chief Keelty abandoned these management meetings due to governance issues with the commission.

By May 2006, the controversy had reached State Parliament, with Greens MP Lee Rhiannon calling, 'as a matter of urgency', for the NSW Crime Commission to be overhauled and placed under some form of regulation. She specifically named Standen in Parliament and his claims that no deaths had occurred from cocaine use.

'This House deserves the opportunity—indeed, has the responsibility—to create the opportunity to bring the NSW Crime Commission up to the 21st-century standard of statutory authorities,' Rhiannon argued.

MP Sylvia Hale then raised allegations of underhand assets seizures by the commission, and suggested Bradley was also thwarting a probe into the unlawful use of listening-device warrants.

A furious debate ensued, with Members from all sides of the House debating the merits of how the NSW Crime Commission operated.

The Labor Treasurer and former Police Minister, Michael Costa, sprang to the defence of the commission.

'The crime commission is well managed and is highly regarded by law enforcement agencies throughout the country,' he declared as he used his numbers to defeat Rhiannon's motion for a commission review.

Officers from the NSW Police and AFP dubbed the NSW Crime Commission the 'untouchables', with more criminal informants, seizures and power than they could ever dream of.

In 2007 Standen bought a property on the NSW Central Coast, a two-hour drive north of Sydney, worth more than $730,000. He borrowed up to 97 per cent of the financing. On his $247,000 a year wage, banks felt secure lending him the money, but they were unaware his gambling had also spiralled out of control.

Standen's addiction was an open secret within the NSW Crime Commission's walls, as it had been to those close to him during his AFP days.

Some said he had lost tens of thousands of dollars at five separate TABs and the poker machines in one infamous long-weekend holiday period. He would laugh off concerns by colleagues and deny he was a gambler, saying he was more an *ad hoc* punter who was more successful than they knew.

In reality, his disposable income each week was about $70—the rest of his wage spent on gambling, repaying debts, or the secret lavish lifestyle he led away from home. Home life was difficult for Standen. His wife had undergone treatment for alcohol addiction. She suffered depression and would often be floridly psychotic, her mood swinging from aggression and anger to paranoia. The problems at home were so significant a psychiatrist would later report Standen's situation had elements of 'battered spouse syndrome', though there was no suggestion that she physically attacked him. Racking up debts worth tens of thousands of dollars became mundane to him in the midst of his difficult home life.

While his wife was sick and in and out of care and not at home to manage or track their finances, Standen was spending his wage and racking up thousands of dollars a month in debt on his credit cards and on an assortment of girlfriends. He would tell his family he had to work back late and would need to stay in Sydney somewhere—since his home was a two-hour drive away—but instead he would take a girlfriend out on the town, and either stay with her or in an upmarket hotel.

He had at least three girlfriends at various times, including a former AFP officer and a model, and they had expensive tastes. He was always a bit showy with his money when he wanted to be charming with the ladies. The incredible self-confidence— almost narcissism—he exuded at work operated in overdrive after hours.

One young girlfriend, Louise Baker, had worked in the NSW Crime Commission's top-secret area of telephone intercepts since September 2005. Standen was almost brazen about his affair with the attractive twenty-something junior colleague, who worked under him in Operation Gymea, and some other officers were concerned.

Baker was completely smitten. He would take her to top restaurants and always pay cash—even when the bill for just the two of them topped $500, which was usually once or twice a month. He regularly bought her expensive gifts. She knew he was married, but he spoke about the apparently failed relationship.

If Standen was worried about the workplace affair and his dwindling finances, he didn't show it. Such was his confidence that he convinced his friend and colleague Tony Newton to take out a second mortgage on his home and lend him the capital—just until his plan to import high-energy drinks came to fruition.

There may have been a dream to move into the drinks business, but it never materialised, and by the end of the whole sorry business Newton would simply find himself $210,000 worse off.

Newton had joined the AFP in 1987, and about a decade later joined Standen in the NSW Crime Commission as an investigations manager. The pair became close friends and over the years would often drive to work in the CBD together, since they both lived on the Central Coast. The long drive would be filled with personal stories about their respective families, and also Standen's desire to start an export business. He told Newton about Bill and Di Jalalaty's meats and fine foods business, and their plans to import goods, including Bavaria non-alcoholic beer and B-52 energy drinks.

It was towards the end of 2006 that Standen told his mate how he wanted to buy his own home and stop renting, but lenders were being cautious. He had seen a $737,000 Bateau Bay property he liked. The 52-year-old Newton offered him a loan of $200,000.

Standen asked if he could make it $210,000, since he needed to buy a flat-screen TV and other furniture. It would only be a short-term loan, and would be paid back in full when Jalalaty made some money from refinancing his business and landing a big import deal. In the meantime, Standen would make the interest payments so Newton wasn't out of pocket.

But the months wore on, and only a few token deposits were made. Newton was initially too polite to mention it; he trusted Standen implicitly.

Standen, meanwhile, went out and leased two new cars, a Subaru WRX and a Toyota Sportiva.

*

Some who knew his demeanour and lifestyle considered Standen a sociopath—it was all about suiting himself, telling people what they wanted to hear, playing people, and doing it all his way.

Many privately believed he would have to come unstuck eventually—if for nothing else, for his 'fly by the seat of his pants' approach to paperwork. Sure, he was the best investigator, but management just tolerated the fact that he constantly failed to adhere to policy surrounding paperwork. When he met an informer, he was meant to complete a contact advice form outlining the time and place where he met the informer, their codename and information obtained. All the reports were then to be forwarded to Phillip Bradley.

Standen just never got around to doing that with his regular informers—and certainly with Hogan he had no intention of doing so.

By the start of 2007, Standen is at least $1 million in debt, with his mortgage and other debts. His family never suspect he is in any serious difficulty—he is so confident, and he also says he has a plan to make them significantly rich.

In reality, he goes to the local TAB and places trifecta bets on races in Sydney, Melbourne and Brisbane. With all his different bank accounts, it isn't uncommon for him to make multiple withdrawals from the one ATM machine near the betting shop. He wins some and loses most, but it doesn't matter: he has friends, some of whom he considers mobile money-dispensers. And there's always that nice stash left in the sports bag at the back of Jalalaty's cupboard.

In January, Standen audaciously agrees to travel to Dubai with

Jalalaty and meet up with Hogan. He makes a mental note not to tell his superiors, a move he knows breaks every rule in the book in meeting up with informants. Indeed, he has already bent that rule a few times.

He decides to take his girlfriend Louise Baker, or his 'Princess' as he likes to call her. Jalalaty agrees to pay for both their flights—business class tickets at $5370 apiece. He tells Baker it is a business trip as part of a blossoming friendship with businessman Bill Jalalaty and they are going to meet potential backers.

Louise is excited. Since August 2006, just weeks after they began their relationship, she has been keeping a diary, titled 'Our Year Together', noting details of her relationship with Standen, and she knows some interesting notations are ahead.

In the journal she has jotted down dinner at one of the world's top restaurants, Tetsuya's in Sydney, as well as stays with Mark at a range of luxury hotels including the Sheraton in the city, and even shopping trips he paid for, including a stopover at a diamond wholesaler. There is also the $1250 Tiffany necklace, handbags, including a Fendi priced at $2485 and a Chanel at $2980, and a $4590 ring. Mark also paid for her accommodation on his credit card for a trip she made to India.

Suddenly her diary moves from just references to Sydney to shopping in Emirates Mall in Dubai, more gifts from her boyfriend, looking out over the Arabian Sea, a facial at a Givenchy Spa, a four-wheel-drive desert tour, and a dinner at the Marrakech Restaurant to meet the mysterious Mr Hogan.

Standen tells her that Hogan had been a crime commission informant but is now a friend, and is in Dubai, possibly to seek citizenship.

On that particular day, 25 January, she writes: 'one and only Mirage for lunch looking over the Arabian Sea. Played tennis then dinner at Marrakesh Restaurant with Bill and [Hogan] (who thought I wasn't to be trusted).' In Hogan's mind, she isn't.

Jalalaty, Standen and Baker are at the restaurant when Hogan arrives, and instantly the mood seems to change.

''Ello lud (hello lad),' the accented Hogan says, extending his hand to Standen, in his standard greeting.

He suddenly sees Baker and regards her as a pointless distraction. She is also law enforcement and Hogan thinks that if it all turns to shit, she'll be a material witness to an important meeting. Bit of a sort though, so Standen is doing okay.

He ignores her from the moment he meets her and speaks to the others as if she isn't there. She notes that he would never make eye contact with her. But the mood changes when all conversations are drowned out by sudden music. There are many patrons in the restaurant, but for some reason they have been seated near a band of Arabian musicians. They laugh at the ridiculously loud music—it is a light point matched only by the poor quality of wine that is then brought out. The group finish their dinner after about an hour and adjourn to a nearby bar. Some work talk is discussed, but not much. There will be other opportunities to talk business during the ten-day trip.

Louise later asks Standen about Hogan and why he apparently doesn't like her. He says it's probably because she is law enforcement and he was once a criminal. She presses him and asks why he would meet up with an ex-informant anyway, and he tells her that Hogan wants to be a legit businessman, and invest in legit businesses such as Jalalaty's.

As she sleeps in each morning, the trio meet downstairs in the hotel cafe and discuss their real business plan.

*

At the same time, Dutch drug traffickers are also conspiring. They had dispatched Hogan to Dubai to have the meeting with the Australians to firm up the plot and discuss in detail their lucrative goal: the re-establishment of a regular smuggling route to Australia.

When Standen returns from his trip he tells his brothers he has met a man in Dubai and has begun looking at setting up an import business with him.

'We're going to bring products, the B-52 drinks, into Australia,' Standen tells one of his brothers. He has spoken about the drinks before, but now it sounds for real.

'That's fantastic,' the brother replies.

'I tell you we're going to make a squillion dollars. We are going to do cement, sugar, timber—we've got all these plans.'

'Wow that's fantastic. Finally someone in the family really made it, too good you, that's great.'

'Yeah plenty, there will be money everywhere, plenty of money.'

'That's so great.'

Another brother then emails Standen saying he has just heard the news that he's venturing into some 'wheeling and dealing'.

'I hope it goes great for you and makes a motza,' he writes.

Standen's buoyancy subsides when his boss Bradley calls him in and questions him about his trip—asking where he has been on his holiday, who with, and what he did.

Standen is anxious, but confidently says he took Louise and met with businessman Bill Jalalaty, who he helps in business from time to time, but there's 'nothing happening' in that area at the moment.

'If he wants you to do anything in the future, or if you intend to do something with him in the future, tell me first. It would need my approval—and that's not likely to be forthcoming,' Bradley tells him.

He then asks Standen about his new home, and whether his arrangements with the mortgagee rely on secondary employment. Standen says it doesn't, but doesn't mention the Newton money.

Bradley then tells Standen he has decided to second Baker to the Independent Commission Against Corruption (ICAC) to work in the assessments area.

Standen is furious. He returns to holiday leave for another three weeks in protest. During this time he continues to see Baker as well as complete a scuba diving course, and continue studying for a law degree that he has spent the best part of a decade trying to finish. His affair isn't bothering anyone—except Bradley, it seems. It makes no difference, he thinks; soon he will have all the money he wants and won't have to work for the commission anymore.

One text to Baker hints at the funds to come. 'Honey you know how to get the most out of a holiday, retain those skills within twenty weeks we will hit Bora or Maldives. I know it's longer than we planned but being realistic. Can't wait though plenty of fun to be had in the meantime.'

Louis Aurik's 'Team 5'—made up of career detectives from the police force and the Dutch tax office—has worked together on numerous other cases. Testimony to this is the number of maps pinned to the walls of the large office in their plain headquarters in the south of Amsterdam.

A map of Europe hangs on one wall; a larger and more prominent one of Turkey hangs on another. Turkey had recently been the target for a large-scale export of ecstasy from Holland, which his team had been investigating. The number of cheap flights and British tourists to the country had created the market there, but the source of the drugs had been identified in Holland and dealt with, and they had got a decent result. There would be more attempted drug exports to Turkey and it seemed the map was almost a permanent fixture these days.

There were operations too in Japan and the Philippines, the former country particularly emerging as a booming target for illicit synthetic drugs.

Team 5's results are always pretty good, but nothing ever to dwell on: you complete one job, hand off a brief to prosecutors, then get told what happens to the targets later. There is little media publicity about the team's victories. Even a big case barely raises an eyebrow here: the public is just bored with drug stories out of Holland.

Aurik has seen many changes within the Netherlands Police Agency (Korps Landelijke Politiediensten) over the years, and specifically to the National Crime Squad—the top department within the agency. It has been evolving as crime itself evolves.

The National Crime Squad in its current state has been operating for only a few years, but attributes its success rate to its unique structure.

Unlike other police forces in the world, the Dutch detective teams do everything themselves, from carrying out surveillance, doing the research, planting and then recording conversations from listening devices, to ultimately making the arrest.

Other forces have separate police sections for different roles, and become specialists in those functions. But the Dutch prefer to keep all aspects of a case within the team holding the case file—better security that way.

When newcomers join his bureau, Aurik often explains why it is so important each member handles all aspects of their case rather than outsource to other departments.

'With detective work, you work on somebody and from that moment you are living his life,' he tells them.

'When you only hear him with tapes, you get one idea of him, but when you are also doing surveillance, you get a complete picture—a complete view of his life—and you can make good decisions. When he says "I'm going over to Mr X's house", straight away, in two seconds, you know and go "ah he's going there and I know why". We combine all parts, everything is live.'

Jan Boersma uses a similar speech when he mentors young recruits.

'It's nice if you are a detective here: you make photos, you make videos, you arrest, you wire them and from all this you get a good picture of what it is you are fighting against,' he tells them. 'That is real policing.'

In recent years, many of those the team has taped, tracked and followed have been exporting drugs to Australia. It is becoming more and more a problem as the drugs market continues to expand.

The team works closely with Cees van Spierenburg, the Dutch national prosecutor of synthetic drugs cases. In the years he has been in the job, he has seen the true emergence of only one country as the world's largest market for synthetic drugs: Australia. Nowhere in the world are synthetic drugs such as ecstasy and ice worth more on the street. Coupled with a growing number of users and general lack of drug, it has become a high-demand product.

He has an encyclopedic knowledge of drug movements and

likes to tell people how it is. The Netherlands and Belgium, van Spierenburg explains, are accustomed to detecting the manufacture of drugs, and the precursor chemicals to produce those drugs, including PMK (methylene-dioxyphenyl propanol). The precursors come from Pakistan, India and China, and are either shipped directly to countries wanting to produce their own drugs, or to holding nations such as Mexico and the Congo, for storage and later distribution. Criminals have to be inventive when it comes to storing their illicit product. There is a Dutch law enforcement saying that criminals producing drugs have two enemies—police and other criminals, with both equally as intent on disrupting their business.

He also explains to the crime fighters why Australia is increasingly emerging as important to their work. Since 2000, both the illicit shipments to Australia of ecstasy and ice, and the chemicals to make them, have increased dramatically.

In 2005, the biggest shipment of ecstasy in history was dispatched to Australia—a record 5.6 tonnes, worth more than $600 million. Police probed the case for three years and discovered that the Dutch-made drugs had been shipped to Australia by the Italian Mafia, based both in Italy and the NSW town of Griffith. It wasn't until late 2008 that arrests would be made.

'The shipments to Australia are increasing, and we are now talking about millions of tablets going there,' he tells colleagues.

'When you talk about shipments of millions of tablets, those are the major shipments in the world. They are all going to Australia because Australians are using the drug—there is a market. If there is no market, there are no shipments. It simply is a question of supply and demand, that's it. But fighting organised crime you need time. If you go for it, the man and the kilos, you can't find the top of the organised crime network.'

On this point Aurik can't agree enough. He now realises the longer the case runs the more complex it appears to get. Merlin was a good operation, but Mayer is like nothing he has ever seen.

He is in some respects secretly envious of the AFP. They know their target. Aurik and his team only have half the targets identified, and even then it is a daily battle to establish who is who on a given day.

The alleged criminals always use codenames for each other and it frustrates Aurik's team. They change names almost daily, and the names are often based on the most random circumstance—a man wearing a suit could be known on that day as Mr Suit. Or the name could be based on the colour of their hair or clothing—Mr Red or Mr Blue. It's like the 1992 Quentin Tarantino crime film *Reservoir Dogs*, he tells colleagues, where the criminals had no real names, just descriptions.

Every day he and his men listen to telephone taps and have to establish who Mr Blond is meeting when he speaks to Mr Brown or Mr Tall and his friend Mr Short, otherwise known as Mr Suit. Sometimes they just call themselves John, Dirk or Daniel, or other random names. It is mostly Loek's idea—he likes nicknames—but everyone plays along. The man the gang calls 'The Shoe' is the chemist for the syndicate, responsible for creating the drugs. Even the locations of meeting places have codenames, although once figured out they are easy to place under surveillance since their codenames did not change. When detectives turn up undercover, they never know who to expect to be gathering for a meeting—except for Loek, a legal arms dealer who often travels the world selling armoured vehicle parts to armies. They have always had a good fix on him, and eventually through wire taps on his phone they begin to form a family tree of suspects. At the top of the tree sit Loek and Foxtrot.

The Reservoir Dogs, as the police refer to them, also use counter-surveillance measures, such as when Jan the sports trainer shadowed François on his mission to Antwerp with flour sacks full of drugs. The group also change mobile phone SIM cards every month. Not that they speak much on the phones anyway—just a vague call with little more than a hello and agreement to meet somewhere. Lots of talk about shipments too, but you can't prove they are anything other than what they are said to be.

The operations of the Reservoir Dogs are essentially compartmentalised, with not everyone in the scheme knowing who else is involved in the different aspects of the plot. Only their leaders, including the principals, know all the players. There are spin-off plots too.

While tracking Mayer suspects, Team 5 had come across another of their plots involving a large amount of hashish. It was a tough decision, but because of the circumstances the drugs had to be seized and arrests made. In any case the criminals themselves would have been suspicious if they were not arrested. But the Reservoir Dog principals were undeterred and continued with their plans for Australia, much to the relief of the police.

After the Mayer case hits a milestone of 250 logged surveillance reports and 100 wire taps, Aurik has to front his boss Boersma to appeal for more time.

'It is very complex, but the longer it goes, the more we know—and I don't think the Australians are ready yet,' Aurik tells his frustrated boss.

'This is important to any court case that we get as much as possible. This is a good job, a long job, an important job—a job that the National Crime Squad is built for.'

'I agree this is what we are built for, but how long can we

realistically let this run for?' Boersma replies. 'I mean there are a lot of other cases we need to look into. We haven't got the luxury to let this run forever. We have a lot of cases here and this is just one of them.'

'Not forever, just for now. If the Australians don't get their man, this is bad for us all and everything is wasted.'

It always comes back to the suspect Standen, and Boersma cannot deny it is a crucial factor in letting the case continue. But he too is under pressure to get results and to move on the backlog of cases building up. He is assured Operation Mayer will be over by August 2007, at least in the Netherlands, and is satisfied for now with that.

Aurik breathes a sigh of relief, but has to make it clear to his Australian counterpart, Peter Bodel, of the need to ensure things progress as quickly as possible. Not only is he under pressure from his superiors, but Aurik knows the longer the case goes on, the greater the chance the operation is exposed and everything collapses.

A small incident had already come close to seeing the heavily invested case come to an abrupt end. At one of the many meetings between the Reservoir Dogs syndicate in a cafe in Almere in the country's north, police nearby listened in through a recording device taped underneath the table. The meeting, and the police surveillance recording, had gone well initially, but then the recording device suddenly peeled away from the underside of the table and dropped to the floor with an audible thud.

'What's this?' the police heard one of the men exclaim as he picked up the device. The undercover officers were initially confused. The man passed it to the colleague sitting next to him.

'I don't know, but it looks like a bug,' another criminal said, confirming to police what had happened. All the men fell silent as the suspected bug was passed around the group. Suddenly a man at the table laughed.

'This is a really old-fashioned recording device—this can't be used by police. I think it was probably used by the Army on a training exercise, they are always around here practising things.'

All the men laughed and threw the bug to the ground. For once, Team 5 was grateful for having such outdated equipment.

When Boersma heard of the incident, he bought Aurik a new roll of sticky tape. 'This is within budget, you may want to use it,' he said, smiling. It was a light-hearted moment between the pair and countered the more heated debates about the operation.

There are no jokes when it comes to discussing the men involved in shipping drugs to Australia, though. While they may be businessmen, white-collar workers or work full time in other industries, they are also seasoned criminals dealing in the criminal underbelly and all that came with it. Some have guns; others walk and talk with hired body-builders or guards nearby. They also have paid informers in the Dutch police, and at least two officers were recently identified as directly involved in the plot to export drugs to Australia, as well as other plots to ship drugs to countries including Mexico, the United States and Canada. These men's connections extended far beyond the world of criminal enterprise and drug shipments.

With borderless boundaries between the twenty-seven European Union members, the Dutch investigators realise the drugs can travel to any European port to be shipped to its final destination anywhere in the world. It is already well established that the Italian Mafia has been acting as an intermediary outfit, having synthetic drugs such as ecstasy trucked to its ports from the Netherlands and Belgium to ship on to Australia. There are no guarantees this next shipment to Australia will not make similar indirect transfers.

Even during the police investigation, their suspects moved around the world freely. They had the money to live comfortable lives, and jobs that would never raise suspicions as to their movements. Those in the sports industry attended conferences and tournaments around the globe, meeting couriers and contacts, while the businessmen simply attributed their continued travel to the Middle East and elsewhere to business deals.

For his part, Hogan would often meet some of the group in Dubai and Aruba in the Caribbean, before returning to his luxury retreats in Cyprus and Portimao in Portugal's Algarve. He also had an extensive network of contacts in the US, Colombia and Venezuela.

In his office, Standen muses about the criminals he has put away over his long career. They are getting smarter, but so too is law enforcement. Yet why is it so many still seem to get away with it, and live a good life? They are smart, that's why.

An intelligence report completed by a colleague in the NSW Crime Commission the previous year concluded as much. It detailed a number of recent seizures of synthetic drugs and precursors by Customs and the AFP, including cases he had been involved in. Precursors were so much harder to detect, more freely available and cheap, but when mixed were worth a lot.

In July 2001, ephedrine was found in a container of ceramic tiles imported into Melbourne from Montenegro. Two years later, in September 2003, pure compressed pseudoephedrine was found in a shipment of 1500 decorative wall plaques sent from Thailand to Sydney. Another two years later the powder was found in

Sydney in ceramic statues from Vietnam, then inside the covers of children's books in Adelaide, sent from Malaysia. Standen knew of all these cases, but they were just the tip of the iceberg.

The intelligence report also cited a few international examples, including a curious one in Greece where 1.1 tonnes of drug precursor was found concealed in a shipment of rice from Pakistan. The report concluded there was 'a proliferation of creative methods of precursor importations with a level of complexity previously only seen for the illicit drugs themselves'.

Ingenious methods and ingenious men behind them, Standen thinks. Standen, like Hogan, believes life is a bit of a chess game—a case of staying ahead of your opponent by predicting their next move. On his bookshelf sits one of his favourite books, *Hunting Marco Polo*. It tells the story of a five-year battle by an American Drug Enforcement Administration agent, Craig Lovato, to bring to justice a charming, Welsh-born, Oxford University-schooled drugs tsar, Howard Marks, who was dubbed Marco Polo because he travelled so extensively. Marks was eventually caught, but not before making millions of dollars from cannabis smuggling and money laundering.

Standen's next favourite book is *Mr Nice*, Marks' autobiography—one of six books he wrote after being released from jail. Bad guys always win in the end, regardless, he thinks. These aren't just paperback escapades, but theses for success in the blurred law enforcement–criminal world.

By May 2007, about a dozen electronic communication intercepts are in place on various phones and faxes. Three months later, listening devices are installed in Standen's and Jalalaty's homes and even mobile phone handsets. Putting a bug in Standen's phone is of course risky, given that he knows what to look for, but is critical to investigators.

However, surveillance teams trailing Standen are becoming increasingly frustrated by the number of codenames everyone seems to be using. The audio on the listening devices and telephone intercepts is often either faint or in many cases inaudible, making it hard to follow. Part of the reason is that the bug placed in Standen's mobile phone is designed not just to pick up calls, but all ambient noise when the handset is not in use. So the voices during face-to-face meetings are sometimes hard to hear over the clatter of cups and saucers, other voices, a background radio or traffic nearby, or even the rub of the phone in Standen's pocket while he is walking to meet someone.

On one occasion the teams question the quality of their tap when Standen apparently arranges a private meeting with someone called Russell Crowe. They think they have misheard, until they hear the name a second time. Sensing a possible codename, they eagerly wait outside an apartment in upmarket Walsh Bay on Sydney Harbour, curious to see what new character is about to enter the plot.

They are then astounded when the Oscar-winning actor swaggers down the road and shakes hands with their quarry. They are then observed talking intently near an arts cafe. AFP superiors are informed immediately of this astonishing development and they want to know more.

Standen is uneasy when he receives an intelligence report handed to the AFP and NSW Crime Commission. Based on informant information, it details a number of 'big time' suspects involved in the illicit drug trade in Australia, but connected to cartels in the

Netherlands and 'Poms' living in Spain and Portugal. It names a number of people living in Sydney's eastern suburbs and notes they may have a 'friend' in the 'feds'.

Standen sees too many similarities to his own situation. He sends an email to Hogan, under the guise that his former informer could assist him in tracking down some detail to flesh out the new intelligence; in actual fact the email warns Hogan about the chatter in the criminal world that needs to be immediately shut down.

They cannot afford these sorts of indirect references to themselves—if indeed this is what it is.

5

Maurice and Myrtle

June 2007

Jalalaty is now in regular phone and email contact with Standen and Hogan, the British criminal and one-time NSW Crime Commission informant.

The trio use free Hotmail accounts and, like the Dutch, always use aliases and nicknames. For Operation Octans investigators, as it is for their Dutch counterparts, it has become almost a game to link the bizarre names to the people at the keyboards.

'Hello Maurice, how's Myrtle, Love Linda.'

Hogan had previously created a Hotmail account and shared the account name and password so the other two on the other side of the world could log in and read messages saved as drafts. He had decided this method was safer than simply sending out emails, which could be tracked and traced. After everyone had read the email in the draft folder, they simply typed over the top of it. This way, there could never be a permanent record. Hogan had been using this method for years, as had the Dutch. He regularly created new Hotmail accounts with ridiculous titles such as tuckedupinbed@hotmail.com or doorbell1996 and saltlunch3pm.

Police track the various accounts and can see they are being accessed from all over the world, including the Netherlands, Portugal, Germany, England, Dubai and Australia.

Hogan likes to use women's names as sign-off codes, including Linda, Jo Jo, Julie, Jenny, Agnes, Rosemary, Susan, Lucinda, Jennifer, Donna, Maureen, Jamila and Julie, and some other names too, such as Hubert and B52. Jalalaty is Myrtle and Leonia or CEO and 'Bruce from sales', while Standen is Maurice or 2IC.

The trio also call the others names behind their backs, so the investigators are in a constant state of confusion when draft emails land. Jalalaty was initially known as Meaty or Mr Meat, on account of his work as a meat wholesaler, but after Hogan met him he said he was more like a Mrs Myrtle Meat, which was then refined to just Myrtle. They often also pretend to be relatives, signing off randomly with 'Auntie Jean' or 'Lorna and Donald', and referring to shopping, sun-baking and visiting beauty salons.

Despite the codenames, Hogan is identified through detailed police cross-checking of references in his emails to actual events. One of his emails mentions a sick daughter with kidney failure and deafness, and the need for a trip to England to visit her in hospital, which corresponds with British police intelligence on his movement. Other emails or draft folder reports are accessed from countries Hogan is known to have been in, or refer to meetings in the Netherlands that the police secretly photograph him attending. Experts also analyse and compare writing and font styles to establish who is who in the email accounts. Hogan can't spell well, and has a habit of double punctuating.

The clincher though for police, however, is a reference Hogan makes to his earlier arrest in Australia, and the close relationship he has since formed with Standen. The three also joke about their week spent together in Dubai. Overseas passenger travel cards are analysed and it now all fits.

And things are starting to move quite quickly.

From its secret offices on the outskirts of Amsterdam, the Dutch National Crime Squad also begins to see a lot more movement of its suspects.

Loek and a colleague called Mike—another central figure from the Reservoir Dogs Breda Group—travel to Dubai for the sole purpose of sending Jalalaty foodstuff samples that they hope will eventually be sent in bulk to disguise their drugs or drug precursors.

They send packages in the mail, as a test run to see whether it would raise suspicion with authorities, but unbeknown to them these are intercepted by Customs in Australia, at the direction of Dutch and Australian police from Operation Octans. Specialist forensic AFP agents open the packages to test their contents, only to find they contain nothing but coconut milk, salt and desiccated coconut. They then expertly seal the parcels, knowing the traffickers are unlikely to detect the breach.

As they will later find out, this 'dry' run will prove significant. The Octans operatives record the find in minute detail in a notebook:

Two pages of *Gulf News* newspaper dated June 10th, 2007
One 500 gram packet of Altaher brand of coconut powder
One 200 gram Emirates Co-op brand citric acid
One 150 gram Eastern brand box of coconut milk powder

One 300 gram box of Eastern brand coconut milk powder
One 200 gram Shama
One 400 ml Golden Prize brand of coconut milk

One small white box is crucial and a covert AFP team is ordered to track it to its end source. It is clearly consigned to BJ's Fine Foods, but not necessarily Jalalaty. Police have still not ruled out the possibility that he is a dupe.

As the surveillance team—a man and a woman, deemed to look less suspicious than two men—tracks the movement of the white box across Sydney, their confidential notes identify a new suspect.

—At 10.45am surveillance begins on Mr Jalalaty at Double Bay, sitting at a table at Indigo Cafe in Double Bay.

—11.23am he then walks to his vehicle, being a dark blue Holden Commodore, NSW registration [XXX-XXX] and drove that vehicle to Bondi Junction. He then parked—he was seen to park that car at 11.37am in a public car park adjacent to Grafton Street in Bondi Junction just underneath Sid Einfeld Drive next to the Westfield Shopping Centre. He was then seen to walk from the car into the Westfield Shopping Centre and went towards the shopping centre and was out of sight.

—Approximately nearly an hour later at 12.27 he was seen to walk from the Westfield shopping centre with an unknown male who was described as being of solid build about 170 cm tall, balding, wearing a large black jacket, they were seen to be talking and then walked towards Mr Jalalaty's car.

—At 12.30pm Mr Jalalaty was seen to walk to and open the boot of his car with the unknown male standing next to the boot. Mr Jalalaty then reached into the bottom and opened a white box which resembled the one . . . examined at the post office. Seen to open a white postal box approximately 30 cm by 30 cm, the box was seen to have blue markings on the edges and the side. The markings on the side of the box resembled a curved symbol and a circle printed in dark blue. Mr Jalalaty was seen to remove a number of items from the box and to show them to the unknown male. He was then seen to replace an item back into the box and close the boot of the car. Mr Jalalaty then entered the driver's door and the unknown male entered the front passenger's door.

Telephone intercepts record Jalalaty referring to the new stranger as Mr Baldy. Police write that moniker on their large suspects whiteboard for later probing.

About two weeks later, with the Dutch Loek and Mike back in Amsterdam, Hogan flies over to meet them and discusses shipping arrangements for the drugs.

Dutch undercover officers, including Louis Aurik, are there and record their every movement. A number of damning photographs are taken of Hogan with the Dutch syndicate, confirming suspicions of his central role in the plot. All the parties are now linked.

On 1 July 2007, at 10.49pm, an email from Hogan to Jalalaty is intercepted:

Hi there, I saw the sales manager yesterday, they are very happy to go on. They raised a few points but I suggest they run everything by you as third hand messages always cause mix ups. They say there is a good profit margin for you to work with so all sounds good. Just one thing, can you please remember not to mention in any shape or form anything to do with your exMrs job or Maurice's business as this would finish the whole thing. Take care love Hilary and Bob

During the email exchange, Jalalaty is excited to see the project will continue. A 'customer' has already been found in Australia for what Hogan has told him will be a shipment of rice. He appreciates the risks, too, of someone realising his wife is an ex-senior AFP officer and that his mate is one of the top men at the NSW Crime Commission, and makes a mental note to never include any references in any email, no matter how oblique.

Hogan and Jalalaty discuss the rice shipment in some detail. It is to be several tonnes. The Blacktown grocer has a business profile of a small-time meats distributor, but it is time for him to make bulk imports and develop a business profile commensurate with the planned large-scale plot.

Four days later he receives another fax from Tara's cafe on the MDL Food and Services letterhead, outlining the expected 'sample' shipment of rice to Sydney in a twenty-foot sea container. In the Netherlands, police record Dutch suspects discussing the sending of the fax.

Jalalaty contacts Hogan and assures him he is '100 per cent' committed to doing business, and is anxious to receive the next test sample shipment before real shipments can commence. They are both excited, but keep the chatter down to a minimum.

There are a number of exchanges, including Jalalaty bragging that the marketing has all gone well and he has buyers, although some are hesitant since they do not know the brand—but a sample will change all that. It is all double talk.

Jalalaty also says he may need some more money to be sent over. Hogan is surprised: his associate, Mr Baldy, had months earlier handed over $1 million for incidentals, and there is no way it can have all been spent. But Jalalaty has not told him about a certain Sydney clairvoyant who failed to see an investment sting.

> I do not understand why you only have 200 available for the account..??? Can you let me know exactly where the rest is as I owe 700 to the people I borrowed the 5 off last time.. everything else is fine I am finished my babysitting and will get busy this week. Lots of love jerry. PS how much did you give Maurice for Jo Jo,,??

Jalalaty responds:

> I gave Maurice 20. I am working on getting more as I am chasing up all outstanding debts. Maurice is helping me with a major one and we are getting close. I am sorry if this is unacceptable but I'm doing my best at this time. I am also sorry for putting you in this predicament with people that you borrowed from. Also I also know that you put yourself out for me and I feel that I have let you down. Maurice has also told me that this is unacceptable and he is helping recover some outstanding moneys. If I can just say that I should have had documents about the groceries but nothing yet. They told me that the goods will arrive on the 22nd but nothing. Did you want me to chase it up? Also I spoke on the phone to the jam people today. Samples will be here in a couple of days. They are ready to go as soon as you give the go ahead.

Hogan is furious, but is keeping his eye on the end game—if his shipments are successful he will be able to cover his debts. He tells Jalalaty to focus.

Agents intercepting messages note a change in tone: there is anger and frustration between the parties, and this is always good for law enforcers as their targets often begin to slip up.

There are other exchanges too. Jalalaty to Hogan on the Hotmail 'bkkshowgirls' account:

Okay you can only do what you can.!! But really Myrtle I find it hard to understand why you are having such difficulties. I was under the impression you were using it to buy stock which would be sold at a profit?? I will make some calls now about the other matters. As far as I know everything has left so chase it up. It would be better if you keep a close eye on them.!! You must check that the babies are always healthy,!! See if they get a check regularly.

I've just had a mail from the girls. They tell me that one has left and will be with you in max 14 days. The other two are sitting there waiting,!! The delays are due to the fact that I have yet to pay the loan I took from them and I still have to pay for the materials. I do not want to be in a situation that I am giving you work in order to be repaid;!! They also say that they are always having trouble with your fax??? Can you get a new one and a new mobile to help stop these delays,?? The jam people are a different group and that is where the future is but you must complete the contract first so that we no [sic] everyone is able to do what they say. About the children you must check that the babies are always healthy.

Jalalaty responds two days later from his home computer:

For what its worth the moneys that I owe you have nothing to do with any business that might occur in the future. I am responsible for all that you have given me including anything that I have given to Maurice. No matter what, nothing will change and you will get every cent that I owe you. I have a number of things happening at the moment and at any time I could get some or all that I owe you. I am sorry if this offends you but it is the truth.

Hogan responds:

Hi there, listen I do not really know you—nobody is accusing you of being dishonest. Maurice has convinced me of that, although I am not happy that you seem to of strayed from the original purpose of my investment . . . it is the fact that the last one was a loan. I explained at the time I did not have any funds there but I do borrow some for a short-term. So now I have gone from investing in you to paying back a loan I secured for you, no matter what way you look at it. It does not make any sense and I am wondering what I have gotten myself into.?? Anyway, apart from that I am okay. I will be with the people on Monday and reassure them that they can rely on you to do your part. Are you 100% that you want to,?? I only ask as I need the test doing before I can start the serious one because there is too much at stake to mess serious people about? Get a decent fax and a phone,!! Give my regards to Maurice, best wishes Lorra and Donald.

About this time, Jalalaty takes a family holiday to Port Douglas and details to his wife the entire plot to ship in the drugs—and most importantly the money they will have. It is the only way to pay Hogan back the missing $1 million, he tells her. She had suspected strange business dealings when the sports bags first appeared in the cupboard.

Also at this time, Dutch police intercept a fax from Tara's to Pakistan, declaring that '300' will cost no more than $93,000. It's a purchase agreement and the money is later telegraphically transferred.

On 5 September, Jalalaty receives an email from Elegant Hosiery Pty Ltd in Lahore, Pakistan, which claims to be acting on behalf of MDL Foods India, apologising for delays and providing details of the container carrying 17,000 kilograms of rice in 5 kilogram bags, expected to arrive in Sydney from Karachi in twenty days.

The delays, the intercepted fax states, are due to regulations for Customs inspections to take place at source in Lahore as opposed to Australia, and therefore the need to renew disinfection of goods and packaging.

Jalalaty contacts Standen and arranges to meet at Cafe Laurella in Wahroonga about a week later to discuss the shipment. Undercover Octans agents are already there when they arrive, ready to record their conversation via a bug in Standen's mobile phone.

It is clear Standen is not happy, despite their business project finally advancing. He can't believe a rice shipment order is being made through a hosiery company, fictitious or otherwise. It doesn't make sense for a hosiery company to send rice—let alone a company in India dealing with national rival Pakistan—and it's that sort of stupidity that law enforcement officers look for when checking imports.

The two are also not even sure the shipment *is* rice, and discuss the fact it could be another product, in which the drugs may—or may not be—concealed.

Jalalaty thinks it is a test run to ensure a smooth process.

'Not much of a test to get some rice. Some rice from where? It's fucking *Pakistan*, compared to getting something out of *Panama*, like they're totally different,' Standen snorts.

Jalalaty seems more worried about what to do with the rice if it *is* rice. Hogan said he had a buyer for 'rice', but he believes Hogan was using 'rice' as the code term for the drugs. The Hotmail draft system may be secure, but it sure is bloody confusing, he thinks.

Either way, Standen tells his friend to find legitimate buyers for the food staple, just in case authorities are watching.

The pair convince themselves the first shipment is just likely to be rice and nothing else, so until it arrives they will simply assure Hogan they are still 100 per cent committed to the project. He seems to require this assurance more and more these days.

For most of the meeting, Standen reveals what is likely to happen to any shipment arriving at port. It would be X-rayed, then perhaps physically inspected by both Customs and Quarantine agents. They would be looking for anomalies in the paperwork, such as a hosiery company apparently selling rice, and maybe later look for money transfers that should have been made by the buyer for the bulk rice. The shipment would also be inspected by Quarantine officials in Pakistan, looking for weevils.

'I don't think the first shipment will have anything in it except rice—particularly if as the first shipment gets Quarantine inspection in Pakistan, it wouldn't have anything in it,' Jalalaty says.

'Unless they have a way of getting to it after it's been quarantined,' Standen replies.

The pair also devise a cover story should they be caught, just in case there *is* something in the test shipment. Jalalaty is to say he has been to numerous countries handing out business cards, trying to establish his food importation business. Faxes and emails between him and suppliers should be kept, so if Customs finds the shipment and police are called, Jalalaty can tell them he had faxes from suppliers and could help police track the criminals posing as hosiery manufacturers.

Standen again tells his colleague he should also now seek buyers for the rice stock, so it will look like he legitimately didn't know it was anything but rice. The rice will be worth about $170,000 on the market. Standen tells him he has dealt with a similar case in the past where a businessman importing a container of drugs was in the clear because he had the right documentation and it couldn't be proved he knew what was in the shipment.

'I will do the same thing,' Jalalaty muses, as if realising for the first time the potential for the shipment to be detected. It all seemed so easy just talking about it, but now that it is actually happening, it is best to be prepared for the worst.

Standen also tells his friend what to do if he is ever spoken to by police. 'Never immediately ask for a lawyer—it makes you look guilty. And then declare your attitude to drugs. You say "If anyone sent me anything they shouldn't have sent me, you need to find and hang the bastards . . . I'll help you hang the bastards and I'll be there helping", you know . . .'

Jalalaty repeats it back. Yeah he likes that. Hang the bastards: it makes him sound like an anti-drugs crusader.

Standen also details what Jalalaty should do to ensure their electronic tracks are covered. He reminds him that when sending a draft email, he should not delete the existing message but type over it.

'If anything goes wrong, your computer should go for a

swim,' Standen says. 'We've followed people into internet cafes if they're doing really dodgy stuff and when they're gone we go and take the—we go and approach the owner and we take the box [computer hard drive] from the internet cafe, download it, because if you delete stuff it's still there.'

The cafe meeting ends with the pair daydreaming aloud about what it will all mean to their lives.

'How much do you reckon it's worth?' Jalalaty asks.

'Depends, but maybe $100 to $120 per kilogram,' Standen replies.

'If 100 kilograms comes in, that's $12 million profit—that's $1 million for each of us: you, me and Hogan.'

A $1 million profit for Standen would ease his ever-growing financial burden. For the first time he talks at length about his financial problems and how they have been growing over the years, and how he had come in contact with Hogan. It's not the first time Standen has referred to his cash-flow problem, but this time it's lengthy; it's clearly troubling him.

The pair also talk again of the Hogan money invested and lost in the Bahamas or the US, or wherever the bloody money was. To the delight of police watching and listening in to their every move, they begin to talk more and more. Still no smoking-gun admission, still always in code—but talk nonetheless for the Octans puzzle. Surveillance teams read between the lines and know things are getting close to a climax.

Around this time, Jalalaty's wife Dianne goes to the Commonwealth Bank in Castle Hill and arranges for $7000 to be transferred to the Pakistani bank account of Elegant Hosiery. It is the first, but by no means the last, transfer.

A few months later she returns to the branch and transfers $22,000 to Pakistan as another down payment for a shipment, this

time to the account of a company in Lahore called Global Biz—
the same one opened by Bob the Builder some months earlier.

A few more months go by but finally, on 1 November, container
PCIU-3985256 arrives in Sydney. Quarantine inspectors look at
the haul, find live weevils, and are forced to remove the 17 tonnes
of rice to have the container fumigated. Nothing else is found in
the container, and six days later the haul is delivered to Jalalaty's
warehouse in Blacktown.

It is just as well the rice has arrived, because Hogan is getting
sick of Jalalaty and his constant questions. Should he sell the rice?
Is he doing the right thing?

In a private draft email to Standen on another Hotmail
account that they purposely have not given to Jalalaty, Hogan
explodes about the 'Mr Bean of the Business World'. It's a term
of ridicule Jalalaty doesn't hear for himself at the time, but will
later use to defend his own ineptitude.

Telecommunications Intercept, 1.58pm, 4 November 2007
(suspect Hogan to Standen)

Hello Maurice, I have not been avoiding you !!!!
I have been waiting for positive news about Myrtle, honestly I do
not know where you found her?? . . . she is a complete Walter
Mitty. Mr Bean of the business world.

We are so lucky to of [sic] discovered our faults now and no
[sic] let her loose with our pension fund. Honestly when I tell you
the stories you will not know whether to laugh or cry, do not say
anything to her as it only inspires her to try and explain everything
away as other people's mistakes and misunderstandings . . .
anyway don't worry she seems to be getting her act together (at
long last)

The one thing that still concerns me is her constant need to talk to anyone who comes into contact with her, but in her defence we have to realise that men are from Mars and women are from Venus . . . apart from that I think that all is looking rosy and I'm hopeful that we can get that long awaited change of profession and well deserved holiday!!!

The weather is unusually nice for this time of year so I am making the most of it and taking a week off, you take care I will put a new number on as soon as I can

Love

LINDA

XX

Jalalaty wants the email address Hogan uses to speak with Standen, but Standen won't give it to him. Hogan continues to fire off emails to Standen and claims Jalalaty has a 'few screws loose'; he is sick of having to deal with him and actually believes he is sabotaging operations because no one could be as stupid as he has been.

Standen responds in civil terms; he has access to all accounts and watches all conversations between his feuding friends, both of whom confide in him. He has the control and that's the way he likes it. He tells Hogan Jalalaty is a little nuts, but he *is* useful—and he does have the wholesaling business.

A week later, after a series of emails, Jalalaty flies out of Sydney for Dubai again, where as previously arranged online he meets Hogan to discuss their deal further.

The pair, along with Standen, had met in Dubai in January that year to discuss the initial stages of their business, but now it is time for the real shipment to be discussed.

Hogan and Jalalaty meet for lunch at the Al Hallab Restaurant in the Emirates Mall, unaware they are being tracked by police. With Hogan is another man—his 'Portuguese mate', also known as Mr Baldy.

Jalalaty and Standen both always knew of the 'shadow', a mysterious other figure in their inner circle, but didn't want to know any more about him. Safer that way. They simply refer to him as Hogan's 'Portuguese mate'—a family man who runs a car dealership in Portugal, but has made numerous trips to Sydney at Hogan's behest; that's all they really know about him. It isn't even clear whether he really is of Portuguese descent—as Jalalaty later notes to Standen, the way the man ate he was more 'pork and cheese' than Portuguese.

Jalalaty details the arrival of the rice container, the weevils and how it had been sprayed by Quarantine, then reassures Hogan he is ready for the next 'real' shipment.

Hogan reveals the next shipment will be sixty 5 kilogram bags of basmati rice, which will conceal pseudoephedrine—enough to make ice worth more than $120 million on the street.

Jalalaty can barely conceal his excitement. This is the first time the real extent of their operation has been discussed in detail. It is good to get it out in the open, to speak freely. Like the others he has been frustrated by the Hotmail drafts and emails, and often misunderstood what was meant or being said in them. Now, in a booth at the back of the restaurant, they are openly discussing a deal that Jalalaty knows will change his life forever. He can't wait to tell Standen. He somehow always feels like just a grocer when he was with him, but now he is an active player in the plot, holding information that makes him a key participant.

This is the big shipment they have all been working towards for about a year. At more than $100,000 a kilo, the pseudoephedrine is worth $30 million in its pure form. But cut and mixed, it would fetch at least four times that.

It will be concealed in rice again, although Hogan talks about how a test run could also be made in canned goods, such as tomatoes or coconut milk.

The men discuss how the plot will proceed once the container arrives in Sydney and is cleared by Customs. Portuguese mate will go to the warehouse and collect the bags to take to the customer, open and empty them at the other location for the customer to see, then return the empty bags to be destroyed. The chemicals have to remain in their original rice bags, so the customers can see there has been no tampering by police.

Jalalaty wonders how the drug will be hidden, but Hogan assures him he wouldn't find it, and if *he* can't, Customs won't. Jalalaty feels reassured.

Hogan also reveals he can travel to Australia on a false passport to watch the drug chemicals being passed on. They also speak of contingency plans should their plot be detected—which, if Standen does his job, they will know about well in advance.

A few days after his return, an excited Jalalaty again meets Standen to tell him of his trip. They can clear their debt to Hogan for the lost monies.

Standen has concerns about customers collecting the original rice bags—if something goes wrong they could be traced back to Jalalaty.

But, Jalalaty explains, Hogan had been specific about what the customer wants: the original bags unopened. Standen thinks it would be better if Pork and Cheese simply takes the inner bags so that the outer skins can be destroyed and never linked back to

Jalalaty. If the bags with the chemical traces are found, they will all be caught. Jalalaty just reiterates what Hogan has told him.

The pair also discuss the possibility of enlisting Hogan's help to recover the lost $1 million, since it was his money anyway. Standen is already nervous about Frank Wheeler—'he talks too much'—and Hogan can probably do it with the right connections overseas. But he says they should leave it all alone for now.

Standen is also not happy with the tinned tomatoes idea, or tinned anything. In 1997 his covert Operation Tamarind had exposed record hauls of ecstasy and heroin in a shipment from Hong Kong of 800 cartons of canned pineapples, after X-rays showed inconsistencies in the tins.

'It's all been done before, mate—it's not new,' Standen says.

No, rice is a better option.

'I'm just surprised they aren't just putting in 10 kilograms in the first container—300 kilograms in one hit is fine by me,' Jalalaty says.

For the next month it is business as usual as the pair in Australia wait for associates in Europe to finalise the shipment.

Through the emails, Hogan tells Jalalaty to pass Standen $20,000 for Christmas to help him with his debts. Monies are always sent to Jalalaty since, they thought, if any financial regulator is watching, it will be less suspicious for a businessman trying to raise capital to expand his business to receive investment cheques than a NSW Crime Commission official. Five days later, Standen and Jalalaty meet, with the latter smiling and handing him a 'Christmas present'.

The AFP check Standen's bank account and do indeed find a deposit of $20,000.

The pair also decide to create 'traffic' to support their cover story of legitimate business, having telephone and email exchanges about random business opportunities—sugar in Brazil, beer from the Philippines, exporting cement to Lebanon, housing projects in Western Australia and Victoria and so on, all apparently for legitimate purposes. The laundering of monies to and from the principals of the drug movements are to be via Dubai, so a plan is also devised for the pair to be investing in a Dubai-based front company, a building materials firm that ostensibly has a contract to assist in the supply of materials for the construction of prefabricated homes and army barracks in Pakistan. All up, police record more than eight hours of conversations between the pair over an eight-month period alone, much of it in coded references to the plot. They also log up to 179 calls from Hogan to Standen on Standen's mobile, and 86 calls to Hogan from Standen and numerous SMS messages, many about seemingly innocent business opportunities. The exchanges in draft emails fill dozens of folders.

About this time Standen rings a Customs contact again and asks simply: 'All quiet on the Western front?'

The officer replies that there is no new intelligence on any suspect shipments and the pair discuss other issues. The call is not seen as out of place by Customs.

Standen reassures Jalalaty that he is checking regularly with contacts to see what big 'jobs' are being worked on and no rice plots have been detected. He says it will be a good thing if Quarantine inspectors check the container first, since it would then be less likely for Customs to double up: there are simply too many containers coming in to warrant it.

Standen is busy at work. There is a lot going on, including scrutinising Maroubra's infamous Bra Boys surfie gang. But

Standen effectively also has a second job—a partnership with Jalalaty and Hogan—and this work load is equally as big.

The AFP logs that their target appears to be increasingly stressed about his financial position. At one point he sends an SMS text to Jalalaty: 'I feel like a stalker but getting desperate to make these payments today. Will incur costs if not paid today. Sorry, but any progress?'

Earlier, Standen had told his friend he was becoming increasingly desperate for cash because of his children's needs, including school fees and car costs for his eldest daughter. There were also some speeding fines. His credit card debt had risen from $87,000 to more than $112,000.

Friends once visited his Bateau Bay home and couldn't believe what they found: a sparsely furnished home, with very simple— almost makeshift—tables and chairs that one friend likened to something you would have found in a poor Eastern European house. They suspected the Standen family had hocked a lot of their belongings to make ends meet. Their fridge was almost always empty, prompting one colleague to buy them groceries. It wasn't a one-off charitable gesture.

The family would explain that things were tight since they were tied up in investments, but those close to Standen at work knew otherwise. Standen himself would claim he was a victim of bad advice from a mortgage broker, and a mistimed gamble on the peaks and troughs of the real estate cycle. He did have an investment property in Bundaberg, but when he sold it, he would say, he would be debt free.

Takeaway meals were the norm for the family—at least when Standen was at home to buy them.

*

In AFP headquarters, the complexity of the case is starting to grind on the agents. Just when they think they have the measure of a particular codename or Hotmail account code, it changes. It is a game that clearly Hogan likes to play.

'Brain teaser I have opened a new one,' Hogan writes on one draft email. He then invites Standen to guess, giving him the clues 'place where you found the computer bag with my papers?', with the password being 'place where I sent someone to see you near where I used to live'.

After some time, Standen responds: 'From rentaspace? How smart am I? Will leave a mail tonight.' And thus the online conversation moves to the rentaspace account.

But the AFP agents scramble through their original records and decode this clue as well. In 2003, when Hogan was arrested, a computer bag stuffed with almost $1 million cash was left in a Rentaspace storage unit in Sydney's east. It was one half of the money Hogan had and would later surrender, with the other half spirited away in a sports bag for later use.

About this time, Dutch telecommunication intercepts record increased mentions of 'The Factory' in Pakistan. Rather than a single facility, as the name would suggest, 'The Factory' is known by law enforcers in both Australia and the Netherlands more as a generic term to describe notorious production houses of synthetic drugs—an efficient criminal enterprise run through a number of factories in the city of Lahore. With corruption rife in the Pakistani bureaucracy, some criminals view the country as a safer haven from which to transit illegal exports than, say, a Third World country like the Congo. Corrupt officials are more predictable here: in Pakistan, turning a blind eye for a fee is just good business.

By now, the planned shipment of the ephedrine is well advanced and Loek speaks almost daily to his contact—the local head of The Factory. Everyone is happy with the deal and negotiations proceed well.

But then the Pakistani head of The Factory dies of a massive heart attack, and the plot begins to unravel. Suddenly the operation is in disarray. There is no natural successor to handle the shipment from the Pakistani end, and subordinates realise the operation is bigger than they have imagined. One local criminal with vague knowledge of the plot contacts the Dutch syndicate and tells them he is now in charge—but then another says he too is the boss, and the Dutch cannot figure out who to deal with.

It is all too clear to both of these new supposed leaders that neither of them can deliver the goods without the working knowledge and experience of their dead boss, and unnamed others. So they decide to string the Dutch, Hogan and Jalalaty along—for as long as possible—in a bid to get more money.

The Dutch are furious and tell Loek and his associate Brusse (Bob the Builder) to sort it out.

By late December, Loek—now almost permanently using the name Rashid—travels to Pakistan to see the shipment ahead of final payment.

After meeting the new principals of The Factory, he tests the product and confirms it is 98 per cent pure ephedrine. Finally, he tells colleagues in the Netherlands via telephone, the shipment will be a go.

He initially thinks about seeing the ephedrine made into pseudoephedrine, loaded onto the ship in the rice sacks, and to note the time the ship leaves the docks. He tells his Dutch counterparts he would personally supervise the ephedrine conversion into pseudoephedrine and the concealment of the haul in rice sacks and their loading onto a cargo ship but changes his mind. Widespread civil unrest and violence breaks out in Pakistan, throwing the plans of both cop and crim out the window.

A month earlier, on 3 November, Pakistani president Pervez Musharraf had declared a state of emergency as unrest swept the country, after the courts looked at invalidating his questionable election. Riot police spilled onto the streets, and there were hints martial law could be imposed. Two days later, Musharraf used the violence and rioting against him to declare emergency rule.

Loek decides he has had enough and flies home to the Netherlands, never having seen his illicit cargo loaded, or the freighter ship leave Pakistan, as had been the original plan.

For the AFP agent on the ground in Pakistan, it is getting hard to keep Pakistani police and resources focused and engaged with Operation Octans.

The Pakistani authorities had not been fully briefed about the case—and certainly not the Standen aspect—as few could be trusted to not sell the information to criminals. Details of such a massive sting would be worth a lot in the local criminal underground. A Pakistani officer could sell it to a criminal contact for a few dollars, who in turn would sell it to a regional crime boss for a bit more, who for a higher fee . . . and so on, until it reached the ears of The Factory and the businessmen in a certain cafe in Amsterdam. The AFP's point of contact in Pakistan—the director of the Anti-Narcotics Bureau—had made a similar suggestion of distrust in some of his own men. He had agreed to assist with surveillance operations and be briefed at a later time—

but he would never receive that briefing, and with all the other troubles, his support diminishes.

As the days go by, all local police resources are being diverted away as the Musharraf stranglehold on power continues to ebb. Every available officer is ordered to weed out perceived extremists, and surveillance resources are redeployed to watch Musharraf's main rival, Benazir Bhutto, who has returned from self-imposed exile to contest fresh elections. Within days she is placed under house arrest by Musharraf and hundreds of police are assigned to watch her around the clock.

On 27 December, Benazir Bhutto is assassinated after leaving a supporters rally, just two weeks before the scheduled general elections. The country descends further into chaos.

In Canberra, Tim Morris is keeping abreast of the situation, but is at a loss as to what to do. It is vital the drugs shipment is tracked all the way from the warehouse containers to the docks and finally onto the ship, but the situation is now impossible. All local police help has ceased and his agent on the ground is now working alone in potentially dangerous circumstances.

As a Department of Foreign Affairs and Trade advisory warns, 'the situation in Pakistan remains volatile, unpredictable and could deteriorate unexpectedly. Australians could be caught up in the violent unrest.'

Morris has never been in this position. He can only advise his agent to try his best to keep tracking the drugs but to stay safe.

'This is ridiculous,' he tells his colleague McEwen. 'I don't think we've ever been up against something like this—an entire country going to shit. We can't count on local help anymore, so we just have to hope that the ship leaves in one piece some time soon.'

*

On 10 January 2008, Standen and Jalalaty again meet at a cafe in Sydney's CBD. He now starts meeting Jalalaty more regularly, usually for small breaks in Cafe Alto or Plato's Cafe near the NSW Crime Commission building, or even the local 7-Eleven.

The pair continue to talk about the Bahamas fiasco and Standen's debts.

'Once I receive the first decent bit of money, I'm going to buy solar heating for my swimming pool,' Standen muses.

Standen says this is not how he had hoped to make his money. 'But the reality is that someone else would be doing it and rolling in the money, so we might as well get a benefit,' he says.

'From something bad comes something good,' Jalalaty replies.

For the AFP agents listening nearby and taping their conversation, it's a defining remark they feel could hang Standen later in a court of law if their case is lucky enough to progress that far.

Standen and Jalalaty discuss how the rice haul has been loaded, and the shipment is ready to leave the Pakistani docks. But to the undercover police listening in, Standen still seems confused about the shipment.

'That's just rice is it?' Standen asks

'No, this is a "live" one,' Jalalaty responds.

'Well I hope it's not just "live" with weevils,' Standen retorts and the pair laugh.

Jalalaty tells Standen that Hogan has told him to be a bit more cautious and to stop using the internet at home at night, and instead always do his online business from random internet cafes.

On 21 January, Dutch police record a conversation between Loek and the sports trainer Jan, discussing how a supplier has sent a total of 600 kilograms of pseudoephedrine, and that 300 kilograms will be soon shipped off to Australia.

The pair also talk about a quality control laboratory certificate of analysis, dated August 2005, for 1000 kilograms of pseudoephedrine hydrochloride, which has been collected by Brusse. This would somewhat legitimise their warehouse stocks should authorities call; dates on paperwork can always be changed if needed.

Hogan sends an email, which is intercepted by Australian police and relayed to Dutch counterparts, in which he says he is going to meet up with the 'girls' and have dinner with their 'mom'.

Dutch surveillance crews find Hogan and all the principal players of the conspiracy meeting at a restaurant in Amsterdam. They are photographed chatting and laughing on the steps. This image will surface some years later in courtrooms in the Netherlands and Australia.

A few days later Loek and Jan send a fax to Jalalaty's home advising that a 20-foot container is ready to depart Karachi, and that the original documents for the rice order will be sent to him as soon as the ship departs. He will need those documents to take the haul off the Sydney docks. Loek had earlier contacted his Pakistani-based cohorts by fax with exact specifications of the shipment.

Jalalaty flies to Dubai again to inspect a warehouse he hopes will later become a staging post for operations. While there, he attends a meeting Hogan has set up, in a large office containing more than a hundred money-counting machines. This is the financial hub for any monies that need to be paid out or laundered. And there's still another $30 million in cash waiting to be counted and sorted.

Jalalaty thinks he and Hogan are getting on like a house on fire. Life is good. In reality, Hogan can't wait to rid himself of the Australian.

6

Getting Closer

Since the start of the year, Tim Morris has devised a new plan on how to keep a close watch on Standen.

It was of course a gamble to have informed the NSW Crime Commission of the AFP's probe, but Morris has been satisfied that the commission has been assisting by keeping an eye on their man. They have in fact provided some valuable insights into the Standen–Hogan relationship.

But now Morris wants to keep an eye on Standen himself, up front, in the form of a regular monthly meeting. Morris will chair these meetings, along with Glen McEwen and another senior AFP agent, Terry Venchiarutti.

The meetings will be held in the commission's Kent Street office, together with Standen and another assistant commissioner, Tim O'Connor, who joined three years after Standen. Sometimes a senior Australian Customs Service official will also attend.

Everyone knows of the friction between the AFP and the NSW Crime Commission, so no one will think it unusual that the investigators on the ground, chaired by the veteran Morris, want to meet to regularly discuss any issues in governance or flow of information between the two crime-fighting groups.

'I want to do this for two reasons,' Morris tells McEwen when explaining his plan.

'One, we can contain *what* he is being told and *how* he is being told, and two, we give him an opportunity to put on the table any jobs he is running. If later he claims that Jalalaty is just an informant he was working, then we can say, "well why didn't you reveal that at all our monthly meetings?"'

During the meetings, Morris deliberately mentions the use of informants, and watches as less than a metre away, Standen shifts uneasily in his seat, or scratches the back of his neck, yet always says nothing.

In fact, Standen contributes very little to these gatherings except to seemingly be obsessed with how much money criminals make and how many luxury holidays they take, how much champagne they drink and the women they have. He also asks the AFP agents if they have any intelligence on any new jobs coming up—for example from the Netherlands. He is always told no, nothing out of the ordinary.

At one meeting in February, Standen asks the Customs official in specific detail how containers are selected for X-ray, and how the actual X-ray and screening processes are conducted. He wants to know it all, from the moment the ship comes in. He raises the issue under the guise of a potential shipment coming into Adelaide that the group had earlier discussed. In many instances, intelligence gathered offshore directed Customs to search certain containers, but Standen wants to know how other more random checks are done. As far as he can see, no one is onto their plot—so if they are to be targeted, it will be by accident through a random check or paperwork. He understands that not all shipping containers can be X-rayed, as the bulk coming into the busiest port in Australia is just too great—so how are they selected, he wants to know?

At another meeting, the AFP watches as assistant commissioner O'Connor genuinely asks Standen about pseudoephedrine trafficking.

For Morris it is like a bizarre poker game, with men sitting around a table keeping their cards fairly close to their chest, each one bluffing in their own way, each one trying to find what the other has up their sleeve.

'I just block it out of my mind,' Morris later tells colleagues when asked how he managed to chair such an unusual gathering eight times, with nothing given away.

'I also don't take anything into the meetings. Nothing, not a diary, not a notepad, I just walk in there with a pen and an agenda. No one wants to be the one to blow it, to accidentally leave something behind that gives it all away. But it is pretty unusual to be looking your target in the eye like that. How often does that happen?'

On a couple of occasions, Standen would be late for the meeting. AFP agent Paul Watt would check later with operatives in the field and find out Standen was late because he was having a lunchtime meeting with Bill Jalalaty to finalise their drug import. The irony was not lost on him.

Mischievously, Morris would ask those at the table—and particularly look in the direction of Standen—if anyone knew what the current value of ephedrine and pseudoephedrine was on the street. Someone would always answer before Standen, who would pull a quizzical face, as if he really has to think about that one.

Morris may have had some fun at the meetings, but he is

Mark William Standen, assistant director for the NSW Crime Commission, in August 2007. Though he doesn't realise it, he is already the major focus of joint Dutch and Australian investigations.

All images are courtesy of the *Daily Telegraph* (News Ltd) and the author unless otherwise noted.

Netherlands National Public Prosecutor Cees van Spierenburg in his office, preparing the briefs of evidence for the prosecution of the men dubbed the 'Reservoir Dogs', suspected of running the largest synthetic drugs cartel in Europe.

Dutch National Crime Squad chief of operations Jan Boersma in the National Crime Squad building, south of Amsterdam, surrounded by files containing the thousands of telephone intercepts and surveillance reports gathered for Operation Mayer/Octans.

Greengrocer Bill Jalalaty posing for a local newspaper feature on his business, BJ's Fine Foods, on Christmas Eve 2006; the image would later attract laughter from Dutch police during an operations briefing on Australian suspects in the plot.

Image courtesy of NewsLocal Newspapers.

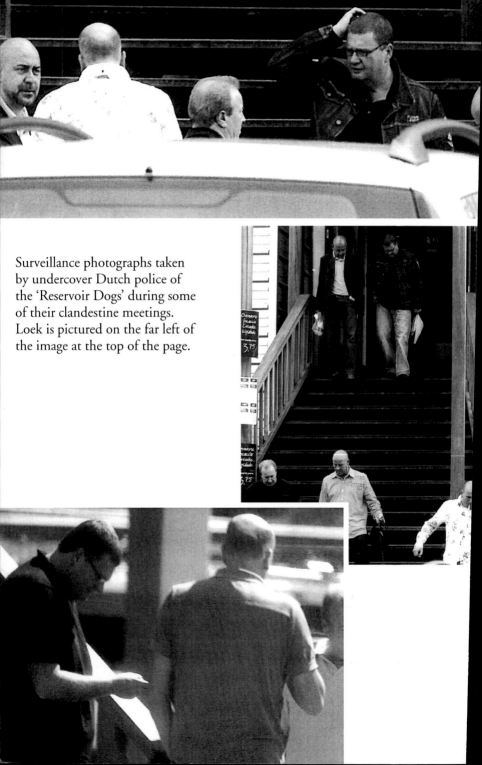

Surveillance photographs taken by undercover Dutch police of the 'Reservoir Dogs' during some of their clandestine meetings. Loek is pictured on the far left of the image at the top of the page.

The hole-in-the-wall Tara Telecom Internet café in north Amsterdam—a legitimate business regularly used by the Dutch conspirators to send emails and faxes around the world to further their drug and money-laundering operations.

Australian Federal Police undercover agents Glen McEwen (left) and Brett Thompson stake out suspects on the streets in Breda in south Netherlands in May 2008.

Undercover Dutch agents follow a suspect driving through Den Bosch, 80 kilometres south of Amsterdam. Their primary target was 'Echo'.

McEwen and Thompson used the cover story of being an advance
security detail for the visiting Socceroos football team to avoid suspicion
as they moved about the southern half of Amsterdam for several weeks
in 2008.

A late night meal for the Operation Merlin Dutch undercover police team and the Australians. (From left) Two Dutch agents, prosecutor Cees van Spierenburg, McEwen and Thompson.

McEwen spent a lot of time working at a Dutch police base in Son near Eindhoven, sending reports back to the AFP Octans team leaders in Canberra.

The Al Hallab restaurant in the Emirates Mall in Dubai, where in November 2007 Jalalaty held a crucial meeting with Echo and his 'Portuguese mate' to plot the importation into Australia of the 300 kilograms of pseudoephedrine.

Stills from police surveillance videos capturing Jalalaty and Standen together during two of numerous meetings in cafés in 2007 and 2008. A bug in Standen's mobile allowed police to listen in on their conversations.

The nondescript NSW Crime Commission headquarters on Kent Street in central Sydney.

AFP agent Paul Watt on his way to liaise with the Director of Public Prosecutions in Sydney.

This photograph, from 30 May 2008, captures the exact moment McEwen is told Echo had received a tip off and had not, as expected, boarded his flight from Thailand back to Dusseldorf where a dozen police were waiting to arrest him. Pictured with Dutch investigator Arjen Cupido at the Amadeus Ribs Restaurant in Antwerp, Belgium.

Undercover Dutch National police arrest a suspect as part of the raids across the Netherlands in May 2008. A total of 14 arrests are made that night, with vital evidence gathered from various homes and offices.

Sacks of rice sitting in Jalalaty's warehouse—without their secret cargo of drugs.

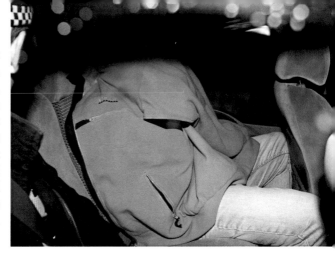

On the afternoon of his arrest on 2 June 2008, Mark Standen cowers with a jacket over his head in the back of an unmarked Australian Federal Police car on his way to questioning.

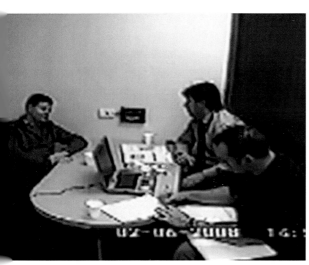

Standen underwent six and a half hours of interrogation by agents Paul Watt and Terry Venchiarutti at the AFP headquarters.

After his interrogation Standen was taken to the Sydney Police Centre in Surry Hills to be formally charged.

How the *Daily Telegraph* broke the world-exclusive story.

AFP Deputy Commissioner of Operations Tony Negus and NSW Crime
Commission Director Phillip Bradley face the media outside AFP Sydney
headquarters on the morning after Standen's arrest.

A markedly thinner Mark Standen in April 2009 being escorted to one of his many court committal hearings. He is wearing a bulletproof vest for his own protection.

On verdict day on 11 August 2011 media gather at one of the vantage points outside King Street Court in Sydney to see Standen's reaction as he is found guilty.

How the *Daily Telegraph* cartoonist Warren Brown recorded the day Standen was found guilty.

The cell measuring
4.3 metres by 3.1 metres
that is to be Standen's home
for the next two decades.

One of the last images taken of Standen as he is escorted from the court a final time to begin his jail sentence.

beginning to lose sleep, with the case constantly foremost on his mind. What if Standen isn't a lone wolf, and there are in fact a whole bunch of law enforcers in on 'the joke'? How much longer can he and his team expect to keep the probe a secret, when already so many people are having to be told in the hope of ensuring their silence? Too much relies on trust. It will only take one person bewitched by Standen's renowned charisma to tell him something is amiss.

The only thing that gives Morris confidence in the operation continuing is the fact that no one is yet asking any questions they shouldn't. The operation's secrecy has yet to be breached. No one outside the Octans or old Statice crew or the very upper echelons of the NSW Crime Commission know of the high-level probe— and more importantly, telephone taps confirm that Standen, too, is none the wiser.

Morris' confidence is jolted in April when a story in Sydney's *Daily Telegraph* points to big shipments of synthetic drugs from Holland set to flood Australian streets.

The small story details the involvement of the Italian Mafia smuggling Dutch drugs, but is enough to set the Octans leaders on edge. The story is from News Ltd's London bureau and is syndicated to all newspapers in Australia. The *Adelaide Advertiser* runs it on the front page and carries another two pages of detail inside, with images of drugs and guns.

On any other day, such a profile of trans-national crime would be welcomed by a police service keen to justify their operating budget to government. But not this time, not now.

Commissioner Mick Keelty is shown the story and instructs his media adviser Kate Bradstreet to immediately speak to the newspaper's London correspondent and subtly establish the background to the story. Specifically, in a roundabout way, she is told to 'suss out' if there was a leak from Sydney, Canberra or the UK.

After an overnight call, she confirms the journalist had made several trips to the Netherlands as part of a wider investigation into the trans-national movement of drugs, that he knows indirect elements of the plot being probed by Octans, and is quickly drawing it all together. She confirms the correspondent has been following a particular line since 2007 and is planning to write more as pieces of the puzzle come together. It is a worry at this very delicate stage of the police operation.

Keelty takes the unprecedented move of visiting the *Daily Telegraph*'s newsroom in Holt Street in Sydney together with Bradstreet to speak directly with its editor, David Penberthy. When told of Keelty's imminent arrival, Penberthy rings the London correspondent and asks for a briefing. He hadn't taken much notice of the first report and didn't know there was to be another.

Keelty arrives shortly after. Forty minutes of discussions ensue. It is agreed that the special news investigation—which had already been going for a number of months, and was to be a front-page exposé of various elements relating to the Standen plot—will not be published ahead of any critical developments or arrests. Maximum security has to be maintained, with discussion of the wider exposé or plot strictly limited, as Octans police telephone intercepts have shown that a number of journalists had been in contact with Standen over unrelated investigations in the past—some in the last few weeks.

One innocent slip from a reporter about a huge exposé being written or canned at the behest of the AFP commissioner could compromise many months of work.

At the meeting, Keelty reveals the news piece actually came closer to indirectly exposing another major drug plot the AFP had been working on. Some months later, it would prove to be the biggest drug haul anywhere in the world: the Italy-based Calabrian Mafia conspiring with crims in the NSW town of Griffith to move 5.6 tonnes of ecstasy into Melbourne in tins of tomatoes.

Penberthy instructs his London correspondent to shelve the special investigation for now and to pursue stories elsewhere in Europe. Penberthy is told by the AFP to come up with a cover story of his own as to why Keelty and Bradstreet were in his office. When curious police reporters in the news room later ask about Keelty's visit, Penberthy says it was a simple discussion about having charges dropped against two of their reporters who were being prosecuted under federal legislation for trespassing at Sydney Airport.

March 2008

'I have met with the girls and everything is on track,' Hogan writes to Jalalaty in an email. The girls he refers to are his Dutch contacts, including Loek and Fat Ron, and the planned shipment is on track.

About the same time, Standen emails Hogan, begging for money to help him through difficult times. He adds that Jalalaty is unable to help him financially anymore, and that it was his birthday the previous week and he is now 51 years old. It's a sad and pathetic email:

Hope all is good with you. I need to ask you something which is pretty bloody rude and bold considering the things that have happened with Myrtle. I won't be surprised if you fall off your chair swearing and saying you can't believe that I'd ask. I seriously will understand if it is no or fuck off or if it just can't be done. No offence taken if it is no and please try not to be offended by me asking . . .

Towards the end of the email, Standen finally states he needs $14,500.

Shamed by his begging email, Standen wakes early the next morning to erase the draft message he left. It is then he sees Hogan has already responded and has wearily agreed to sort it out. Standen then sends him another message saying he feels wrong about asking, but adds 'many thanks'.

Hogan then emails Jalalaty:

Maurice needs some expenses and says you are not in a position to help?? Nobody has yet explained to me what has happened to my investments??? Love Jill

Jalalaty responds:

Maurice has extended himself so much and borrowed more than he can handle. I gave him your Christmas gift and much more. He is living beyond his means. I am selling stock for people to help him pay his debts. He is supposed to be trying to help me get my money back from my investment people. If he does I will give him more money than he can ever spend. He has interviewed people here at his office and then he traced the money overseas. There is 7.5 million owing to me. Most of that was meant for you as the money is a combination of my assets and savings as well moneys from you. They call me every week telling me that they are going to pay me and then nothing happens.

To the Briton the exchange is troubling and he realises he has a problem with the both of them. He is almost a puppeteer, with his two marionettes now independently reporting to him about each other. He sends a message to Standen and the pair agree Jalalaty is a Wally, but someone they will use for now.

Standen, meanwhile, barely has enough food to feed his family. He even goes to the trouble of looking about his car console for spare change. He finds about $5 in small coins, many of them 10 and 20 cent pieces.

Standen then texts Jalalaty and complains about money. 'Hopefully not much longer but I have to survive that long. If you can work some magic it will repay itself soon enough,' he texts.

Jalalaty would have texted him straight back, but Loek is now texting Jalalaty.

All the while these texts are being captured by recording devices placed in Jalalaty and Standen's handsets.

The high volume of intelligence flooding into the Octans/Mayer investigation creates a frantic pace. They are now tracking suspects and suspected drugs across more than a dozen countries including the Congo, Pakistan, Belgium, Dubai, Germany, Spain, Portugal, Australia and the Netherlands. The number of intercepted communications between Jalalaty, Hogan and Standen is massive. In Holland, extra police are brought into the probe. There are now references to foodstuffs and other goods from all over the world, including shipments of cans of tomatoes, coconut milk, jam from Panama, crockery from Malaysia, goods from China—and neither the Dutch nor Australian police can tell what is real or code for narcotics, although they suspect some of the references to South America involve veiled cocaine shipments.

During another meeting in the city, Standen gives Jalalaty a long description of how Customs works and how they choose which containers to search. It is still fresh in his mind from a meeting just a few days earlier.

Jalalaty is surprised to hear that Customs checks very little incoming cargo but wants to know how they choose which containers to inspect.

'They just profile it—like look at it to make sure,' Standen tells him. 'They might X-ray it, might just check the documents, have a second look at them, make a quick, make an inquiry, make sure the factory exists or something you know, do that sort of stuff.'

Hogan, meanwhile, continues to worry about Jalalaty and tells Standen as much:

To Snodgrass, I need you to keep an eye on Myrtle as she is young and naïve, talk soon and I am looking forward to hopefully seeing you. XXX Big Sis

On 31 March, container TTNU-282498-0 leaves aboard the ship *Bunga Delima* from Pakistan, bound for transit port Singapore, then on to Sydney.

In the Dutch National Crime Squad headquarters, Jan Boersma has a meeting with Louis Aurik.

Boersma is not happy and wants to take Operation Mayer through to its resolution: that is, to make arrests and end the investigation.

'We have to stop this, it has gone on for too long,' Boersma tells his subordinate. 'I mean we have enough already to make arrests—we have other crimes that need to be looked at. Shall we go on, yes or no?'

'Yes,' Aurik simply replies.

This is not the first time they have had this conversation, and he knows to let his boss let off steam before making his case.

'Louis, give me some evidence of the container. I trust you, but is the container coming, yes or no? All I hear is talk. We're not sure there is even anything but rice in there—you are not sure are you?'

'Well I didn't put it in there so no, I'm not sure.'

'Six months, yes, this is normal. You ask for a year and I say yes okay, if you think it makes Merlin and Mayer a strong case for court. But now we come up to two years? Two years, Louis! This is one of the longest cases in Dutch law enforcement history.

'I know the Australians are important to you—to us—but we can make a case here already. They don't know what's coming. As far as I am concerned this case is closed. We have a lot of evidence, we have a lot of other cases in Holland, and this is just one of them.'

For Aurik these discussions are becoming harder and harder. His boss is right on all counts. But it is not just about the drugs or their relationship with the Australians, who he is now in contact with at least three times a week. It is about protection of law enforcement.

'I have done a lot of cases with heroin and these drug things, but I think for police in total in the world, this is one of the most important cases,' he tells his boss finally.

'Somebody in police is involved, and that is like a deadly sickness to a police body; somebody corrupt on a level that is corrupt for all police forces in the world, not just Australia.

'Because anyway, you can do a lot of investigations—all these other ones we have—but when something is not reliable between police forces, all the effort is gone.'

'Australia is the linking pin for this case, yes?' Boersma asks.

'Their man is deadly for any police organisation in the world.'

Boersma stares out the window. The commissioner is a smart man and knows Aurik is right, but it's part of his style, his relationship with his men, that he can challenge them and get confirmation of what he thinks privately. He does want to shut Operation Mayer down and move on, but agrees to give Team 5 a little more time. Coincidentally, on the opposite wall of the meeting room, is an old image of 'Ayers Rock, Central Australia'. Yes, Australia is central to everything, he thinks.

He looks back at Aurik and says: 'We have come this far. This is a case the National Crime Squad is built for.'

Aurik rises from his seat and smiles. He has secured another victory, bought more time. Each argument, he knows, could be the last for the case.

He returns to his men and gives them the thumbs up. There is little more they can do except continue to live the lives of their quarry and hope to hell the drugs arrive in Australia and the AFP can wrap it up.

Meanwhile, Dutch agent Casper Prenger is given the daunting honour of collating the tens of thousands of intercepted telephone calls, looking for the ones most likely to be relevant to the Australians, and the ones related just to the Dutch. Hundreds of lever arch folders are brought into the room for him to begin the evidence split. He will later directly liaise with AFP agents and play back hundreds of telephone calls stored on discs to help identify the voices. Aurik will be present for those playbacks also.

*

There are now hundreds of emails, but one particularly captures the attention of agents sifting through the exchanges. Standen is sitting in his office at his computer when he picks up a draft from Hogan.

> Hey listen. You know what would be a very smart move from your intelligence service for your intelligence service?? Would be to let someone do some laundering as it would bring a wealth of info. And every so often bingo they would get some terror stuff. Everyone is scared of Pakistan at the moment and looking for other routes. I have good China alternatives. Something to think about. You would overtake the US and UK very quickly, Love Linda.

Standen responds, 'very good reasons to be scared of the Pakis at the moment'.

Hogan replies:

> I only mentioned the laundry as every time I am near people in that area I hear enormous amounts of goings on. Not all is relevant but as was shown last time with the greedy Singapore one a controlled operation can lead to whoever is working big in any areas. Anyway gotta dash Love Renee.

Police perform 'controlled operations' all the time—that is, they allow an unlawful act to occur, in order to allow an investigation to progress. They study Hogan's file and realise the Singapore reference is to particular Pakistani cash-dealers working there and in Sydney. AFP agents conclude 'last time' refers to the job Hogan did with the NSW Crime Commission in 2003, when $300,000 was laundered.

Agents surmise Hogan, who is spending a lot of time with Pakistanis, is suggesting another money-laundering operation could attract intelligence that expands into terrorism. The importance of this reference will not be realised until some years later.

For Jalalaty, the wait is a major frustration. His natural instinct is to call and talk to somebody and find out what is happening. He knows the news and hears about all the troubles in Pakistan, but needs to know that all is on track. Hogan says they are, but Jalalaty wants to hear it for himself.

Jalalaty starts to make phone calls of his own, rather than follow the agreed procedure to put communications via Loek or one of the agreed Pakistani contacts. He speaks to anyone who picks up the receiver of the phone number he has been given. When that phone is engaged, he even rings the telephone number in the letterhead of the faxes that have been sent from a front company. Because he does not refer directly to the illegal drugs shipment, and complicated by broken English on the other end of the line, the telephone calls police listen in to are confused, to say the least. Instantly police recognise they are dealing with amateurs, in both Pakistan and Maroota, NSW.

Jalalaty never knows who he is dealing with from one day to the next, but as instructed begins to transfer money to facilitate a shipment.

Realising there is potential to make more money off the shipment from not only Hogan and the Dutch, but also now some fool Australian who has contacted them, the Pakistani criminals decide to withhold the bill of lading documents that will be needed at the other end of the shipment to get the cargo off the Australian wharves.

Jalalaty sends the Pakistanis a $20,000 cheque in the first instance, thinking he will get his money back from the Dutch when the shipment arrives, but then they ask for more.

Embarrassed by what he has now created, the hapless grocer from Blacktown lies to the Dutch syndicate and Standen when they ask if he has had any contact from anyone in Pakistan or sent them any money.

1 April 2008

Undercover AFP operatives follow Jalalaty from his home in South Maroota to College Street in the heart of the city.

It is 10.30am and the area is busy, but Jalalaty stands on the street looking about. The agents expect to see Standen's face in the crowd—but instead another man walks up to Jalalaty, exchanges only a few words, hands him a red bag, then walks on. The exchange lasts less than thirty seconds.

Half an hour later Jalalaty meets Standen and hands him $25,000. He says he only met the man briefly, but the shipment must be close and the money a gift from Hogan and his Dutch mates. Standen takes only a portion of the money and says he will return for the rest when he needs it and that Jalalaty should keep the rest safe.

Jalalaty reveals that there is a new Hotmail draft from Hogan and how he has advised again on what to do 'if it all turns to shit'.

'I don't want to hear those words,' Standen replies, but agrees he will read the draft for himself.

They speak about the need to be more careful. Standen reinforces his fear about reading and sending emails from home, and ensures Jalalaty is checking emails from internet cafes and not from home.

'Something must be close now,' Standen repeats in desperation, before again complaining about his money situation.

'It is—I'm just waiting on the bill of lading and then I can trace the container's movement on the internet,' Jalalaty replies.

They discuss a lengthy draft Hogan had written from his home in Portugal days earlier, in a new Hotmail account. In it he advised Jalalaty on a cover story. It is, he wrote, his 'insurance' if it all goes wrong.

Jalalaty says both he and Standen should read it, then erase it. They do—but not before police also read the draft.

In a nutshell, Jalalaty is told to admit he knows Loek, who uses the codename Rashid, as an importer, and they have a fight over the first consignment of rice. A second is organised, but the supplier has changed, so payment gets forwarded on. This means Loek looks like the 'strange one' in the plot using Jalalaty.

In the 'subject' line of the email, Hogan writes 'paypal'.

Has the girl rung you concerning Maurice? This is important for you, this is your insurance, if by any chance there was a problem. Okay listen this is important for you, this is your insurance if by any chance there was a problem here is the scenario: You have been working with Rash & Co, you had one consignment, there was a lot of arguments about the product and the factory (all true) okay. You sent payment for a second consignment. You were contacted by Rash & Co and told that they were changing to another supplier and that your payment would be credited to the new company!! But you had to reorder the goods, and they also had a customer for you but as yet they have not contacted you so you have done nothing wrong. Clever bit is Rash did not take the money back from the first company so on paper you have paid for stock and for some reason Rash did not ask for it to be sent to

you (do not contact the old company). So inquiries will show that
Rash & Co are the strange ones and should anything go wrong
you are in th [sic] clear. Everything looks good but always best to
have the answers even if they may not be needed.

Jalalaty replies he understands the scenario and will keep it as
insurance.

Four days later Jalalaty meets Standen and passes him the other
portion of the $25,000; he is surprised that it is needed so soon.
He again thinks to himself that this man is living beyond his
means, and wonders how much of it will be put on the horses or
into the poker machines. Clearly it's not being used on his wife
and four children.

On 8 April a fax arrives at the Jalalaty home. It is from MDL
Food and Services, sent from the Tara cafe north of Amsterdam.
It is a bill of lading for container TTNU-282498-0, which
confirms 537 bags of rice—in 15 kilogram, 25 kilogram and
40 kilogram sizes—has been dispatched from Karachi.

He texts Loek, who sent him the fax, and thanks him.

Jalalaty can hardly contain his excitement. This is real, this
is happening. He meets Standen the next day and, almost to
reassure himself, revisits the same conversation about how
Customs couldn't possibly check all the containers that came in.

He had had legitimate food orders come in from overseas
many times before—soft drinks, fish and of course rice—so his
latest order under BJ's Fine Foods will not raise suspicions. He
also has a clean criminal record working in his favour. No, there
is nothing to throw up any suspicion, he thinks.

Standen tells him if the authorities do look, they will see all the money that went through the psychic Bruce Way, but all he has to say is that it was his savings built up over fifteen years in business as a grocer and wholesaler.

Loek later telephones Jalalaty and agrees to send him the original bills of lading by air courier.

AFP investigators Glen McEwen and Brett Thompson fly into Amsterdam to get on the Hogan trail and work closer with the Dutch police.

It is being rumoured the Socceroos will play a friendly soccer match against the powerhouse Dutch team ahead of their campaign to qualify for the World Cup 2010—so the pair use these unofficial reports as their cover story. The match is to be played in Eindhoven in the country's south in September, so naturally they are here as an advance party analysing safety and security ahead of the Australian team's arrival.

The pair immediately go into undercover mode. They never stay at a hotel longer than two or three days, and are constantly on the move about the region of Eindhoven—only a few kilometres from Hogan's semi-permanent base in the city of Tilburg. They also travel about the cities of Den Bosch and Breda, trailing suspects.

Their primary mission is to take a leading in-country role in the case and pass on critical intelligence being gathered by Dutch counterparts. They are looking for any hints that could identify more suspects in Australia and bolster a case against Hogan and the others.

On Morris' instructions, their other critical role is to encourage the Dutch to stay interested in the case. There were grave fears, based on past experience, that the Dutch would move on from the case—understandably, considering their massive case files, given that their country is the synthetic drugs capital of the world. Other investigations and nations were also demanding their attention, and the Dutch had already given a great deal of assistance to the Australians.

McEwen and Thompson meet a number of times with both Boersma and the national prosecutor Cees van Spierenburg, but generally work in with Aurik and the other undercover Dutch police tracing and tracking the movements of Hogan and other key suspects.

The trip is supposed to be for a matter of weeks, but a month later McEwen and Thompson know they cannot go back anytime soon: the conspiracy is bigger than anyone had imagined. When they do leave the country, it is only to travel to Germany, then Dubai, London, Portugal and back to Holland. Crucially, they establish that many countries do not recognise drug precursors as an issue.

McEwen's regular telephone and written briefs back to headquarters are usually in code, although not as elaborate as that being used by Standen, Jalalaty, Hogan or the Reservoir Dogs. All suspects are given a phonetic alphabet code tag for quick reference. Hogan is Echo (which police think appropriate since he has an ego with a capital 'E'), and Dutch contacts are Alpha, Bravo, Charlie, Delta and Foxtrot. Each is matched to a physical characteristic of the suspect. One is large, so he is codenamed Foxtrot (or just Fat Ron); arrogant suspect is Alpha; a crazy Dutch man becomes Charlie; bald man Bravo, and so on. Standen is given the codename Zulu, because he is a warrior—but the pair also use the code Rupert, which is what agents back in Australia are calling him from the children's story book character Rupert the Bear, after their target spoke about the character in one of the many hours of eavesdropping tapes.

It all makes for confusing times. So many codenames, so many *Reservoir Dog*-style descriptions, and so many players in the plot that they have to constantly remind each other who is who.

The AFP pair even struggle to maintain their cover as forward security scouts for the Socceroos, since at times they are in a fortified ancient Dutch town that has no sports field. Most Dutch hoteliers suspect they are perhaps just two gay men on holidays, shy about their status, and ask no further questions—it's the Netherlands after all. Fine by McEwen, but he jokingly warns his burly partner not to get any ideas about taking that guise too far.

One morning, the pair wake up in Oisterwijk, in the country's south, and know the day will involve a lot of waiting around. Dutch intelligence from various wires suggests the syndicate will meet at a specific restaurant. The pair dress casually to sit the meeting out, but soon realise they stand out in the crowd far more than they had imagined. It happens to be the Queen's Birthday, or Koninginnedag, a national holiday, and everyone—*everyone*—is wearing the national royal family colour: orange T-shirts, orange dresses, even orange painted faces and orange hair. The streets are full of people waving national flags or orange flags. It's the only day of the year people can trade on the street without a licence, so the many cobbled roads are cluttered with impromptu street markets and parades and the atmosphere is festive.

As they sit at a crowded pub across the road from their target restaurant, hoping they are just ignored or written off again as out-of-place tourists, a silver Porsche pulls up. Fat Ron ('Foxtrot') steps out. He looks directly across the crowded street at the two men and a faint smile creases his face. Shit, McEwen mumbles to his partner. It's too obvious he was looking straight at them. Maybe someone gave Foxtrot the heads up, but either way their cover is blown.

Nothing else to do but order another beer, then move on.

Luckily for them, Foxtrot writes off the sighting as just another pair of hapless Dutch undercover agents trying to rehash the Merlin inquiry.

It's an embarrassing slip by the pair.

7

Rice Man

Police are watching as the *Bunga Delima* arrives in Singapore and container TTNU-282498-0 is offloaded. Then watch as it is loaded onto the *Sinotrans Shanghai* to complete its voyage to Australia.

The vessel docks fifteen days later on 26 April in Sydney's Botany Bay, and the container is offloaded. Jalalaty has been tracking the ship and container via the internet and knows it has come in. He wants to contact Hogan immediately about the exciting development, but the Briton has been very clear in his instructions. He now only wants to hear from Jalalaty when the cargo has been cleared from the wharf—then the men can discuss what to do next, including which portion of the drugs to give to whom. A saved portion has to show there has been no tampering; any sign of tampering and the whole deal will be off.

'Everything is looking good,' Hogan thinks to himself.

But it is far from looking good, as they soon discover.

Jalalaty does not receive the original shipping documents

needed to get the container off the docks. Instead, he receives a ransom note of sorts, demanding further payment before the originals will be released. The Pakistan controllers now want $65,000 in US currency for the documents.

Jalalaty is incredulous. He texts, then rings, Loek, and demands to know 'what the hell is going on'. Loek blames *him* for the bullshit and tells him to sort it out. Jalalaty then emails Hogan and says he cannot believe how stupid people can be.

For his part, Loek suspects Jalalaty is the fool and is out of his depth. He has already done an online Australian Securities Investment Commission search of Jalalaty's business to build a profile of him, not convinced he is a solid businessman. He decides to get tough with the Australian and they go on to have some fiery exchanges.

Hogan replies in an email:

> Let's see what unfolds in the next 24 hours at least now there is positive proof that the main problems are from their side keep me posted I am on their case in five minutes.

Jalalaty responds:

> Getting unprofessional and too ridiculous, I have kept the note just in case I am hoping that tomorrow something will happen problem is I can't get Rash before 4.30 our time that only gives me 30 minutes to do something I will keep you up to speed.

Hogan replies:

> Hey listen, with Rash and Co we now play hard ball, tell them that you are really not happy and they have been blaming you for all the

mishaps and telling me that you do not know what you are doing.
Tell them I have been bollocking you unjustly for their mistakes.

Jalalaty stores what he calls the 'ransom note' in a drawer in his home office; later he will wish he had thrown it away.

Hogan has no idea there is any real issue and has already flown to Dubai and is preparing to fly into Australia.

Jalalaty continues having conversations with men in Pakistan, but most of the time has no idea who he is speaking with. Loek tells him to tell freight officials that the documents are lost. Jalalaty has to stall until everything can be sorted out.

Jalalaty reports to Hogan via email:

Something smells and I have until tomorrow before the container is picked up and sent back. I can confirm that the guy asking for the money has the docs. If I can transfer by Western Union within one hour I will have the docs at MISC in Karachi. I have contacted Rash and he is to follow-up.

Standen too worries about his friend. His desperate calls and texts are over the top. For the first time he fears Jalalaty could crack and let something slip that gets back to the commission. Dianne's knowledge is also a problem. He knows Jalalaty is a necessary burden, the syndicate needs his food business as a front—but what a fool he is.

Standen, now also extremely worried about money, rings a Customs supervisor to see if there has been anything of concern on the docks. The telephone call is again not out of order as the men often speak about what's coming in and out.

It all seems okay, but just to be sure, Standen then rings a colleague in the commission, who acts as its liaison officer with

Customs. Again, the liaison officer suspects nothing from the call and the pair chat about recent seizures.

Only then does Standen send a blank SMS text message to Jalalaty, as previously arranged, to signal all is clear.

Jalalaty is still in a flat panic, though, and calls and emails everyone again—including Hogan, Loek, syndicate members in Pakistan and legitimate freight forwarders. Without the bill of lading, the goods will not clear and he can't work out why everybody seems to now be holding out for more cash.

In his mind he tries to clarify the who's who in the picture. Mohammed is from the rice factory, but there is also a Mohammed and an Abdul, who are the Pakistani-born Dutch citizens working with Loek, and the go-betweens with Khan and Ali, and also the bloke Mubashir who looks like Manuel from *Fawlty Towers*. But he struggles to establish clearly who is the legitimate rice producer and consignment handler, who is using a codename, and who the drug conspirators are. But they all contact him claiming to have not been paid for their legitimate or illegitimate part in the plot, and demand more money from Jalalaty.

Even when Loek rings and tells Jalalaty it's Rashid calling, Jalalaty confuses the voice and thinks it is really a Pakistani calling, and talks about demands for money which Loek can't understand, but Loek plays along with, thinking it's all part of the covert conversation.

It is now 8 May and the consignment has been on the docks almost two weeks.

'I thought you blokes know what's going on there,' Hogan angrily tells Jalalaty.

'Yes, in normal business I know, but the people in the office override other people in the office. What do you want me to do? I've made fifty fucking phone calls to Pakistan in the last two days, what do you want me to do?'

'Okay, okay, don't get your fucking knickers in a knot.'

The pair go on to discuss options, with Jalalaty explaining in detail what he has been through with the various bureaucracies.

'You are supposed to know all of this shit,' Hogan concludes. 'Pull your socks up.'

'Mate, I only know the general rules—and stuff like this sort of bullshit and fraudulent and all this stuff that happens, bugger that. How the hell can I control that? If you need me I'll be in Pakistan tomorrow and I'll fax it, the document, delivered there. Someone at the miscellaneous office changed all the rules, they took the document and gave it back to the bloke and he went away with it. Luckily he kept it. All I need is this fucking document, this is the original bill first and second. Once I get that it's clear.'

'Just get it sorted.'

Standen starts to think Customs will get suspicious that the container has not been collected. Things like that get red-flagged on a computer. Anything out of the ordinary usually pops up fairly quickly, and a food order just sitting there is starting to border on the weird.

From his office, he telephones a colleague on a different floor and says he is about to send him a blank fax to see what, if anything, appears on the top of the page. He has already trialled this and knows that when he sends a blank fax, the receiver receives a blank fax with no header. He wants to send a message to Hogan at the Le Meridien Hotel in Dubai, but can't risk anyone seeing on it the letters 'NSWCC', or worse still, the acronym spelt out in full.

A minute later the unsuspecting colleague calls back and says the test fax was fine and no letters appear, just the time and date.

Two hours later, Standen sends Hogan a blank fax. It is another coded message about concerns. Hogan emails Standen back and simply asks 'how are the children?' He is not referring to Standen's family but rather Jalalaty, who he suspects is getting increasingly agitated by the delay and carrying on like a child having a tantrum. Hogan and Jalalaty have just had an animated discussion via email, in real time, while they were both at their computers, and the tone was one of panic.

'The kids are all good and behaving themselves although some are saying too much,' Standen replies.

Hogan says he has heard another shipment of MDMA is on its way to Australia from China, hidden in bath salts. Its detection could throw off any potential heat on their rice if the information is passed on to the appropriate people.

Standen rings Jalalaty for the latest. The pair talk in code, as always, and discuss the purchase and pick-up of a new car (shipping container), and how to get the right papers to ensure collection. Where are the papers and why is it all taking so long?

At 4.43pm on 9 May, Jalalaty receives a call from a man who will only identify himself as Shaun.

Shaun tells him he wants to buy the container of rice, and asks why it has not cleared the wharves yet.

Jalalaty doesn't know how to answer. He doesn't know who

Shaun is, or whether he really wants to buy rice, or what he thinks the consignment is hiding.

After he hangs up, he immediately emails Hogan and tells him of the call. He also says he shall start to investigate how to *steal* the container off the docks. He is in financial trouble himself now and needs the cargo.

'This is supposed to solve our problems, not make them bigger,' he says.

He rings a Customs Agent and bemoans all the bureaucracy and paperwork, and jokingly suggests he would have sent the container of rice back if he had not already paid for the product. It's a call he hopes will provide him with some cover and relay to Customs that he is as frustrated by the delay as anyone. It is all about arse-covering now.

'I will fly to Pakistan myself,' he half-jokes. Half-jokes because he is indeed considering flying there. He knows that every day that goes by raises more questions. Storage costs have also blown out to $9600, and a good Customs officer would soon ask why no one has come to collect a food product.

Jalalaty rings Standen and tells him the same, adding he is happy to pay $500,000 to a corrupt Customs officer, although he doesn't know any, to help have the container released. He is in a sweaty panic.

Standen has been around too long to entertain such nonsense, and he stands to lose the most—namely his home, lover and family—through his mounting gambling debts, so he calmly tells his hot-headed friend to calm down. Bringing anyone else in is far more dangerous than just working patiently towards getting the container released legitimately.

'Nothing beats just ordinary cargo, because there is so much of it. We shouldn't let anyone else in as every new person is a risk, and if they were caught they may try and trade their way out of it by providing information about the shipment,' Standen explains.

Four days later, a second unknown company tries to requisition the container with its supposed rice haul. Standen is told by Jalalaty and immediately knows something is wrong: there could be a double-cross on the books. Either way, having a second company try to requisition a shipment is highly suspicious—exactly the kind of thing staff at storage facilities are trained to look out for. And it would take just one person with an inquisitive mind to make the phone call that would end it all.

Hogan emails Jalalaty and tells him to pretend to be interested, but not put himself in a position where someone could take possession of the rice.

On 14 May, Hogan asks Standen, through the Switzerland-spelt-backwards Hotmail account, to check the container is still free from law enforcement scrutiny. He also wants reassurance about the apparent added interest and kids 'gossiping'.

Standen responds:

Hi Sweetie, no big deal, just lots of kids saying they are expecting presents soon etc but all different stories. None worthwhile. Just shows though kids should learn to wait patiently and not get so excited that they tell all their friends what they are getting for Christmas or their birthday etc. No big deal. Otherwise the kids are fine. Can you tell me the China stuff on the normal Yahoo please. Any time frame for getting it here? Love as always regards to Herbert and the girls Norma.

DECEPTION

Telling Hogan to email him on the Yahoo account is critical. That is the account Standen uses overtly to contact informers, so getting Hogan to send his tip—albeit a phony distraction— to that account will allow Standen to show the NSW Crime Commission his source.

Jalalaty, meanwhile, sends another $65,000 to Pakistan in the hope of having it all sorted out. It appears to him that if he pays Mr Khan, who had the initial ransom note, assuming he is legitimate in his claim, then he will pay the rice makers, and freight forwarders, and ephedrine farmers, and whoever else is bloody well asking him for money.

Hogan writes:

Are you 100% about the authenticity of the guy (Khan) and do you think not that once paid he will ask for another payment . . . So who is Khan? How did you get his number? Why did we pay him? What relationship is Khan to Mohammed? Mohammed must have a land line or an address for him or a way to contact him or an associate unless this is all bollocks and Rash was correct?

Jalalaty responds:

Khan is the guy that paid the supplier for the rice. Legally he owns the rice. But the guy has also an investment in the matter and has gotten a little spooked as calls were made to the shipping agent from your side (you) and he wants to check that it is not a trap of some sort.

Soon after, police intercept an email sent from Hogan's email account to mstandenau@yahoo.com, stating that a shipment

160

of MDMA has been sent from China hidden in bath salts or crystals. It states: 'all I know the shipment was sent. It is very close or maybe it has arrived. It's from China.'

This overt email from Hogan to Standen's Yahoo account was one of 140 Hogan had sent since leaving left Australia in 2003.

Hogan goes on to suggest Dutch people are involved in the shipment and asks that he not be compromised with his tip, 'as they are heavy people'.

At first it is not clear to agents reading the emails whether it is part of a cover—an informer pretending to tip off a contact, in case anyone is watching—or an actual tip-off. But police discover there is in fact a suspect container coming from China, although it is not clear whether Hogan is in any way involved, or has simply heard about it. In the criminal world, most syndicates know what rivals are up to.

Standen later contacts Customs and tells them that a source, 'who's given us some good stuff in the past', has tipped him off about a possible shipment of crystal methamphetamine or ice coming in a container from China.

On the advice of Standen, Jalalaty flies to Dubai to meet up with Hogan. Standen wants to get his friend away from Sydney and his crazy ideas about stealing whole shipping containers off the wharfs or paying Customs officials, but he is also keen for Jalalaty to personally make Hogan aware of Standen's now dire financial situation.

He has no more money to spend and is getting desperate. He can barely make remortgage repayments or contribute to his family's basic household needs.

At 5.45pm on 16 May, Jalalaty calls Standen and in a jovial way asks, 'Do you want to say hello to someone' and passes the phone to Hogan. For a very brief moment all three talk on the phone at the same time, and this will later be significant to police: it links all three for a common purpose—a plot to import 300 kilograms of a precursor drug chemical.

In Standen's mind, everyone's tone has changed. They don't sound drunk but simply happy. Something has happened, and maybe he can finally get some cash flowing again. He doesn't like to ask Hogan directly for money and waits until Jalalaty comes back on the line. He tells him he urgently needs $10,000.

By the time Jalalaty flies home to Sydney, a DHL package with the original bill of lading has finally been sent. A fax sent from the Le Meridien Hotel in Dubai to Jalalaty's home also includes copies of the first and second bills of lading. Hogan has clearly been successful in his phone calls, Jalalaty thinks.

Standen doesn't care anymore and just asks when his pay cheque is coming. It takes the wind out of Jalalaty's sails; he has just spent days in Dubai securing what he needs to move the issue forward, and all Standen does is talk about money and how little he has. Bloody idiot, he thinks, it's his own fault for being such a pathetic gambler, or whatever it is he continually loses his money at.

'I just hope there is enough stuff in there that he [Hogan] won't want to do this again,' Standen finally says, before wearily adding that no, law enforcers are still not looking at the container.

Standen describes how he intends to launder the proceeds through one of his unsuspecting brothers. He knows he has to watch how he moves the money about, to avoid any scrutiny from the Police Integrity Commission.

He says one day they will all look back and laugh and wonder what all the panic was about.

'In all honesty I would be happy if I get $100,000, as then I would be able to breathe,' he says.

Jalalaty, being secretly recorded, replies that he has been assured they will get paid before the product is manufactured into anything else.

Standen just snorts, 'This is getting ridiculous.'

'We're right, as soon as we get paid first, we get paid first before anything happens like container [indistinct]. We get paid tomorrow whether there's stuff, stuff or not we get paid. I said to [Hogan] "mate we're in dire straits",' Jalalaty replies.

Standen is not convinced and cuts his friend off. His next words, recorded by police and later transcribed, are damning and desperate and will ultimately provide police with what they feel is clear motive.

'I'm in worse than dire straits. I emptied my bank this morning so that they couldn't take it out in fees, alright, I've spent $5 already, I have $85 exact to my name and an empty pantry—empty but not empty—but close to empty. My kids they're going "Dad, why aren't you shopping, why haven't you got a shop done?" I said, "Oh I'll do a shop soon."

'My daughter this morning wanted to make—before I went to work, she was going to school—she wanted to make a chocolate. I normally have Milo right, no Milo, nothing. She was making me a chocolate drink out of my son's Army-ration powdered chocolate because he went to the Army Reserve—he had a container of like Army stuff like, um, condensed milk and things. She's looking through the pantry for something to make, she's looking to make something and found an Army ration pack—powdered chocolate in an Army bag, making herself a drink of that. She said, "Dad, when are you going to do a shop?" I always shop, I do the shopping.'

'I was going to ask but I couldn't bring myself to do it,' Jalalaty replies sympathetically to his rambling friend.

'She said, "When are you going to shop?" I said "Ah". Out of food in the cupboards and the fridge and I can't even do a shop. I've got $85 till next Tuesday night.'

Standen is in trouble and he can barely keep on top of it all. His American Express credit card, Citibank Platinum Visa, Westpac MasterCard, ANZ Visa, Police Credit Union Visa and GE CreditLine ATM card from Harvey Norman are all maxed out, and his equally numerous bank accounts are overdrawn and cheques dishonoured.

He laments he has to travel to Wagga Wagga with his son for an Army parade and he has two birthdays coming up that he can't afford, and has had to ask Citibank to extend him more credit. If he defaults, 'they will fucking ruin me', he says.

'Everything alright with the container?' Jalalaty asks again, changing the subject.

'Yeah.'

'Heard anything?'

'No, it's right. What are we going to do? I was really hoping that he [Hogan] was going to say "okay here's something" out of his pocket.'

Police listen on as Standen starts to swear. His desperation is obvious. For a split second, Octans agents feel sorry for him. But then they think what will happen if he successfully manages to get the precursors in the country and how many lives will be ruined. Also it didn't have to be this way, but he has chosen his own path.

The recordings suggest Hogan is as frustrated with his Australian friends as he is about the shipment not going through. Nope, no one listening in to the conversation believes Hogan will be flicking over any more money any time soon.

'I just want to know it's rice, rice, rice,' Standen demands.

Jalalaty responds, 'I've got everything covered my side, because people have rung me telling me that that Pakistani's given them my number—said they'd take the whole container no worries. "What's your name and number? I've got it down", know what I mean? It's fine, but really it's booked into quarantine, the guy wants to check the crap and chemicals. They said to me even if it's selected for an X-ray, he said "it's no problem". All I'm thinking—unless they have a tip-off, unless they're sure something's in there—we're right.'

'But they're not, there's nothing happening, but I don't . . . ah don't even tell me,' replies Standen.

'Because they won't tell you anything?'

'Ah they'd tell me that though . . . my mate would tell me that, um—all I, all I want to know is that there's a pay cheque coming.'

'Unbelievable, fuck. They said to me "don't get your knickers in a knot, just settle down". I said "settle down it's three weeks sitting here, three weeks". Oh these things happen . . .' Jalalaty trails off.

'Hopefully there's so much stuff in there that he won't want to do it again that he might just part with enough money to tide . . .' Standen says.

'No, not enough money for us to retire on . . .'

Standen starts swearing again about his 'fucking bills'. He then tells Jalalaty how the previous year he had told his brothers that he had linked up with a man in Dubai and was going to start importing energy sports drinks and other products into Australia and be rich. He even took a sample case of that B-52 drink into work and all his colleagues were drinking it thinking he was going to be a big-time importer.

Standen then reveals how he plans to ensure the money he does eventually make doesn't raise any suspicions with authorities.

'They keep saying to me now, "What's happening?" Um, ah, they think I was supposed to make a squillion dollars like a year ago. We haven't made five fucking cents, so what I was thinking of saying to the brother here that I talk with, that I finally got some things happening—made some money—but work doesn't want me to, like work wise, I'm not allowed to get involved in another business, and I don't want to jeopardise the job because it is too good here and you know?'

'Yeah, yeah,' replies Jalalaty.

Standen continues: 'So I wanna use the money, but I can't just pull it out of nowhere, so I was going to say, what if I could get my brother in Hong Kong to send me like, um, the family home—the father lives in it, and we've all got one big share in it, you know.'

'How much is that house?'

'Probably about 200,000 bucks each, you know. So I'm saying if I can get the money to my brother somehow, I'm saying can my brother send me the money from Hong Kong, cos they'll never be able to get there and check all of this stuff in Hong Kong. So he sends it to me, as him buying me out [of the house] because I need the money.'

'He gives you $100,000?' asks Jalalaty.

'I don't get nothing yeah and just . . .'

'Two hundred will get you out of the shit?'

'Yeah yeah.'

Jalalaty understands the plot, and agrees he can send Standen's share of the money they make from the illicit import from Dubai to Standen's brother in Hong Kong, who would send Standen $300,000, or whatever his future inheritance share was for the family home. Jalalaty then details how he has a relative who has a private lending company, which works in with the National

Australia Bank. He suggests he could run the money through his money, through accounts held by his unsuspecting relative, and the bank would pay a handsome monthly interest.

'Ah look, as I told you, 100 grand gets me out of the shit, 200,000 makes me really, really happy and 300,000 so that I can [indistinct] around the world.'

'Just got to do it slowly,' Jalalaty replies.

'Yeah I'm in no rush, but at the minute like at the moment, $500 makes me happy.' Standen sighs and again mentions how his daughter had to make a drink from an Army-ration sachet.

'I've got to do the shop. Every time I go to the shop, every time I go to the shop it costs me like $600.'

Standen then remembers he has actually withdrawn $90 from the bank, but has already spent $5 during the day on a drink. He then remembers the $5 in loose change in the car.

'When you see a kid in the pantry pulling out Army . . .' he trails off.

Jalalaty tries to console him that everything will be okay, but Standen can't see it.

'Fucking ration packs, to make a chocolate drink, and they're used to me shopping, you know? They're saying why aren't you doing a shop? I went on the internet about half an hour ago and my savings account, like, I had it was 90 bucks positive right. I had 90 bucks positive. Yesterday I had a dishonest, I mean dishonoured transfer. I looked at it about like 40 minutes ago and minus $369.70.'

'Really?' asks Jalalaty.

'On my savings account.'

'Fuck.'

'Savings minus $369 and 70 cents, lucky I took out the 90 bucks.'

'Yeah that's pretty . . .'

'So I'm just going backwards—so yeah, alright, I just hate doing this, I'm telling you. Hate it, hate it, hate it.'

Standen says his only objective in life is to get rid of his loans and get back on track.

'Get rid of these fucking loans. They're like a noose around the neck—like a noose around the neck, you know?' he says.

Jalalaty adds, almost in sympathy, that he understands his mate's predicament. 'At least now you know what it is like to have money, when you've got it, you appreciate it. Like me, I'm converting my car to gas, that'll save me $5500 a year,' he says cheerfully. He has more than one car and his main drive is a Mercedes.

'Know what it's like, know what it's like,' Standen agrees humbly.

'That's great, now you know.'

To the AFP agents listening in, it seems all the discussion of profit has blinkered the men to the danger of getting caught. But no: for Standen and Jalalaty, it is a constant threat that simply doesn't need to be stated all the time. Although they again discuss the process of cargo being checked at Sydney's docks.

'The only way—only way, only way, only way, only way—they can catch us is if they . . .' Jalalaty begins.

'Open it,' Standen offers.

'Unload the whole container and check the bags. That's the only way they can do it. X-ray? Not a problem. But there are fifteen per bag, the bag's sealed, they're in those bags.'

'Of rice.'

'Yes.'

'It's all rice, it's all rice, I just . . . it's all rice.'

Jalalaty reassures his friend that Hogan values them more than the container. 'He said to me "I don't give a fuck about this container—you're more important to me than this container. Fuck, this container is becoming an absolute shit fight. When it comes through, then it's sweet, no problem."'

'Well he's got so much money here, why can't we get some of that?' Standen asks

'I don't ask . . . if they found this one, like it would be all over the news.'

'They haven't. It's out of Customs, finished Customs—well it's not finished, but I mean yeah world news, ah la, la, la, la.'

Standen tells his friend the chemical is like crystal.

'The product itself won't do anything to anyone—like you opened it won't do anything. When you mix it with something else, then it becomes something else,' Jalalaty offers.

'They're making something, where ever, we don't know,' says Standen.

'Yeah they've, they've, they've made it my warehouse. The guy was there but he's finished. Before they make it we get paid and I will make sure that I remove the bags, transfer it into a plain brown box, tape them up and hand them over to my Portuguese mate and I get them back and I burn them so there is no trace of that bag. I said "look I'd rather do that cos they know I'm in control".'

'Hmmm then his [Hogan's] bald mate must be close?' asks Standen.

'Well he can't cos he said to me, "sit on it for two weeks, take a holiday I don't care what you do, just go away, enjoy, don't do anything, leave it there for a couple of weeks". Let him get his mate over here, find an apartment . . . we're sweet, my work. I can do in one day and I can go there in about four hours.'

'Without helpers?'

'On my own I can do it in about four hours.'

'Don't want to use helpers, you know?' emphasises Standen.

'No, no, on my own, no one do anything. I can do it myself.'

'Helpers is where things go wrong you know?'

'Yeah, no, I don't involve anybody, four hours.'

Octans agents record Standen as he goes into a lengthy explanation of what is to happen once the consignment is cleared. It's one of the longest conversations the pair have shared. The AFP agents listening, and later reading the transcripts, believe this conversation alone proves the conspiracy, as it shows Standen giving advice.

'As soon as it clears, we will have money in our pockets and we can get on with our lives,' Jalalaty says.

'Does your wife know what is in the container?'

'My missus said she had suspected it. I had to tell her, she is now clued up,' Jalalaty says.

'She's alright now, she hasn't said anything?'

'Yeah no she's fine, she's fine and I said to her "after this it's just smooth sailing". She's fine with it.'

The men pause to think before Standen again launches into his woes. Then, not for the first time, he concludes the future looks bright.

'I just hate doing this, I'm telling you—hate it, hate it. But one day we'll look back and we'll laugh. We'll go that was silly, you know.'

Jalalaty reflects on this, then says he's glad it's not in small packages 'hidden inside the rice', but full bags.

Just then the audio begins to drop out, and the AFP agents

listening in curse. The recording quality isn't great, but as long as the conversation keeps running, it is all incriminating stuff. This will form the basis of the charge sheet, they think. For whatever reason, the recording audio comes and goes. But they don't realise how bad it really is until the playback and transcript.

'[inaudible] . . . so you might get [inaudible] bags [inaudible] hide the [inaudible] in the bag . . .' Jalalaty is recorded as saying.

'Hmmm, need a good clean-out afterwards because the most minute particles get picked up by these little chemical swabs, you know—minute little air particles,' Standen says.

'Ah good after I mean [inaudible] put the container.'

'Massive clean out, major.'

'What do I use?' asks Jalalaty.

'I don't know.'

'[inaudible].'

'Oh I mean, um, just need to wash, I mean you can't put water inside the place can you, you can't shhhhhhhhhhh.'

'Yeah I can,' replies Jalalaty.

'Can you?'

'Yep.'

'Ah, be happy just to hose it down, hose it down,' Standen says.

'I can Gerni it out—I can get a Gerni in there and put some, ah, detergent. Yeah I'll pop some detergents, rub it in and foam it up and squeeze it out. Yeah I can do that, I'll do all that,' affirms Jalalaty.

'Okay, well, if we can feed the little hungry mouths by this weekend, it's starting to sound sad isn't it? *If* we feed the hungry mouths. But it's like that.'

The 45-minute conversation ends, and the agents tell Octans chiefs, including Tim Morris, they reckon they've got the goods.

'It was all there—not a great recording, but all there, talking

half in code and Standen telling him what Customs and AQIS
[the Australian Quarantine and Inspection Service] will do,' a
surveillance agent tells Morris.

Morris will hear, then later review, the transcript—pages 4128
to 4142 on the ever-growing pile of listening-device recordings—
and realise he still needs more. The conversation was largely about
the Standens' pathetic home life. Hell, even Jalalaty, who seemed
to be doling money out left, right and centre, was whinging
about his finances.

They need more evidence.

About this time, Standen receives another email from Hogan,
again expressing worry about Jalalaty.

'I am so happy you are keeping an eye on Myrt and the kids,'
it begins, with kids being code for drugs, 'as I was really getting
worried. She didn't seem to be coping that well.'

Standen responds in code that he's on top of it. Hell, he thinks,
for the first time in a long time Jalalaty even sounds a little less
stressed, although just as crazy as ever. It almost feels like he is
actually enjoying this excitement. Standen recalls that at one point
Jalalaty joked to people—in front of Standen, at a cafe—that he
was an undercover agent. He then even parked his car in a marked
police zone, calling out to a nearby officer that he was undercover.

Then there was the conversation the pair had where the
grocer, as far as Standen could make from the jumble, told him
he had met a truck driver who had invited him into a mosque in
western Sydney, and Jalalaty had begun working 'undercover' for
law enforcement to uncover possible terrorist plots.

It was all fantasy stuff.

*

As the weeks wear on, with no actual sign of drugs in Australia, in the Netherlands Jan Boersma's impatience grows. There are now just too many variables that can sink his case.

He could arrest Hogan immediately and charge him in connection with Operation Mayer, then move on the other fourteen local suspects. This whole protracted exercise could end.

He calls his subordinate Louis Aurik into his office yet again. He tells him he has been patient too long and the case has to be wrapped up.

'This thing, it ends now, let's go,' he demands.

There are not even any guarantees that there are drugs in the consignment, or that they will ever be released from the docks. Aurik nods and excuses himself to make calls.

Understanding his boss's frustration, Aurik rings Bodel and makes it clear the Australian end has to provide some evidence that there is still a valid reason—other than a guarantee drugs are being shipped to Sydney—to let the case run. After all, both police teams already have enough for conspiracy charges.

Bodel confirms the AFP wants the drugs to arrive and be collected by Jalalaty, or at least directly linked to him and Standen, for a watertight case. The AFP will not budge without the drugs moving off the wharves and into Jalalaty's hands.

Bodel, in turn, later passes Aurik's concerns to Tim Morris. Until now, they have managed to get extension after extension from the ever-obliging Dutch police—but it may be time to get the top men negotiating directly with each other.

Morris sends a letter to the head of the Dutch National Crime Squad, Tom Driessen, explaining the situation. He asks the commissioner to ensure his subordinates do not move on their targets early, namely, until the AFP is ready.

He is given his assurance.

Driessen then rings Boersma, who listens, grips the telephone tightly, but accepts his superior's orders. Incandescent with rage, he then rings Bodel at the Australian Embassy.

'Don't fuck with me with this letter—don't fuck with me!' Boersma yells at Bodel.

'We have a frank and open dialogue—and going behind my back with this letter to my chief is . . . fuck . . . I'm the guy in charge and you can deal directly with me!'

Bodel is stunned and grimaces. The Dutch don't normally lose their cool; they rarely show emotion like that. And Boersma is one of the most in-control men he has ever met.

'We just need that container . . .' is all he can muster, as the man on the other end of the phone continues to make his point clear. Bodel doesn't get a chance to say that he had actually tried to telephone him in advance but couldn't get through.

Boersma then calls Aurik into his office.

'I know when you work in international affairs, if you work with Australians, they have their goal, and we have our goal, and it's good management that brings these two things together. I can bring these two things together, we have good cooperation—also I know the importance of this guy [Standen],' Boersma says even-handedly.

'But this letter—this letter—there was no need. I'm not impressed.'

Aurik now has to provide Boersma with an update every day, including a summarised copy of serious calls being made among the group. Bodel also has to bring in a translator to read daily reports he receives from the Dutch investigators.

Bodel begins meeting Aurik in person a little more too. During one drive to the Dutch police headquarters, he looks at the odometer and chuckles. His work-leased Audi A6 was new when he arrived, and he has already clocked up more than 10,500 kilometres, predominantly on this one job. 'It's not even that big a bloody country!'

This job has gone on too long, he thinks.

Still in the Netherlands, McEwen and Thompson also begin to feel their position is less tenable. They are checking into the same hotels in the same towns now too often. Hoteliers and locals are surprised, but simply ask them, 'Ah, back again?'

The Queen's birthday slip was bad, but now the 'advance security party' story is starting to wear thin on those around them.

Then, a bit of luck. The pair check into the Sofitel in Eindhoven, to find the lobby full of sport types and fans. They discover that the Dutch soccer team and the visiting Danish side are staying at the hotel, ahead of a match at the Eindhoven stadium the next day. It, being so busy, means they will not stand out as much as normal—but then one night on the way out to dinner, their exit from the hotel coincides with the Dutch team leaving the hotel for the tour bus. McEwen accidentally walks out with the players and managers into a flood of cameras from TV networks and other media. He is jostled and pushed next to two large players he doesn't recognise and is peppered with questions in Dutch from the excited media. Later Dutch police laugh and tell McEwen he is all over the TV news, walking out with none other than Dutch striker Klaas-Jan Huntelaar, more commonly known as The Hunter, and Ruud van Nistelroy, one of the best football players of his generation, who only months earlier had announced his retirement from international football.

'You look like one of the trainers,' the Dutch police joke with the barrel-chested McEwen.

'I didn't know who they were, I was just walking out of the hotel to get a feed!' he replies.

Still, the wide media publicity of the team helps McEwen and Thompson with their cover for a few more weeks. Some months later the Socceroos would play the Dutch squad in a friendly match at Eindhoven—but by then McEwen and Thompson were nowhere to be seen.

The incident spurs everyone on, not least of all the undercover Dutch, who do not have the same appreciation of Hogan's reach across the world. The secretive British Serious Organised Crime Agency does, but they are strangely uncooperative, so suspicion turns on whether Hogan is a paid informer for them too.

To the Dutch, Hogan is just another foreign player, like Standen, in what is largely a Dutch conspiracy. Each time Hogan can't be found or gives police surveillance the slip, Dutch agents switch focus and get back on the trail of the other suspects, leaving McEwen and Thompson to pick up Hogan's trail again, by ringing various airlines and officials at various ports.

It is frustrating and time-consuming work and the pair are getting weary, but they know they cannot leave until the case is resolved. Their colleagues back in Australia are also asking questions more regularly now as to where they are. A loose word now could overturn all the good work they've done to date.

The line goes out that they are overseas working on an aspect of the Melbourne underworld killings, and specifically on a suspect who is hiding out in Europe. It is known that a key criminal-turned-police-informer from the Melbourne 'underbelly' slayings is in Amsterdam and talking to police about a controlled return to Australia, so it's a solid cover story for now.

Back in Canberra, Morris is thinking the same as Bodel and Boersma. It's all just going on too long.

Privately, for the first time since 2006, he wonders whether the whole operation has been a waste of time. He knows of course it hasn't been. The imperative has always been to find the rat in the rank, and at worst they already have enough to charge Standen and the others with a conspiracy to import.

But it has just been so frustrating, and now his undercover team tells him Jalalaty—jokingly or not—is talking about sending the container back. Not for the first time, the officer muses about how an intelligent man like Standen could get into bed with these amateurs. The desperation of a man in deep financial woe, he thinks to himself.

Morris' habit of standing by the window and scratching his chin during meetings with his AFP team, as he ponders the complexity of the case and where to take it next, becomes his 'shtick'—providing team members with parody material for some much-needed moments of light relief in the Octans investigation room. Their Morris impersonations, however, are all in good humour.

Just as the men on both sides of the world believe the plot can't get any thicker, they discover the Dutch businessmen—obviously equally as frustrated with the delayed shipment to Australia—have been coordinating a second Australian shipment, with another Sydney-based criminal group.

It is the Lacerta team that has uncovered the plot, which has apparently been revived, shortly after a Dutch sports trainer named Jan had come into the country with a drugs sample but left without a trail. Through telephone taps, the AFP Lacerta team now manages to not only identify the when and wheres, but the whos as well.

A prominent Australian sportsman, who apparently knows the Dutch sports trainer Jan, and another Sydney man agree to smuggle in pseudoephedrine—again to be made into ice—in food cans. Once converted, the haul would have a street value of more than $50 million. The same six key Dutch names that had cropped up in the Hogan–Standen plot are now also in this plot. Their shipment is coming direct from the Congo, to be repackaged in Dubai, then shipped to Sydney.

For Morris, it is like someone has tipped an old jigsaw on top of the current one he is working on, messing up all the pieces. It is clear that the Australian plotters in each conspiracy have no knowledge of the other.

Morris cannot believe that the Lacerta operation is now again linked to Octans. Another 'double Dutch' conspiracy.

May 2008
Standen uses the Switzerland-spelt-backwards Hotmail account to contact Hogan. He heads the email 'Fashion House' and in the subject line types 'Subject: Skirts'.

Hello sweetheart. Missing your funny stories and warm cuddles. Couldn't find the clothes from China that you wanted. So much comes here it is not funny. Will look in case I find the style you're after. Have you heard of Chanel E designs before? Take Care, love to all Boyd

To the AFP, the China reference relates to the (true or otherwise) tip Hogan had given Standen in an overt email to divert suspicion from their own cargo. The 'E', they believe, is ecstasy.

Hogan replies a short time later.

Sorry you missed the boat from China. Never heard of Chanel. I have nothing to do with design wear and try to avoid the top 10. I sorted everything out for Myrt yesterday and she has not read her mail correctly. She really is hard work. Back to you later.

Meanwhile, Jalalaty has changed the locks on his warehouse for better security and anxiously waits for his container to clear Customs. It's getting close. The truck with his container is in a queue of rigs waiting to pass through the inspection shed, but it won't clear inspection before the end of the working day.

He rings Standen to tell him of the 'longest day of my life' waiting. He is told it will be released on Monday, as inspectors don't work on weekends. Another anxious weekend to wait—but at least this will be the last, he thinks.

He had earlier told his wife that once this one came through, he was through with Hogan.

'That's the one we want. When this comes through hopefully we will be debt free doesn't matter what's on it, we will be debt free from those people—and I reckon that if it doesn't get through and he's nice enough he will say "Look that's enough",' Jalalaty says.

'Well then let's hope he's got . . . he's very bloody reasonable and he takes off everything that you have given Mark, which is a lot,' she replies.

*

DECEPTION

Louise Baker lives with her mother and stepfather, so when she wants to spend the night with Standen, they often stay in luxury hotels such as the Sheraton, InterContinental or Four Seasons, or the Somerset Apartments near the NSW Crime Commission building.

Money never seems a problem for her boyfriend and she loves being showered with gifts. She offers to pay for things, but he always insists on paying. Since she moved out of the NSW Crime Commission their relationship has blossomed, and they are more comfortable being a couple. They do trips together, including one stay at Barrington Tops.

She asked him once about his money and Standen told her he had invested some with Bill (Jalalaty), who she had met in Dubai, and he was paying him back. But that didn't account for all the phone calls she had indirectly overheard from banks and other financial institutions chasing him for payments.

'I'm hopeless at paying bills,' he would simply tell her.

Standen would visit Louise at her parents' house from time to time. On one occasion he used her home computer to look up his Hotmail draft account and make contact with Hogan. He used the tuckedupinbed account, but failed to erase the account address when he switched the computer off. Louise's mother saw the address when she later switched the computer on and became curious, asking her daughter about it, who in turn asked Standen.

He thought he had deleted it from the Hotmail memory. It was sloppy, but he laughed it off with Louise.

Jalalaty's wife, Dianne, however, wants this whole affair to end. By January 2008, their liquidity is down to $18,000. What had been a profitable venture with plans for expansion twelve months ago can now barely pay the bills, despite the money Hogan has provided.

It is a constant source of friction between Jalalaty and his wife, who now bristles every time her husband refers to his 'little mate' Standen.

'I thought we had a hundred thousand stashed somewhere else, I thought we had a hundred thousand stashed away,' Jalalaty tells his wife.

'No,' she replies. 'You've given seventy-something to *you know who*.'

The police record similar angry confrontations about the money coming in—and particularly going out to Standen. Jalalaty had given the vast remainder of the money in the sports bag back to his Portuguese mate on the orders of an angry Hogan.

'How long is this relationship going to continue?' she asks.

'Once we get this first one through, then we'll decide. I spoke to my little mate, he said, "You tell me when to stop", he said to me, ah, and I said, "I'll do as you . . ." and we'll stop it—is that what you want to hear?'

'Ah I just wanted, wanted to know that was all bull—would've thought that, seeing as how the last one was rice, they'll get in the next one.'

'Yeah but this one's gotta come in . . .'

Dianne knows the greed of her husband's 'little mate' will ensure this whole business will go on. She remembers Standen asking her for money once—about $10,000—and when she refused he wouldn't speak to her for months.

There is more money coming in from Hogan soon enough: he wires another $25,000 with instructions to pass it on to Standen. Jalalaty tells Standen he has some more money for him, and to meet him out the front of the crime commission.

Jalalaty pulls up a short time later. Standen reaches into the car and takes a bag with $24,000 in it. Jalalaty says he is keeping $1000 as a tip. Standen, feeling generous, smiles and tells him to keep it.

Standen is spending close to $3700 a week on gambling, his girlfriend and other goods. He himself is concerned about his spending, but knows soon enough all his debts will be wiped.

He tells himself once he is a success, he will not get himself into such a position again. He and Jalalaty even joke about buying matching luxury cars.

It's getting so close now.

8

Last Drinks

On 23 May, almost a month after the container arrived, the bill of lading documents are handed over to Customs. TTNU-282498-0 is moved from Patrick Terminal to Customs, then to the Australian Quarantine and Inspection Service examination facility.

Morris has earlier ordered one of his team to contact Customs officials and ensure the cargo has passage through their care and is not touched. He risks a suspicious Customs officer making a mental note of the unusual request and inadvertently telling Standen when he calls, especially as Standen seems to be calling more regularly these days. But things are moving quickly, and detection of the case now is a risk Morris is willing to take.

The Quarantine officials look for bugs, not drugs, and Jalalaty knows it is close to coming off.

So too do the AFP agents from Octans who, in their backroom office, cheer when they are advised the consignment has finally moved on.

'They've finally got their shit in one pile—these blokes are a joke!' one agent says to another in their Sydney office.

'Now we go in and find some rice in our bags of ephedrine,' another responds jokingly.

Over one weekend, for twelve hours each day, twenty-five AFP agents working in shifts covertly go through all 537 bags of basmati rice—meticulously ensuring that their opening of the canvas-type sacks, stacked on pallets and wrapped tightly in shrink-wrap plastic, and their hand searches of their contents will not be detected by the criminals.

As each bag is resealed and the agents call out that nothing is found, Morris begins again to worry. There is no mistaking the batch is the one sent to Jalalaty; it has his company logo all over each bag, next to the proud declaration 'Product of Pakistan'.

Finally the last bag is resealed and the agents slump about the warehouse, looking exhausted and shaking their heads.

Not an ounce of the drug precursor is found. Just tonnes of basmati rice. The agents can't even find a forensic trace that a precursor chemical or a drug has ever been in the consignment. They use an IoScan device that can pick up a minute particle of substance.

Nothing. Negative readings.

They record their search on a handycam camera and take various photo images of the search, expecting the evidence to be key in any later trial. They needn't have bothered.

'Bullshit, look again,' Morris tells his crew in exasperation more than anything. After almost two years of investigation it appears this is another red herring. Just like Operation Lacerta, just like Operation Skysail, just like all those other money-laundering and drug operations that involved the NSW Crime Commission, or the Dutch police, or both.

To Morris it seems incredible. Somehow, somewhere, the drugs have been offloaded from the ship—if they were ever loaded in the first place. With all the chaos in Pakistan there has been a surveillance gap. There is no doubt, based on all the intelligence and communication intercepts, that none of the crooks themselves suspect there will not be something else in the rice.

All the coded correspondence points to this being The Big One. The angst and infighting between Jalalaty, Hogan and Standen—that couldn't be faked . . . and even if it was, why would they bother?

No, it was something else, thinks Morris. Someone in Pakistan, probably from The Factory, had found and offloaded the chemicals, and paid someone off to never deliver them.

There is no other explanation.

That night, Morris speaks with McEwen, who is still in his hotel in the Netherlands, and asks his opinion.

'Everything pointed to this being it. It was not meant to be a trial run or a dummy run—this, as far as the crooks were concerned, was it,' Morris says emphatically, after instructing his electronic intercept surveillance teams to double-check they haven't missed a coded word or phrase.

No, the double-checking shows they have all been double-crossed.

McEwen thinks to himself that the emails and telephone calls may have looked and sounded like double Dutch, but Octans knew the plotter's codes, and everyone was expecting there to be more than just bags of rice in the shipment.

He rings his AFP partner, Brett Thompson, who is at the Australian Embassy in The Hague, already reading translated transcripts of Dutch police wire taps for new leads, and tells him the bad news.

'This makes the brief just that little bit harder,' he tells his colleague. 'Without product it's very open. This will provide the defence with a number of opportunities to create doubt over all the conversations on the LDs [listening devices]. This is a new level of complexity.'

'It will only take one juror to disagree with us,' Thompson adds.

For the first time in a year, they fear their efforts are perhaps all wasted. Both are bitterly disappointed, but discuss what to do next.

On the police log of the search, the AFP officially records the failure in a single, simple term that belies the frustration and anger they feel or the efforts they have put in since 2006: 'Inspection of the bags failed to locate the presence of border controlled precursors or drugs. The consignment was repacked for delivery onto 24 pallets.'

The Octans agents hastily convene a crisis meeting and discuss what action to take next. There is evidence of a conspiracy, but nothing to show for it. Legally they can still make a case, but it won't be as strong without the actual product. Doubts will be raised.

Yet there is little other option. They cannot go for another two years waiting to catch Standen and the others trying to make another run. They may not even *attempt* another import, after this disastrous experience.

For the first time, doubt even grows in their minds. Could they all have been so wrong for so long? They don't think so.

The Dutch will not cop another delay: the operation has already taken too long and they have made several calls urging the AFP to act now.

It is decided there will have to be a change in the charges, from importing precursors, to conspiring to import the precursors. What that precursor is—ephedrine or pseudoephedrine—they have yet to decide. A move to arrest the men will also have to be made now. If the drugs had arrived, police would have waited until the mysterious Portuguese mate or perhaps the unknown Shaun or the other customers turned up—but that's not an option now.

The only other thing Morris can tell his team is to ensure the telephone intercepts and other surveillance remain in place. They may not have the drugs, but they can get incriminating evidence when Jalalaty comes and finds nothing. Morris is sure he will be as shocked and dismayed as them.

'We can go for the strongest, most incriminating, no-dope conspiracy brief ever seen,' he tells his assembled team.

'In one sense we will get a stronger brief when they try and work out what went wrong. You know they love to talk, and no doubt will be as surprised and disappointed as we are.'

27 May 2008

About the same time, Standen and Jalalaty discuss convening a meeting of their own.

The Australian Quarantine and Inspection Service has advised the consignment is still with them and is undergoing inspection. Standen had a day earlier telephoned the NSW Crime Commission's Customs liaison officer and again asked him if there were any new drug targets about.

No, just some illegal shipment of 510 kilograms of iodine tablets. The focus at the moment, the liaison officer said, was first-time importers, and so far nothing had popped up.

Jalalaty has imported product many times before, and this is always going to work in his favour, Standen thinks. This at least is good news, but Standen also thinks it is unusual Quarantine is unpacking the goods.

He and Jalalaty speak again in code via email, and it is clear the latter is getting jumpy and is eager to collect the container.

Standen emails him:

> I'm disappointed you are pulling out of the big tennis match I have been watching the tennis in Germany and now France on TV and am ready to kick butt. Are you pulling out completely or just delaying your return to the court? How are the immediate plans coming along are you still expecting a healthy collection? You don't want too much but a manageable number is always good especially for the pressies my guess it will be because as usual as the end of the month approaches we will make up for this later on.

Jalalaty tells him they should meet and talk in person; he is over this bullshit coded talk.

Hogan is also emailing Standen, asking whether Myrt has any news. Standen replies in email and directs it to 'fusspot'; 'Subject: Old woman'.

> Hi, she shits me at times. She told me earlier she had a bad day at work then she runs away and told us without talking to anyone and makes herself uncontactable. I have no idea what she's doing about arranging holiday. Lorna XX

Hogan responds:

> You'll now experience a little of the frustrations she has caused me. Nothing is ever clear cut with her and always she has someone else to blame. I'll try and contact her in the morning. XX

By the time Standen meets Jalalaty, the latter is extremely nervous and believes the Quarantine inspectors know something.

'The container has been fully unpacked—why would they do that unless they suspected something?' he asks Standen. 'They know something.'

Standen tells him that this isn't Quarantine's job—they look for bugs not drugs—and that his contact in Customs has told him there are no fresh drugs jobs on law enforcement books.

'How do you know that guy is not lying?' Jalalaty asks.

'He wouldn't need to,' he replies.

'Unless he knows there is a connection to you,' Jalalaty chimes in.

'That's giving them too much credit, and they are never *that* good,' Standen retorts.

Standen suggests his friend calm down and telephone the Sydney-based freight broker and ask her what is happening.

Standen and Jalalaty then discuss another cover story—a fresh take on their 'insurance'—should anyone make a connection between them, as well as what to say if they are caught.

They can argue they are innocent pawns and simply buying bulk rice to corner the market; they have no idea there are drugs involved and can—on request from police—help by providing faxes and emails from MDL and/or the Pakistani hosiery company.

Jalalaty will say he has travelled about the Middle East and Europe handing out his business cards to find potential buyers of his produce, and has no idea who he's got involved with.

'I'm not worried about myself, I can get out of it—but I'm worried about you,' Jalalaty tells his friend, in all sincerity.

But Standen just waves the concern away. He already has a cover story that involves how he came to meet Jalalaty through his wife Dianne, the ex-AFP agent, and how they came to be doing rice imports together to make money and were pawns caught up by criminals.

Standen would rather pretend to be embarrassed at being duped than admit to anything else. He could also tell police he was deep undercover and suspected a drug import was on the cards, and was simply doing what he was trained to do—lure in and catch criminals. Yes, he could say he was just playing along to catch the mastermind criminals.

He could, maybe, throw Jalalaty a life line and say some of the things he did—like buy acetone all that time ago—was at Standen's behest, to catch another criminal drug producer. He even already had some Yahoo emails from Hogan that would make it all make sense.

'Would someone let you know if you were in trouble?'

'Yes, some people would,' Standen replies confidently.

As Standen again laments his financial hardship, Jalalaty's phone rings. It is a freight forwarder broker, advising his container has cleared Quarantine and is ready for collection the following day.

Relief washes over the pair, who now have something to smile about. It is great news. Standen particularly knows the quick turnaround means nothing unusual was found, since police would normally want a longer period of time with a container if they were involved in any inspection.

From his own experience with Operation Mocha, he tells Jalalaty that it is extremely rare for a consignment of drugs to be allowed by police to run 'live' as a controlled delivery, so it appears police are not involved in looking at the cargo. If they were, they would have to replace the hidden haul with an inert substitute and then wait and watch for it to be collected. This usually takes time and the AQIS turnaround was relatively short.

Standen says the shipment would also be X-rayed and if anything was found his man would have contacted him.

'This looks good for us,' he says confidently, before adding he will ring another friend in the AFP surveillance branch under the guise of just catching up, and find out if there is anything being looked at.

Jalalaty is told not to talk near the container in case it has a microphone, but to start making calls to sell the rice. He is reminded again that when he moves the product, he should also give the warehouse a good clean-out, because the smallest particle could be detected. A hose-out with detergent is a good option.

If it is a set-up, the container will be tracked, so Jalalaty is told to have it collected as normal.

'Get the consignment to the warehouse and go about business as normal,' Standen says. 'I will safely sniff around as much as possible. You should go to the cafe and send [Hogan] a message and say you had a virus but you are now feeling much better . . . he is stressed.'

Standen knows that listening devices only usually have a one-week life span, so he says the container should be collected and left in the warehouse for at least a week, just in case.

'Go about your normal business, the bugs won't last longer than a week,' he says. 'Police would have tried to buy more time if there was something wrong. It is very quick for them to have done any work on it. The only way something could be wrong would be if they hadn't tested the samples yet and it came back as something wrong. Anyway, I would have heard something if they had done all that.'

The pair again discuss the man known to them only as Shaun, and wonder whether he wanted to actually buy rice, or whether he was 'the buyer' they had been expecting.

For weeks, Octans police have also been trying to work out who this person is and whether he is a food or drug buyer. The daily running sheet produced by undercover Octans agents and sent to Morris records the confusion of both officer and suspect.

> Jalalaty stated that they could give the lot to SHAUN who had called him earlier [9 May 2008] and STANDEN replied that he might not be a real rice buyer but might be 'the' buyer. JALALATY said he didn't know who he was and STANDEN stated that he could be a baddy for the other side and that JALALATY wouldn't want to sell it to them.

Jalalaty feels relieved. He goes off to find an internet cafe to send Hogan the coded message as suggested.

Police record a flurry of emails, and with time differences are confused by the sequence and reference. Yet the tension between Hogan, Jalalaty and Standen is clear.

Hogan to Standen:

> Hi Gal I just heard from Myrt, she seems a little worried about her exam results. I told her to relax as she cannot change anything. Anyway keep your eye on her as you know she is a drama queen. I will check the mail later. Love Swizz.

Standen to Hogan:

> Hi Swizz she was feeling ill but I met her and after seeing her she didn't look that bad. Her eyes were a tiny bit bloodshot that was all. Gets a cold and thinks it's the flu every time. A cut is like a leg amputated, she needs quiet times, we're all different. Jules

Hogan to Jalalaty:

Sorry to hear that you have not been feeling too good. Hopefully it will clear up fast and you will be up back to normal. I spoke to Maurice he says the children are all doing good at the new school so let's keep our spirits up, talk soon lots of love Danny.

Jalalaty to Hogan:

To: Chicken pox.
Subject: Getting better.
The kids are coming home tomorrow. They have been completely undressed to check for any spots. I will look at them tomorrow to see if there's any change. I am not sure what condition they are in. I will know a lot more tomorrow. Thanks for your concern, give my love to June. Love Peter and Joan

Hogan to Jalalaty:

Get well soon. I was talking to Maurice. June was telling him that children are on the mend. Just some bug going around. Best take medicine and keep them in bed until fully fit. I'll call you on way home from work tomorrow to see how they are. Take care lots of love Sally.

Hogan to Standen:

Thanks Moss. I was getting a little worried for her as we know she's a bit of a hypocondriat [sic]. Just had a mail from her she seems a little calmer. Take care love always Lorna.

*

28 May 2008

At 4.36pm, undercover AFP agents watch and record on a handycam as 537 rice bags on twenty-four wooden pallets are delivered and unloaded at BJ's Fine Foods warehouse in Chicago Avenue, Blacktown.

Jalalaty, expecting the delivery at 11am that morning, had physically vomited when it didn't turn up. By way of apology he tells a co-worker that waiting for the shipment of rice has been like waiting for a baby.

But it is here now and he wastes no time.

Another hidden camera inside the warehouse films Jalalaty on the forklift carrying the pallets, with an associate helping to direct. This is it. After months of heartache and frustrations, his delivery is safe in his warehouse. He looks relieved but anxious.

He decides to simply store the cargo for the next day: there is too little light left and he doesn't want to flood the warehouse with lights and draw unwanted attention. He also wants to see if there are any hints someone has tampered with his cargo.

Jalalaty goes home and sees a very short message from Hogan on his computer. 'Dear Sir waiting' is all it says.

He sits down and replies at 7pm.

To: long at the office

Subject: Dark side of the moon

Home now after llllong day at the office. Finally got the kids home. They look okay will need to keep an eye on them for a while. By the time I got them home it was very dark. Better look at them tomorrow. Thank you for your good wishes. I have aged 10 years worrying about my precious kids. I will update you tomorrow on their progress. Love Judith.

To: Rebecca winner
Subject: Long day
Darling so happy to hear from you. I was worrying. Nice to hear
that little Johnny and Sally are home. Tell June to put them in
bed until Doctor Maurice says they are fully recovered. Thankyou
again for your concern and all your help. Mail tomorrow. Lots of
love Sathonlunch

Jalalaty reads Hogan's email at about 7.30pm—about the same
time paramilitary police are gathering at police stations across the
Netherlands, Belgium and Germany, to be briefed about a mass
coordinated raid.

Hogan now emails Standen:

Just heard Myrth is home from the doctors. She says children
feeling a lot better. Can you advise her to keep them off school
and leave them in bed as long as possible. Better not remove
bandages until doctor says. Mail tomorrow. Love Auntie Jean

29 May 2008
At 1.36pm, Standen and Jalalaty meet again at Plato's cafe near
the NSW Crime Commission building. An AFP surveillance
squad is nearby and records the meeting. Both men look content.

Jalalaty is excited: all the bags were there, packed normally
and intact, and he says he is '75 per cent' confident everything is
fine. The bags have his brand stamped on the outside of the big
bags, but he will go out and buy forty cardboard boxes, double-
line them with bags, tape them up and put the smaller bags of
rice inside—and then meet Hogan's Portuguese mate.

Standen doesn't share his friend's enthusiasm. He tells him
that a bank called him and asked if they were speaking 'to A Mr

Mark W Standen'. He said it is odd that a bank would call him out of the blue and again they should shore up a story about money transfers between themselves. For a fleeting moment he wonders if police have been doing financial checks on him; he knows they can do that.

Standen can't pass up the opportunity of talking about his dire financial situation, and asks for another $10,000 to tide him over.

He has no idea how much his friend Jalalaty has loaned him, either directly or from Hogan, but knows its somewhere over $200,000 by now.

Jalalaty tells him he has no more money to give, but Standen asks him to ask a neighbour for some. Jalalaty has helped the neighbour out with some work at his property, so he should be amenable to a loan of a few thousand dollars. Standen suggests maybe $60,000.

Jalalaty is non-committal about the money. Wife Dianne will have his guts if he gives Standen more money. He moves the subject on and tells Standen he plans on putting the consignment in his car and driving it out of the warehouse to another location.

Standen uses his experience to caution his colleague on the move. If police are watching and listening, they will see all that, he tells him. He has to go about his normal business at least for a week. At least until the listening bugs expire.

'You should still treat everything as if it's still bad,' Standen cautions his friend.

Jalalaty says he has been—and even when he speaks to his wife Dianne about it now, they go outside. They are being very careful.

*

Police are already worried about the lack of drugs in the shipment, but on the other side of the world a bigger problem is being created.

A letter sent to a defence lawyer in Holland threatens to scuttle the entire two years of work by police, both in the Netherlands and Australia.

Unbeknown to Australian and Dutch police, prosecutors in Amsterdam—oblivious to the sensitive, heavily invested joint police investigation—have decided it is time to prosecute the principals in the Merlin case (known as Tahoe in Australia), based on new evidence that has been gained.

This is a grave error the Dutch prosecutors could not have known about at the time. The deadline for the appeal period for Merlin is about to expire, and if a prosecution is to proceed, any new information or evidence has to be served on defence counsels. Now prosecutors hope to hang a new case on some point-of-law technicalities.

Inadvertently, however, they have also collected the top-secret evidence and reports McEwen has been gathering in recent months, which focused on Hogan and went to the heart of the Standen conspiracy. Worse, the prosecutors then hand the whole lot over to defence lawyers representing the Dutch businessmen caught up in the 2005 drugs case—including their ringleader Foxtrot.

When the defence lawyers discuss the evidence with the Dutch businessmen, they are all staggered and confused. There are all these allegations seemingly based on new intelligence, printed on Australian Federal Police letterhead—and the dates are contemporary. This does not appear to be simply a re-interpretation by the Dutch prosecutors of their five-year Merlin case, as there is new evidence and information as late as 2008, against the members of the Reservoir Dogs. And furthermore, it involved the AFP who, to their knowledge, had never had anything to do with the case in their country. Alarm bells ring.

The businessmen call Hogan as he is packing his bags to fly from Bangkok to Dubai then Germany, before driving across the border to his home. He had considered flying into Australia first to oversee the sale of the haul, but decided not to test Sydney International Airport's passenger and passport screening abilities.

When he receives the call he has no idea what the Dutch are talking about. As far as he is aware, the AFP had investigated him years ago for Operation Merlin/Tahoe, dropped the charges, and had since learnt he was a paid informant of the NSW Crime Commission. There is no new case against him, that he knows of. He even remembers meeting a couple of agents more than a year ago and assuring them he was clean. To him, the recent dates on the legal papers don't add up—there is no new intelligence on the case, he thinks.

The Dutch are worried, but agree to convene a meeting in two days' time to discuss what it all means. If police were investigating Merlin as late as this year, then they must have stumbled over the fresh plots to export to Australia. They think that even if Australian police are not aware of the latest plot, then jailing them now will impinge on their drug operations. Business can still be carried out from jail, but it is cumbersome, time-consuming and costly.

Either way, it is all bad news. It is too late to stop the pseudoephedrine export to Australia, so perhaps they should all disappear for a while. They are all independently wealthy, so it won't be hard to move about borderless Europe.

*

They never have that chance.

In police compounds across the Netherlands, Belgium and Germany, more than 150 heavily armed members of six SWAT teams don balaclavas and bullet-proof vests for a series of raids on homes and offices.

They are backed by dozens of uniformed police, as well as detectives who have waited almost two years to see their work come to 'resolution'.

Moments before the police trucks roll out of the compounds, Jan Boersma has time for a series of telephone calls to Australian counterparts to warn them of what is about to happen.

He feels the timing is not ideal, but their hand has been forced by the prosecutors' inadvertent blunder. He calls Tim Morris first and tells him the operation has entered a 'critical situation'.

'We have to move—I have to do this, this is my decision,' Boersma says, almost expecting an argument from the Australian. 'It is in everyone's interests to stop them contacting Hogan. We are going right now, right now.'

But after hearing about the accident with the court documents, Morris agrees. He knows there is now no choice. He immediately calls his key people to warn them they have less than twenty-four hours before the first direct arrests are made and they should prepare to swoop on people of their own.

'It's a miracle we've managed to keep this going this long,' he tells colleagues, including lead case officer Paul Watt.

'That has been due to a little bit of luck, but also testament to the way you've worked. Operational security was critical, and through diligence you've ensured no one else has been in on the joke.'

Morris thinks back to the day he stood in a Canberra hotel almost two years ago and saw the young faces of the assembled AFP agents.

'This has been the most sensitive case ever undertaken by the AFP, and one of the most complex and protracted. The stakes were high. I wanted the best team and I got it. Now let's finish it.'

The emails between Jalalaty, Standen and Hogan continue.

How could they know that paramilitary police in the northern hemisphere are now checking their weapons and equipment in the back of vans that are pouring out of police compounds?

Jalalaty responds in email first to Hogan:

All good here. I incurred a large hospital bill. I managed to put it on credit cards. The last two weeks were very dramatic and expensive. Everyone has been paid and there are no angry creditors. I think we are over the worst. Thankyou for your concern.

Hogan later to Jalalaty:

Thankyou for your email. Sorry to hear that you had more than expected expenses. I have spoken to head office and have been assured that you will be reimbursed. I will try and arrange that you get an advance as soon as possible. I am busy reorganising things at the office and as I said when I saw you there are going to be a lot of changes and also fines for those who were responsible for this calamity. As we discussed have no more conversations with anyone and refer everything to my office and I will deal with it. Again I thank you and Maurice for your support in this matter.
Kind regards Simon.

Hogan later to Standen:

> Hi Doris, just to let you know, you know, that I am thinking of you,
> I have had a very nice time here and am a little sad to leave. But
> we cannot be holiday forever or can we. I look forward to catching
> up. Give my love to Myrt, love always.

Hogan had been in Dubai when he spoke of leaving his holiday,
but he has landed in Thailand when he next touches base with
Standen:

> So happy you are keeping an eye on Myrt and the kids as I was
> getting worried. She did not seem to be coping that well. I had a
> mail from her today and she sounded much more relaxed but I
> have told the office she will be staying on leave until she is fully fit.
> So no worries for her. I also am really looking forward to a catch
> up and it feels forever since we last had coffee and even that
> was not really a chat on our own. I will keep you posted as to my
> moves, lots of love Swissy.

Eight minutes later Standen replies to Hogan.

> **To:** Skiing season
> **Subject:** Boot hire
> Dear Swizzy, nice to hear you are relaxed and happy. It's a quiet
> time here for a while and it's nice to kick back and relax and
> do nothing. Always good to recharge the system before again
> tackling the problems of the world. I agree that 'coffee' or cocktail
> is long overdue and yes last time was not quality catch up. Too
> rushed and noisy. We will make better plans for next time. Please
> give my love to uncle John and also to 'Bruce' haven't seen him

in ages. Will pass on your regards here to everyone. Kids are
well. Cheryl is her usual crazy self and Myrt is fine too. Take care,
love Mel.

On the other side of the world, the Dutch swoop goes without
a hitch.

All those arrested are shocked, but do not put up any
resistance. One businessman is driving home in the early hours of
the morning and is stopped in his street by police, then watches
as they smash down his door to look for him. Instead of fleeing,
he tells the barricade officers that it is *his* house and is promptly
arrested. Such is his confidence that he may have thought police
were breaking into the wrong home by mistake.

Others are asleep in bed when police come calling.

In all, twelve men and one woman, all aged between thirty-
five and sixty-six, are arrested in Almere, Amsterdam, Zaandam,
Alphen aan de Rijn and Zwaag in the Netherlands, and one
person in Germany. Six weapons are found, as well as a large
amount of cash, laptops and only a small quantity of drugs: the
men are too experienced to store their product at home. A large
number of mobile phones are also found, and will prove useful as
court evidence for tracking other operations and suspects.

In the second-floor attic of one raided home, police find a
SanDisk memory stick. On it are dozens of documents—and
critically, photographs of the products, including the coconut milk
and citric acid that Loek and Jan had sent Jalalaty years earlier.

When Loek is arrested in his home, police find on him a
1 gigabyte memory stick, with further evidence of contact
between Loek and Jalalaty, as well as between Loek and the
hapless Rene Brusse.

In the home of another suspect, Dutch police find other BJ's

Fine Foods material, as well as a photograph of Jalalaty taken by the *Blacktown Advocate* newspaper in 2003.

One of the men arrested is a Dutch police officer. Although he is fairly young and junior, it still comes as a surprise to many—none more so than Jan Boersma, who has made his career by busting internal corruption in young officers before they progress up the ranks. Some peripheral suspects are not at home during the raids, but will be rounded up later. By this stage police know where their wives, mistresses or friends live.

Boersma is present during the raids, despite the fact his pregnant wife has gone into labour. For him, this birth has been nine months in the making—but the police operation has been more than twice that. The birth can wait a few minutes more.

News of the arrests in the Netherlands does not filter down to the southern hemisphere. There is a small news item on Dutch National Radio, and a short news brief in the newspapers, but there are so many busts and raids in the Netherlands that it just doesn't rate as a big news story.

Curiously, the names of those arrested or fronting court after being charged are never handed out by the authorities or courts in Holland, and certainly never published and broadcast by media outlets. The AFP is counting on this when they hear the Dutch have conducted their raids.

There is real pressure now to wrap up the case. The AFP will keep listening and intercepting communications to the last minute, but they know it is all but over, and local arrests will have to be made.

The shot clock has started and the game is almost up.

*

30 May 2008

At 1.29pm, Jalalaty buys the forty cardboard boxes and bin liners.

Twelve minutes later he meets up with Standen, who gets into Jalalaty's car in Sydney's CBD.

Jalalaty hands his friend $10,000 he has managed to scratch together, and tells him everything is on track.

31 May 2008

The next morning, at 10.13am, Jalalaty goes to his warehouse and stares at his rice consignment, pondering how the drug chemicals were hidden. The bags are still sealed. Listening devices inside the warehouse record someone moving things around; he is seen leaving thirty-three minutes later.

Jalalaty also replies to Hogan's email with a coded response, saying his 'kids' love playing hide and seek, and once he has the 'toys' in his hand he will hide them again. But he again asks Hogan to send someone to help him find the toys.

Hogan, as he reads that email, has no idea the Royal Thai police are watching him, and that they have been following him around Bangkok at the behest of the AFP until they can get their own man there to arrest him.

Then, at 3.59pm, Jalalaty reads an email from Hogan that mentions the arrests in the Netherlands. Hogan can't confirm how many have been arrested or even what for; he wants to believe it was for something other than what they were up to, but couldn't be sure. In the back of his mind, Hogan believes the arrests could just be for Operation Merlin, but the information he is hearing is so scant, and other underworld contacts he speaks with on his mobile are too fearful for their own positions to bother looking into it too carefully.

Hogan says either way it will be wise to check with Standen

on how to move the haul to a safer place. He also advises he will not now come over to Australia.

All this is conveyed in code, but the urgency is clear.

To: Removal

Subject: ASAP

Hi there. I do not like to bring bad news. I just heard that Rasheed's mum and father were involved in a serious crash a few days ago!! I am not sure who they were driving for! They are both in the local hospital. As yet I cannot find out how serious it is. I do not know if they had any copies of the insurance papers with them or at home but I am trying to find out so we can see if they have cover for private health care. Can you ask Maurice for advice on moving the children. I think it would be better if they went to stay somewhere more quiet as soon as possible. Other than that everything is fine. Maurice said it is quiet at work so has more time to relax Sorry to bring bad news. I will let you know immediately when I hear how they are Love Sathorn.

Three minutes later, at 4.01pm, a second Hogan email tells Jalalaty to buy a few cheap metal detectors to go on a 'treasure hunt' for 'toys' that could be hidden in the consignment. They will be wrapped in tin foil and easy to find.

Hi April, John was thinking to buy a couple of cheap metal detectors and organise a treasure hunt for the kids. He is going to wrap the toys in tin foil so they can find it quite easily. He tells me you know a nice secluded place for the kids to play that would be great. And I, we look forward to see you Sunday maybe better to travel in the night to miss any traffic Lots of love and kisses Sathorn and Nad family.

Jalalaty writes back at 4.07pm, saying he has already gone through many files, looking for 'pictures of the kids' that he has apparently been sent and found nothing in 'files' one to fifteen, but there are so many '25s and 40s' and he can't search them all.

'I checked more than 50 per cent of all files in the 1 to 15 and saw nothing.' And he doesn't know what happened to the Portuguese mate, who was supposed to help.

Hogan has no time to offer any other advice.

The AFP know it is only a matter of time before details of those individuals arrested, as opposed to the raids, might leak through the internet to the southern hemisphere.

Morris is at home when he is told of the raids. He immediately switches on his computer and begins trawling for news of the event. There is nothing.

Then, before he goes to bed, he does one last search and sees a small item on the Dutch *De Telegraaf* website. Just three paragraphs about the arrest of a well-known sports identity, Jan. No mention of the 50,000-plus pages of evidence the Dutch police have amassed in the lengthy investigation or the links to Australia and a certain crooked hat.

But he fears it may be just enough to tip someone off.

1 June 2008

The next day Morris hastily convenes a meeting to draw up the final plan for the arrests of Hogan, Jalalaty and Standen. The men are now under constant surveillance, and the police hope to make the arrests in daylight—less room for error and logistically much easier.

They decide to move on Standen first, then Jalalaty, and wait

206

for Hogan to fly into Germany, where the local police have been alerted and an arrest warrant already secured.

But as Hogan sits in the international lounge at Bangkok airport waiting to board his flight, he receives a call on his mobile. It's from a neighbour in his hometown of Tilburg, who says plain-clothed police—'some speaking in English'—had broken into Hogan's home. He didn't know any further details as the police weren't very helpful, the nosey neighbour says.

Hogan now begins to sweat—under the heat of suspicion rather than the notorious Thai swelter—as he stands in the air-conditioned airport lounge. Looking around anxiously at the blur of faces—passengers walking towards, behind and around him—imagining they are all looking at him. A couple of security men walk by, giggling at some joke, and barely give him a glance. Then a passing airport official brushes his arm and continues to walk on.

In reality, only the eyes of several Thai security police a discreet distance away are fixed firmly on the now panicked criminal.

Hogan decides that even if police are swooping, there is no way they can know where he is. He has taken all the right precautions. Hell, he is even travelling via Dubai, just in case. He decides to get his bags off the flight and retreat back into Bangkok to make calls and find out exactly what is happening. He thinks quickly how to do this and decides to feign an illness.

'I can't travel, I can't travel!' he yells in desperation at the Emirates airline staff waiting to take his boarding pass. Extra airline officials gather at the commotion. He puts on a big act, talks of feeling ill, of a fear of flying, and rather than delay the flight further, ground staff agree to remove his bags from the plane.

Hogan's mind is racing. He can't understand how it could have all gone wrong *now*. It is impossible. He has been betrayed by someone, he thinks—probably that useless Jalalaty. In private emails to Standen he had expressed his concerns about the weak Lebanese grocer. But then in private emails with Jalalaty, the grocer had expressed fears about Standen and his growing desperation for cash as Standen continued to live beyond his means.

They are as bad as each other, he thinks, as he races back towards the airport's main hallway.

McEwen, having earlier raided Hogan's Tilburg house with AFP colleague Brett Thompson—removing a number of pieces of potential evidence, including laptop computers and mobile phones—sits down to a meal at the Amadeus steakhouse in Antwerp.

He is expecting Hogan to come home the next day and thinks about what he will say to him. He feels he knows the man, having spoken so often about him during his many months in Holland, but also his years within the AFP and NSW Crime Commission.

It will be satisfying to finally meet Hogan. Will he be as expected, or something else entirely, McEwen wonders.

Thompson knows exactly what he is going to ask him.

It is a celebratory dinner of sorts for all those involved in the European side of the investigation. Hogan is on his way to the northern hemisphere and police will pick him up about the same time Standen was expected to be arrested.

'The goose is almost cooked,' McEwen says, before having to explain the phrase to the off-duty Dutch police he is sitting with, who wonder why he would talk of goose when he is about to eat some fine barbecued pork ribs.

McEwen just starts pulling apart his 'ribbekes' when his mobile rings. He initially remains at the table as his friends joke and laugh, and even take photos of him on the phone. 'Always working, that man,' they think, cheering loudly in the background.

But he quickly moves away from the noisy table. He is then told by a colleague that Hogan is not on the flight. McEwen is stunned. He looks back at his table as the police raise their beer mugs in a toast.

Hogan, meanwhile, is rushing out of Bangkok International Airport towards a taxi rank to return to the luxurious Grand Hyatt Hotel where he had previously stayed.

He quickly checks back in, before rushing to an internet cafe attached to the hotel and begins trawling through websites for information. He fires off emails to contacts, but thinks his own research more likely to come up with something ahead of reply emails, particularly given the time difference.

There is nothing on any news sites to worry him. He thinks perhaps he has overreacted. The raid on his home could have been a case of mistaken identity. As for the English-speaking cops his neighbour had mentioned, well, it was unlikely they would be from Australia, where, after all, he had indemnity from prosecution.

In Canberra, the extradition unit of the Attorney-General's department hastily puts together a brief for an international arrest warrant in Thailand. It has to be translated and wired to the embassy in Bangkok overnight. All stops are pulled out.

The document is created and sent, but when hand-delivered by an embassy official, a Thai magistrate rejects the warrant: it's all happened too fast for the magistrate's liking. These sorts of

things take a minimum ten days—a month is more common—
to discuss, and here is one written and awaiting his signature
in twenty-four hours. The magistrate declares it 'suspicious' and
refuses to sign it.

A rash of telephone calls are then made from Attorney-General
to Attorney-General and then Police Commissioner to Police
Commissioner. It helps that Mick Keelty plays golf with his Thai
counterpart and has a personal relationship with him and many
other senior Thai officers. Keelty appeals to his Thai colleague to
accept his personal word that the details in the arrest warrant are
legitimate, and that this man, Hogan, has been a target for more
than a year, and how important he is to a wider conspiracy.

The Thai Police Commissioner agrees to look into it, the
documents are relodged the next day, and a different magistrate
accepts them.

Undercover Royal Thai Police are ordered to arrest Hogan in the
Starbucks cafe near the hotel. They have been covertly filming
him tapping away at the keys, and even manage to zoom in on
his screen—to the point that the words he is typing can even be
read. This will be crucial evidence later.

The two uniformed senior officers, both of whom speak English,
approach Hogan and without any fanfare tell him he is under arrest.

'It's for the Australians,' one officer adds.

The AFP is nervous about where Hogan could go and
disappear to but then get a call advising of his arrest.

Hogan is incredulous and initially attempts to bully the
two local police into backing away. It is harassment from the
Australians, he explains—something that happened years ago.
Steadfast, the Thai officers order him to come with them.

Hogan looks down and thinks for a moment, then asks them to wait, to stop and think for a moment.

'Let me go—you let me go right here and now and you've got $2 million US, just like that. It's yours if you let me go right now,' he says.

It had been earlier impressed upon the two officers how important the arrest was. This offer of money—more than the two combined could earn in a lifetime—reinforces in their minds the stature of the criminal sitting before them in the hotel cafe. He is a big fish.

Without hesitation they drag him out of the hotel, where other armed officers escort them back to the central police station. Other officers may have been tempted by Hogan's bribe, but these two were too senior and professional to bother, despite how the offer could have transformed their lives. They suspect he didn't have any money anyway.

Meanwhile, at the Amadeus steakhouse in Antwerp, McEwen never finishes the pork ribs on his plate as he rapidly explains to his colleagues what has happened.

McEwen cannot believe Hogan is now in Bangkok. He had originally thought he would be arresting Hogan at his home in Portugal, then his other home in Tilburg, Holland, and then finally Germany, where several German police officers had been placed on standby. Just in case, arrest warrants for Hogan had been taken out in these countries as well—all very time-consuming and expensive.

But Bangkok? Shit. The death penalty in Thailand always made it hard to have someone arrested there on behalf of Australia. He hopes Hogan wasn't found with any 'samples' or they'd never get him out.

McEwen races to the nearest airport for a flight to Thailand. This job has already been one of the most expensive he has been involved in: what's another international flight now?

He and Thompson arrive a day after Hogan has been arrested and take a taxi directly to the central police station, where Hogan has been brought up from the cells and is waiting for them, handcuffed, in an office.

'How are you?' McEwen asks, to the blank, furious stare of Hogan.

For the Australian officer it is satisfying to finally see his prey up close. Hogan looks expressionless, if not a little mad.

McEwen, who has had a long time to think about his opening line on the flight from Antwerp, uses a code Hogan would understand well.

'We've just locked Myrtle up,' he says.

Hogan slips a little further into his chair. The use of the name 'Myrtle' shows the prisoner they are onto everything—the drugs, the accomplices, the farcical codes and women's names used for months by conspirators.

Nothing is said by either man for a moment, before Hogan looks up.

'Off the record?' Hogan asks.

'Yes, no problem.'

'So what's this all about then?'

It is a laughable moment of parley that continues for about twenty minutes as McEwen gives the man a thumbnail sketch of the case.

'How can you be going me for something from 2002? I got off that,' Hogan says, still not understanding the full picture, and apparently keen to concentrate on the Tahoe matter, rather than the Octans case against him.

'No you didn't, you had charges withdrawn in relation to a small matter—but I'm hitting you up for 1.5 million tonne.'

There is silence again as Hogan thinks about it. Clearly the AFP not only know about his plot with Standen, but also the previous shipments—only one of which, the Tahoe brief, has ever been known by authorities. And if Standen has been nicked, then it's every man for himself.

After what seems an eternity, Hogan breaks the silence.

'I tell you what, I'd be willing to do 10 to 15,' he says, acknowledging jail was now likely.

'We're not in a position to discuss . . .'

'I know, you just searched my home, that was you, yeah?'

'Yes.'

'Righto . . .'

'I've put you at the top, from our organisation, you are a very important person to us,' says McEwen. 'Basically I can assure you that it's a very tight brief of evidence we have got on you. I like having all my cards on the table and as I said we've got Myrtle locked up.'

Hogan puts his cuffed hands to his chin and thinks about what to say next. He has little to offer.

'Well it might not be as bad as you say, it might not be as bad as you think,' Hogan says finally. 'How 'bout this then—I will keep my cards close to my chest and you will keep your cards close to your chest and until I see someone, I'm not interested in saying any more.'

'That sounds fair enough, I can understand that,' replies McEwen. 'Obviously we have an extradition process to go through—what do you think will happen?'

'How long will it take me to get back to Australia?'

'Maybe six months.'

'Oh okay, I know you are only doing your job, thanks very much.'

And with that the conversation is over. As Hogan stands to be led away by the Thai police who have now come into the room, McEwen turns and asks him one final question.

'What's that tattoo on your knuckles stand for?' he asks.

'Don't you know?'

'I have a fair idea.'

'Well, I'd say you would probably be right,' Hogan smiles broadly as he is led away to be formally charged with seventeen charges relating to conspiracy to import a drug precursor, and a host of other charges related to 2005, including money laundering.

On his knuckles are the letters 'A C A B'—All Cops Are Bastards. McEwen smiles; his question was aimed at prompting Hogan to recognise his predicament, remind him what he was thinking at the time he had the tattoo etched many years ago, probably after he was nicked for an armed robbery.

McEwen walks away to ring Canberra and report in about what he describes as a 'roller ride' of a case.

The next day, McEwen and Thompson again visit their prisoner to explain in more detail their plan to extradite him to Australia. Thompson this time gets a chance to meet the man—again.

Thompson smiles at Hogan then says, 'Do you remember me?'

'No, should I?' the sullen Hogan responds.

'Yes. Don't you remember me from Sydney in 2002?'

In 2002 Thompson had been tailing Hogan in his car from Quay Street in The Rocks during the Tahoe operation, when the pair stopped at lights at the intersection of Alison Road and

Avoca Street in Randwick. Hogan waited for the lights to go red, then screamed across the intersection to the blare of horns from other drivers.

Thompson followed in his unmarked surveillance car, but by the time he had crossed the intersection, Hogan had done a U-turn and his car was pointing in the opposite direction. Their eyes met as they passed, and Hogan smiled. That was the closest they had come until now.

To Thompson's disappointment, Hogan doesn't remember him. The officer wanted to tell his prisoner of another occasion, also six years earlier, when he was watching Hogan load a large amount of cash in a box into the boot of his car, parked in a multi-storey hotel car park, and how he had to jump over a balcony and hang sixteen storeys up from a railing after Hogan turned around and almost spotted him.

Yes, Thompson thinks to himself, it has taken six years for the hunter and the hunted to meet up, and he is deflated that Hogan won't play ball and admit their long game of chase is over.

A warrant is then requested to raid Hogan's Portimao home in Portugal. Again a magistrate there rejects the warrant as being too rushed, and initially refuses to sign it. He does so twelve days later, by which time the AFP find someone has gone through the place and cleared it out. Probably the 'Portuguese mate', who police confirm is no longer in Australia.

They do find some valuable intelligence, however, including several bank accounts, deeds, laptops and a large number of mobile phones, all of which will prove to be valuable for tracing incoming and outgoing dirty monies.

*

Unaware of Hogan's arrest, Standen reads Hogan's earlier email and replies he will remind Jalalaty to buy the metal detectors for the treasure hunt.

On 2 June, Jalalaty deposits a draft email saying the kids love playing hide and seek, and once he finds the toys he will let everybody know. But he is confused about Hogan's metal detector line.

> **To:** On Line
>
> **Subject:** Give me time
>
> I do not understand the second message. Is this why I can't find what I am looking for or is it something else? I am sorry if I am not understanding what you are trying to tell me. Give me a time you are on line and I will wait for you. My kids love hide and seek. Once I have my toys in hand then I'll hide them for the kids. Can you send someone to help me find some nice toys. I'm having a little trouble finding the right toys, any ideas???

But Hogan never replies.

At 1.56pm that afternoon Standen finds out why. Forty-eight minutes later, so does Jalalaty.

Incredibly it is five days since all the suspects in the Netherlands have been rounded up and formally charged. Such is the nature of the business arrangements between all the parties that no one was overly concerned about the lack of communications during that time.

2 June 2008

The AFP does not want to cause a scene at the offices of the NSW Crime Commission. Relations are already strained—some might say explosive. It is decided Standen will be arrested off-site, or at least away from his desk and colleagues. Discreetly, with no fanfare.

The selection of the arresting officers is also carefully considered. It has to be someone Standen—who held most of the agents from his former force in contempt—could respect and listen to. Veteran agent and former AFP liaison officer to the Australian Embassy in The Hague, Terry Venchiarutti, is chosen, along with case officer Paul Watt, and 29-year veteran of the AFP John Beveridge, who is the AFP's liaison officer with the NSW Crime Commission.

Watt and Venchiarutti, it is decided, will also be the interviewing officers. Watt has been a team leader throughout the investigation and knows the brief well enough.

The arrest has to go smoothly, the men are told—strictly by the book. No commentary, no extras, just tell him he is arrested and read him his rights—in full—no matter how weird they sound on a former colleague. Watt is armed with a tape recorder to capture the moment.

Beveridge would often have coffees with Standen after official crime commission meetings so the phone call he makes shortly after lunch on 2 June doesn't arouse suspicion. As they often did when they went out for coffee, Standen and Beveridge take the elevator to the basement of the NSW Crime Commission building.

They are about to walk out the back door of the basement when Venchiarutti steps out of the unmarked AFP car in the basement car park.

Watt is also there, as is NSW Crime Commission executive and solicitor John Giorgiutti, invited to witness the arrest.

'Mark Standen!' Venchiarutti says firmly.

'How's it going?' replies Standen.

'Do you know Paul Watt?'

'Hello, Paul, how you going?'

'Good,' Watt responds.

'Mark I want you to listen, I want you to listen to me very carefully okay? We're here to arrest you for conspiring to import into Australia a commercial quantity of border control precursors. Do you understand that?'

'I hope you're kidding me?'

'I'm not, mate, I am deadly serious, do you understand that?'

'Is this a gee-up?'

'No it's not, do you understand that?'

'Yeah.'

'You are now under arrest. You are not obliged to say or do anything, as anything you say or do may be given in evidence. Do you understand that?'

'It's got to be a gee-up . . .'

'No it's not, the tape's running.'

'Yeah.'

'You're now under arrest, do you understand that?'

'Yeah.'

'Alright, next thing I have to tell you is your rights. You are able, you are allowed, to communicate with or attempt to communicate with a lawyer, alright. Do you understand that?'

'What are you talking about?' Standen says, looking about now.

'We are talking about a conspiracy to import into Australia— a conspiracy with Bill Jalalaty—to import into Australia a commercial quantity of border-controlled precursors. Do you understand that?'

'Yeah I know Bill, but . . .'

'Alright I will finish reading your rights.'

'Ok, alright I'll listen.'

'Are you Aboriginal?'

'No.'

'Alright, are you over the age of eighteen?'

'Yes.'

'Alright now, I will repeat again what I said to you before. You can communicate with or attempt to communicate with a lawyer of your choice. Do you understand that?'

'Yes.'

'Alright, you can also contact a relative or friend and let them know of your whereabouts. Do you understand that?'

'Yeah.'

'Alright, what we propose to do now is, ok, we are going to conduct a search of you, ok, and then we will be taking you back to our office to an interview room, where we will be giving you the opportunity to take part in a tape-recorded record of interview. Do you understand that?'

'Yeah.'

'Okay.'

'I hope there's a good reason for this, Terry.'

'Yep, Paul is now going to conduct a search.'

As Watt frisks the suspect, other police emerge from the shadows of the car park. A couple of other bystanders from the commission are inadvertently listening nearby, hiding behind a car, poking their heads up and down as another law enforcer, oblivious to the action, walks through the car park, past the men, whistling loudly.

'Do you know about this, John? My God you got enough people, um, this is very bizarre, Terry,' Standen says.

'Okay?'

'Is that your mobile phone?' Watt asks Standen, showing him the device after removing it from his pocket.

'Yep.'

'Yep, are these just coins?'

'Yep. Obviously something has happened but I'll wait and hear it.'

'Do you have any keys or anything on you at the moment?' Venchiarutti asks.

'No, can you give me a clue?'

'I have.'

'I mean a real clue.'

'I have.'

'Bill's done something wrong obviously.'

'*You* have, at this stage we are talking about *you*.'

'Ok we will leave it at that at this stage, alright then, yeah . . .'

'Alright, what we are going to do now is we'll go back to the office in our car ok. Paul is going to put the cuffs on you.'

'Really?'

'Yes.'

'Why?' Standen asks, as Watt goes to move the suspect's hands to his back.

'At the front,' Venchiarutti instructs.

'Why?' Standen asks again, almost pleading now.

'Because you're under arrest,' Watt gets in.

'The time is now . . .' Venchiarutti interrupts. 'Time is . . . uh . . . two o'clock on the second of June 2008.'

Watt walks off to get the car as the others stand in silence, waiting. They then walk slowly towards Bradley's car spot adjacent to the elevator when the mobile phone inside the plastic evidence bag rings.

Venchiarutti looks at it and announces, 'It's your daughter Simone calling.'

'Can I talk to her?'

'No. Some of our people will speak with her. I know they are making contact with her. We have some people up, they are going to do a search warrant on your house in Bateau Bay.'

'That could be a problem, that may cause some difficulties with my wife.'

'We are liaising with the crime commission and we will deal with it as best we can. We're also conducting a search of your office, and the crime commission is assisting us with that as well.'

The phone stops ringing.

'So come on, Terry, tell me, did Bill actually do something?'

Venchiarutti doesn't respond with words, but nods slowly.

The phone rings again and Venchiarutti sees it is Simone again. No one says anything this time.

Watt then pulls up in the unmarked police car. Standen is ushered into the rear passenger seat, while Venchiarutti walks around the car to get into the other back passenger seat. The pair in the back have a short conversation, with Standen asking his friend how much was allegedly imported, then what was the actual commodity?

He can't believe this is happening to him. His heart is racing as quickly as his mind is to process the situation and work a way out of it.

As the car leaves the basement car park, senior NSW Crime Commission managers several floors up call a staff muster. They then tell colleagues Mark Standen has been arrested on conspiracy to import.

There is initial shock, then several women burst into tears and comfort each other. Whatever his faults—and his colleagues know he has a few—Standen is a popular member of staff. Several in the commission already knew the arrest was on and had been thinking about the implications for their organisation.

Staff are then told the building is in 'lockdown' as AFP agents prepare to go through and seize documents, and anything else of relevance to their investigation. It is an unprecedented move for the NSW Crime Commission—indeed, rarely does *any* law enforcement office get locked down by other law enforcers.

Some police officers in the building rush to the telephones and immediately call colleagues outside the building, including the NSW Police Force—for while the lockdown is unprecedented, so too is the arrest of one of the most senior and powerful men in the building, and in law enforcement generally.

The arrest car drives along Kent Street, turns left into Market Street, before stopping at a red light at the Market and Sussex street intersection, alongside the Shelbourne Hotel. They are the third car back from the set of lights.

Standen breaks the silence. He turns to Venchiarutti and asks: 'So, what was brought in—what did you mean when you said border-controlled precursors?'

'Ephedrine.'

'And how much is involved?'

'Between 300 and 600.'

'Oh it's that serious then.'

The lights change and the men drive on in silence towards the AFP Sydney Headquarters on Goulburn Street, Surry Hills.

It will be another twenty-four hours before Standen learns from his lawyers that nothing in fact was found; by that time it is all too late.

Some time after Standen arrives at Goulburn Street, AFP agents tear his life apart for evidence.

Principally they seize both his home and work computers, and several Spirax notebooks in which he would jot down daily thoughts while at his desk. Among the unrelated crime-fighting notations, they find many damning references of interest to Octans, although these are disjointed and will take weeks to unravel. It is a case of joining the damning dots of words—'Dutch', 'Atone', 'Fat Guy', 'Belgium', 'Ron' and 'B52'. Wheeler's famed business card is there too; AFP agents have heard about it and its curious message but it is great to see the real thing.

The code for 'Switzerland' is found in Standen's car. In his home, telling bank statements are uncovered—a dishonoured cheque, demands by credit agencies and banks for immediate payments, arrears for council rates for his investment property in Bundaberg, Queensland.

In Maroota, northwest of Sydney in the Lower Hawkesbury area, Jalalaty is contemplating the continued email and telephone silence—not only from Hogan, but now from Standen—when there is a firm knock at the door.

He opens the door and three AFP agents announce who they are and tell him he is under arrest. Very little is said, other than Jalalaty expressing his genuine surprise.

As they drive him away, he can't imagine that just a day earlier, one hundred friends had gathered at his home to celebrate the holy communion of one of his children. It had been one of the happiest days in his life.

Jalalaty is taken to the AFP headquarters for formal interview. During his recorded conversation, Jalalaty goes into a lengthy explanation of his import business. Yes there was rice, but it was just rice, and oil shipments also planned, and cigarettes from the Philippines. He had all sorts of imports but nothing bad.

'I've never seen drugs in my life—only drug I've ever seen is Panadol,' Jalalaty says. A short time later he adds that if Mark has done 'something wrong', he doesn't know anything about it; he certainly doesn't know anything about drugs.

'I have a friend, Mark Standen, sometimes I chat with him, he's a good mate, I like talking to him, he is very knowledgeable,' Jalalaty says, before adding they spoke about all sorts of things, including tennis and travel, and that Standen recently advised him on a legal matter.

And as for money, no—Jalalaty says it was all his to invest from a life as a successful small goods businessman.

As the interview goes on, Jalalaty appears to become more anxious and talks faster, but with more faltering. His hands gesticulate more, and overall his body language becomes more animated, almost agitated. In pleading his innocence, he asks why, if he is guilty, he didn't run when police came to his house?

He changes his tune slightly and acknowledges that if there are drugs in his import of rice, it is because he is considered a good, clean businessman and is 'a soft target' for the criminal milieu.

'That's about the only thing he has got right,' Octans agents say while watching the recorded video of Jalalaty's interview in another room.

Jalalaty initially denies knowing Hogan, or ever receiving money from him, and says he had only lent money to Standen over a six-month period.

He said he used the Hotmail email system to contact his friend as a cost-cutting exercise, and had only ever contacted a man named Rashid in Pakistan in relation to the importation of rice. It is all an unconvincing performance, and police do not bother going over all the evidence with the man or playing all the tapes.

But they do reveal Standen has also been arrested, and suggest to Jalalaty he cooperate and save everyone time and money.

Shortly after being interviewed, Jalalaty rings his wife to tell her he is being taken up the road to the Sydney Police Centre to be formally charged. Dianne tells him she's already had a visit from the Australian Crime Commission.

'Okay, I've got no legal representation, I don't know anybody, eh? I didn't tell them the truth because . . .' Jalalaty says, before his wife cuts him off and tells him she has a couple of names of lawyers.

Jalalaty tells her he has been charged with attempting to bring into Australia a chemical precursor. 'It's front-page news,' he adds in exasperation. 'If you put the TV on, um, the guy here said that they've, they've cut a couple of stories and got Mark's face on the front page of the news tomorrow morning. Front page and my name in there everywhere, so if they charge you then you've gotta fight for your innocence.'

'Yep, okay.'

It is a short call and Jalalaty is told he can call his wife again soon, after a few formalities. He is also told that Standen is also downstairs, now being charged.

He has no idea that Standen has just spent several hours blaming him for the conspiracy, and accusing him of pretending to act like a 'dumb Leb'.

9

Fallout

Within an hour of the NSW Crime Commission's headquarters going into lockdown following Standen's arrest, police outside begin to leak to the media that something big is going on inside the Kent Street offices.

The *Daily Telegraph* editors decide the story can't hold as a newspaper exclusive for the next day. Instead, they break the story of Standen's arrest on their website a short while later, just before 4pm. It is only a teasing six short sentences, with a pointer to buy the next day's newspaper for the full story behind the plot. By day's end, the online splash attracts more than 40,000 hits.

Other news outlets follow suit and rush to post a Standen story on their websites, citing the *Daily Telegraph* just in case the details of the arrest are wrong.

It is a sensation.

Television stations immediately send TV crews to Kent Street, the AFP headquarters in Goulburn Street, and to the nearby Sydney Police Centre in Surry Hills, where those arrested are usually charged, processed and detained overnight, ahead of an early-morning court appearance at Central Local Court on nearby Liverpool Street.

Channel 9 also immediately dispatches a TV crew from London to Amsterdam to pick up the drugs trail, sensing this is a story that will only get bigger.

There is still confusion over the story, and most news crews in Sydney are simply told to photograph or film any movement outside the NSW Crime Commission headquarters, the Sydney Police Centre and the AFP headquarters until the authorities can confirm what is now being reported widely on websites and radio.

Meanwhile, oblivious to the frenzy outside, Standen is being interviewed in a secure area of the AFP headquarters. By the time he arrives there, no more than twenty minutes after being arrested, his bravado has returned.

'I don't need a lawyer, I can clear this up right now,' he tells officers as he walks into an interview room and sits down.

The interview is done by Venchiarutti and Watt, with a video recording the start time as 2.36pm. After reading Standen his rights again, Venchiarutti asks his first question, as to whether he understands the allegation put to him, to which Standen responds 'yes'. When asked what he can say about the allegation, Standen wastes no time branding Jalalaty a bit of a storyteller who just talks about things, but doesn't really do anything.

Venchiarutti stops him and asks him to go back and describe his position at the NSW Crime Commission and provide a brief detail of his background.

Standen launches into a confident defence; he was well rehearsed. Rather too much so: he has no idea that police had already secretly recorded him and Jalalaty rehearsing exactly the lines he is now rolling out. For Watt, who is also sitting opposite Standen, it is gold.

'I certainly never, never, for a nanosecond thought that Bill would import any drugs of any sort,' Standen declares.

'He talks anti-drugs, he talks about hanging the bastards. That's one of his favourite sayings. He asked a lot of questions. I never, I never think too much about it, and I never told him anything he shouldn't know, but he does, he certainly asks questions—but, like he's in the, he's in the import, export business.'

When told about the shipment, Standen again sheets it home to Jalalaty. He secretly fears his simple grocer mate has capitulated and rolled over, telling police everything, so he lays the groundwork on Jalalaty's state of mind.

'Yeah, yeah, I have no knowledge of that, no involvement. Got a big interest in it, obviously now, but never been a party to any discussion about any drug component, drug anything in this thing,' he tells his interviewers. He then continues:

If you know Bill, which you probably do by now—hopefully you do—you never read too much into what he says or does, or how he behaves. He's an unusual fellow. He's very likeable, again, perhaps the world's biggest liar in a funny sort of way. I've often thought it was pathological, but nothing—nothing that's sort of too harmful. And it's disappointing when you have plans that didn't work out. But he's close, he's probably as close to a pathological liar that I've ever met. He lies about things he doesn't need to lie about, and absolutely no reason to lie about a whole bunch of things. And he just does.

The interview gets bogged, with Standen providing lengthy responses to things he knows, like the business of Jalalaty.

Then comes the moment Watt has been waiting for. Venchiarutti announces that the AFP has had some listening devices and telephone intercepts in place, and he is now going to play a few.

'I usually enjoy this moment in an interview; this thing's a lot different,' Standen says, for the first time showing some concern.

He slumps further in his chair as the tapes are played, stopped, he is questioned, then the tapes resume. He is told there are 170 contacts between him and Hogan.

Standen brands some alleged coded conversation 'irrelevant frog shit' or just 'talking crap', and denies the Hotmail draft system was anything unusual, or that it was suggested by Hogan. It was all 'ducks and drakes' conversations that had no real sinister meaning, or even a meaning at all.

'I've done nothing wrong here,' he declares confidently.

Standen admits he went on a holiday to Dubai with lover Louise Baker, and that their airfare was paid for by Jalalaty—but it was simply that, largely a holiday, where they happened to also catch up with Hogan for dinner and talk about some export business prospects. He agrees that, yes, he and Hogan were in regular email contact on various accounts, including one which was spelt Switzerland backwards, but they were 'superfluous' messages designed simply to stay in contact.

'We used draft folders within the Hotmail email system for no real reason other than mind games and general silliness,' he tells investigators, still hopeful his months of line rehearsals will hold.

When police say they have recordings of Standen giving Jalalaty Customs and police advice, Standen responds that it was simply innocent information in relation to dealing with imports of rice; his friend in return would pay him a bit of money—about $20,000, over a number of years.

Standen says he never got any money from Hogan, but knows Jalalaty received about $800,000 from him for some business venture they had.

'I don't know what they are . . . my dealing with both men is legitimate,' Standen says.

As the questioning continues, Standen's resolve diminishes. Even to his ears it all sounds ridiculously unbelievable. He had begun his interrogation by describing his friend Jalalaty as harmless, an importer who made a lot of bad investments. In the final stages of his lengthy interview, and after one particular damning recording, he claimed Jalalaty may have taken advantage of him by asking about trafficking of illicit goods.

Ironically, midway through the interrogation, the fact that Standen has been arrested pops up on one of the bank of television screens in a 'situation room' adjacent to the room in which Standen is being interviewed. Many AFP officers are stunned that on one screen they are watching Standen being spoken to on camera in a locked room—and on another, featuring breaking news, is the story of his arrest in full.

Everyone who worked in law enforcement knew Mark Standen. He had been around so long his contemporaries were superintendents, commanders and assistant commissioners from various national law enforcement agencies, and no one can believe what is being reported online as 'breaking news'.

Finally, Standen slumps in his chair. He is beaten physically, mentally and emotionally.

At 7.30pm, Venchiarutti applies for an extension to Standen's custody for interview purposes. He is formally granted by a magistrate another eight hours. By this stage, solicitor Gordon

Elliot has turned up and is allowed to sit alongside Standen in the interview room.

Standen now clarifies:

> Um, just before we proceed ah, um, my position remains the same. I'm happy to answer questions, um, give my version of events, because I can see that our views, our view are at odds with each other ... Regardless about what we talk about and how, how it, how it goes um, my position I've stated earlier is, is the right one—that I know nothing about any ephedrine or any other drug, um, that may or may not be here. It seems that it is.

He goes on to say how troubled he is that Elliot, his solicitor, has shown him the reports of his arrest already appearing in the online newspapers.

But the interview progresses, and at one stage Standen asks if he can be 'unarrested' so he can go home and return tomorrow to finish his story.

'Why do you laugh?' he asks as Venchiarutti and Watt grin and shake their heads.

Just on 9pm, former AFP agent-turned-barrister Paul 'Chewy' King, drives his Aston Martin up to the front doors of the AFP headquarters and declares the interview over.

Standen then tells his interviewers:

> Paul has told me in no uncertain terms that even though I may well believe I'm—I know I'm innocent and I've got a story to tell—um, that his advice is that um, ah, I should follow his advice and not, um, continue with the interview at this point at least. And I should leave my options open. I've said to him that I'm quite happy to leave my options open, that at some stage, um, I'd like

to finish the story. He suggests that now at the end of a long day it started for me at 4.40 this morning when I got up—um, that at the end of such a long day it's not the best time to be dealing with um, an important story, um, in an important matter like this. So um, despite not having changed my view about wanting to cooperate, I'm happy to do it at some stage. But I'll follow Paul's senior legal advice, I respect his opinion.

The formal interview concludes at 9.06pm.

Outside the interview, Octans agents discuss the interview.

'He's still playing at different levels. He still thinks he is more clever than everybody else,' one agent says to his colleagues.

'He has always worked to his own rules, and if they have to coincide with the rest of the world that's fine—but if not, he doesn't see that as being a problem.'

Observers who saw Standen walk in, and then walk out so many hours later, reckon he has aged ten years. He is exhausted by the revelation of the extent of the AFP operation against him.

Crucially, neither Standen nor Jalalaty realise no drugs have been found in the container. For all they know, the large shipment of pseudoephedrine or ephedrine is where it should be, and that is how it has been traced back to them. For the first time they wonder whether the email silence means that Hogan has also been arrested.

The fact that no drugs were found was not mentioned by police for some time, in the hope one of the men would crack and confess. Standen and Jalalaty were both given the option, but neither of them do.

Police do eventually reveal the extent of Operation Octans: the hundreds of hours of recorded conversations between the pair, and even more intercepted and coded emails, and the tracked trips abroad, involving the assistance and cooperation of more than a dozen foreign police forces.

The revelations leave Standen gutted. Backed by thirty years' experience as a crime fighter, he had bragged to Jalalaty that his colleagues were not smart enough to trace their operation, nor decipher their coded messages—only to find out that they'd been onto him for years.

Later that night, a demoralised and handcuffed Standen is helped into the back of an unmarked police car and then taken to the Sydney Police Centre to be charged and detained overnight.

The police car makes no attempt to avoid the media camera crews that have been camped outside the Sydney Police Centre for more than six hours. Instead, it stops by the roadside to allow the blaze of flashes and television camera floodlights to splash the vehicle.

Standen covers his face with a jumper, but it doesn't matter— his public profile means media organisations already have images of him on file. The car finally drives into the building, with Standen's head between his knees.

At the Sydney Police Centre, King spends the night with his client, who is understandably confused and stressed by the day's events. He has seen that look in many clients, but perhaps none as high-profile as Mark Standen. King is angry that the arrest of the officer has already been made public, and is starting to attract what he sees as prejudicial remarks.

But he will be even more furious the next day, when the full story explodes across the front pages of newspapers around the country, and again leads radio and television news broadcasts.

'Top Cop Busted in Ice Cartel' shouts the front page of the *Daily Telegraph* in Sydney, with two full pages inside detailing the activities of the alleged plotters, from the early days in the Congo through to the proposed drug run from the Netherlands to Australia via Pakistan.

The *Sydney Morning Herald* declares, 'Drug Cop Accused in $120m Bust', and quotes colleagues declaring Standen's arrest must be 'crap': 'It is just unimaginable, it's a pretty frightening development,' a Standen colleague is quoted as saying.

News of Standen's arrest is even picked up in the Netherlands, where the Radio Netherlands Worldwide station begins broadcasting details of his arrest, and links to the previously under-reported fourteen arrests made six days earlier. The Radio Netherlands news report comes after Dutch police issue a press release and formally suggest local media monitor the *Daily Telegraph*'s website in Australia for more information. This is the first significant public mention in the Netherlands of the key Dutch suspects in the plot—but with pseudoephedrine rarely seized in Holland, Dutch police have to ring their local media outlets and explain that this raw material can be used to make methamphetamines.

Part of a lengthy press release states:

In Australia, the Far East and America the use of meth-amphetamine is a large social problem.

Methamphetamine is known under the names Ice or Crystal Meth.

Methamphetamine is especially used in this way in Australia, the United States and several Asian countries. It hardly appears in Europe, only in the Czech Republic. In the Netherlands the use of ephedrine and pseudoephedrine as raw material for methamphetamine is only found on isolated occasions.

Commissioner Mick Keelty is away when the Standen story breaks. He is honouring a long-standing commitment to walk the Kokoda Track with the sixteen-year-old son of a former AFP colleague who had been killed in a plane crash two years earlier. At various points, however, messages are relayed to him via satellite phone on the progress of the Octans case.

So it is down to his deputy, Tony Negus, to front the cameras and attempt to restore public confidence in law enforcement in Australia.

Keelty had, before he left, made it clear to his senior managers how he wanted the matter handled in the public arena. 'The message to get across is this is international and the investment we have made in that over time,' he had told them. Further, he explained:

Each jurisdiction has its own priorities and you can never assume what is important to the Dutch or what's important to the Thais is important to Australia, so the ability to get them to understand our priorities is a real advantage to the AFP. That's the message I want to come across.

If you've got relationships offshore, you can have better capacity to understand what is happening when it comes to Australia, and why it's happening when it comes to Australia.

Important features of this case, once we briefed Phillip Bradley at the NSW Crime Commission, meant commitment from the domestic and international side of things to ensure the whole syndicate in the Netherlands, right through to anyone who was involved in Australia, were going to be identified. And that is really the crux of organised crime—that you be patient and it is one of the AFP's strengths, in keeping patient in these complex and long-term operations. It will be before the courts, so we can't talk directly about Standen or what we think he did.

Negus carries the message clearly in his press conference, held outside the AFP's Sydney offices the morning after the worst day in Standen's life:

> This was a very well-planned, very well-conducted interception of the individual. Nothing was left to chance.
>
> This was kept very tightly within the Australian Federal Police and at the most senior levels of the NSW Crime Commission, and the operational security to keep this quiet, in this environment, for over twelve months, is a testament to the skill of the investigators involved.
>
> Other than the Commissioner, myself and the Commissioner of the NSW Crime Commission, there were very few people advised of this.

Negus purposefully steers clear of the facts surrounding the case, since a few hundred metres away Standen is about to face court, but praises agents involved in the lengthy operation:

> One of the skills this individual possessed is, he knew police methodology, and for our surveillance people and our technical surveillance people to be able to cover him as they did for over twelve months, without being compromised, is a tribute to their ability.

Standen and Jalalaty's appearance at Central Local Court is short, with the pair not required to sit in the dock, and instead remaining in their cells below the Liverpool Street courthouse. They do not apply for bail. A single charge sheet reveals the pair are being charged with conspiracy to supply a large commercial quantity of a prohibited drug; conspiracy to import a commercial quantity of a border-controlled substance; and conspiracy to pervert the course of justice by using privileged information in relation to the judicial power of the Commonwealth. The charges carry a sentence of life in jail and/or a $600,000 fine.

The court is told the offences allegedly occurred between 9am on 1 June 2006, and 2.45pm on 2 June 2008: roughly the moment of the pair's arrest.

After the hearing, Standen and Jalalaty are taken to Long Bay jail, where the former police officer is placed in isolation. He is told that for his own safety, he will not be allowed to mix with other prisoners and will spend most of his time in his cell alone. There are many criminals in the jail who he had helped put away, and who would no doubt like to see their nemesis again.

Meanwhile, at his NSW Crime Commission headquarters, Phillip Bradley prepares for his own media conference. He has been warned by the AFP that the *Daily Telegraph* has been investigating the drug trail and Standen for several months.

He and most of his 150 staff are stunned by the detailed revelations that follow the arrest—some of the Dutch aspects particularly, which the commission has not been fully aware of.

Bradley had gone to enormous lengths in the past to avoid any sort of public profile—he once asked not to be filmed at parliamentary committee meetings, and reportedly also asked a magistrate if he could use a back door when appearing as a witness at a court case, to avoid the media recording his identity.

But on that Tuesday morning, a clean-shaven Mr Bradley, who once sported a beard, is forced to front the cameras for the first time in his career and allow scrutiny of his organisation. It is a humbling experience. The ferocity of the media against his organisation is stunning, although not surprising.

Bradley has no intention of resigning, but privately knows

the buck stops with him, and the NSW Crime Commission is unlikely to ever be the same again.

'It's a very damaging blow for the crime commission, there's no doubt about that,' he says.

'But this is an isolated incident, one person engaging in alleged crime.'

Both Negus and Bradley dismiss concerns the investigation could have jeopardised convictions made by Standen, or that the officer is involved in any other criminal enterprises.

They are prepared for the denial, since lawyers had been on the radio all morning claiming clients arrested by Standen may have grounds to appeal. The former National Crime Authority chairman, Peter Faris QC, had summed it in a few words that morning: 'the fallout from this will be massive'.

Bradley disagrees.

'We had a great deal of coverage of him [Standen] through both physical surveillance and electronic surveillance, and that gave us some confidence that this was the only crime that he was involved in,' Bradley says.

'Obviously we used our insights through the electronic surveillance to contain anything else, and I think we've succeeded there.'

In reality, Standen's arrest had sparked panic in law enforcement agencies across the country, with the NSW Crime Commission's top officer's work not confined to just the state of NSW.

The AFP, along with state police forces, privately begin drawing up lists of cases and criminals Standen may have come in contact with.

'Any time an investigation ends up in a result like this, we actually need to review those other matters that might be affected,' Keelty had earlier warned colleagues.

The Victorian and Queensland police, as well as the Queensland government-backed Crime and Misconduct Commission, almost immediately begin reviewing cases that involved the NSW Crime Commission.

Publicly, Keelty is cautious not to comment about the case, but does admit it is the toughest one he has experienced in his career. Via telephone from Papua New Guinea, he tells the media:

> The complexity of this is something that is very difficult to describe, given we had to coordinate the law enforcement agencies in the Netherlands, in Portugal, in Germany, in Pakistan during the coup, in Thailand and obviously Australia.
>
> It just shows the value of building up relationships with law enforcement agencies and the investment that is made in that.
>
> The regrettable part of this is that someone from law enforcement is alleged to have been involved, because it tends to detract from the serious and organised networks that exist in the world, who are capable of large-scale importation at a time when, for example, a presidential candidate is assassinated, like what happened in Pakistan.
>
> These drug syndicates will stop at nothing to peddle their commodity around the world, and it is vitally important that operations we do, target entire syndicates, and not just one end of it.'

Meanwhile, Bradley's day is going from bad to worse, with critics lining up to call for the ultra-secretive NSW Crime Commission to be shut down, or at least face the same scrutiny as other law enforcement agencies.

The Criminal Defence Lawyers Association president, Phillip Boulten SC, tells the media that the scandal engulfing the commission now demands a Royal Commission-style probe.

'The NSW Crime Commission isn't sufficiently accountable,' he says.

'There should be an immediate investigation into their operations by someone with the powers of a Royal Commissioner. There should be a standing inspector who has the same powers to ensure that their powers comply with the law—even ASIO has to do that.'

The usually politically cautious NSW Police Association also demands action.

'We call on the NSW Government to establish a standing oversight body for the state's crime commission,' Association Secretary Peter Remfrey says during a hastily organised press conference. He adds:

> Police are entrusted with special powers to enable us to do the job of protecting the community. With that comes proper oversight in the form of the Police Integrity Commission, as well as the Ombudsman, so the community can have faith that those powers are used properly.
>
> The crime commission has been granted extraordinary powers which are critical to their role in investigating organised crime. These powers go far beyond those entrusted to police, and accordingly it is even more critical that the crime commission should, as a matter of public policy, be subject to a standing oversight body to ensure those powers are not abused, and they too are held accountable for their actions.

University of Sydney criminologist Mark Findlay says the commission's tight-knit culture is its own worst enemy. 'It has been said in the past that it was more open to corruption due to its internal and rather protective organisational structure,' he remarks.

The President of the Law Society of NSW, Hugh Macken, joins the demand for change. 'Every other police investigative body has an oversight, or is overseen by a body such as an inspector general, and it is time for the NSW Crime Commission to also be subject to oversight,' he says.

In NSW Parliament, the question of oversight and accountability is asked—but, not surprisingly, the ever-defensive Premier Morris Iemma remains non-committal.

The issue does not leave the front pages of the newspapers all week, with one revelation appearing after another. Bizarrely, disgraced former cop Roger Rogerson joins the media frenzy, writing a 1000-word opinion piece, published in the *Daily Telegraph* under his name, about why good cops go bad. It is a personal piece based on his own experience decades earlier, but relates to current events.

Ironically, a day later, Rogerson's own indirect involvement in the case and that missing $500,000 is revealed by the newspaper.

By Wednesday, it is time for the Independent Commission Against Corruption to front the media, when Standen's connection to one of its employees, Louise Baker, is revealed. Although there was no suggestion she had done anything wrong, the commission had to comment.

'Senior management has been kept informed at all times about the Australian Federal Police investigation, including her involvement with the subject officer,' was all its Commissioner, Jerrold Cripps, would say on the matter.

The scandal is moving fast and no one is sure what will surface next. There has not been a story like this in a long time, and certainly none involving such a high-level public servant.

Three days after Standen's arrest, the NSW Crime Commission's investigations manager, Tony Newton, is forced to resign. Newton has told Bradley he is personally and professionally compromised, since he wants to stand by his friend Standen. This makes his position with the commission untenable, and he is given the option of resigning ahead of being sacked. He is not, however, suspected of any crime except wanting to loyally stand by a mate.

Newton defies an order by Bradley that no one should have any contact with Standen, and visits his friend in jail. He also sits at the back of the courtroom the day Standen makes his first court appearance.

Newton had worked with Standen over three decades in both the AFP and NSW Crime Commission and, as a friend, had lent the increasingly desperate Standen money. He now realises he is unlikely to see his $210,000 again.

Others at the commission, mostly women, also want to stand by Standen, who they believe has been set up, but fear losing their jobs.

'He's the best investigator I've ever worked for—you've got the wrong guy' one colleague declares, before refusing to provide the AFP with a formal statement of their observations of Standen over the past few months.

The NSW Crime Commission has never been challenged in this way, and the siege mentality within its Kent Street walls is obvious. Some at the commission have to be threatened with court action to get statements from them. This will not be the only attempt by some in the commission to stymie a probe into its operations. The commission began to recognise its power was diminishing by the day and was unlikely to ever be the same again.

By Thursday, NSW Premier Morris Iemma and his Police

Minister David Campbell—who had been given a confidential briefing of the Standen case a few months earlier—announce a 'landmark move' to have the Police Integrity Commission oversee the NSW Crime Commission's operation.

The move does little to placate the critics of the commission, or the media's pursuit of the story.

'The [NSW] Crime Commission and the Police Integrity Commission have far too much shared history for anyone to believe one could investigate the other without bias or compromise,' Liberal Opposition police spokesman Mike Gallacher says of the announcement. Furthermore, he declares:

The refusal by the Premier and Police Minister to set up a new, independent body to look into claims against the crime commission shows they want nothing more than an expedient end to yet another crisis of their own making.

This move by the Iemma Government has simply allowed the perception of one of the secret Police boy's clubs looking into another to become even further ingrained.

This ham-fisted changing from one investigative body to another does little to restore public confidence in the commission, or the Iemma Government's ability to handle serious matters such as this.

The only way to ensure the crime commission's ongoing investigations are not compromised while still getting to the bottom of allegations levelled at it, is to have an independent body with the powers of a Royal Commission conduct the investigation, and to make recommendations for the future.

A day later, five days after Standen's arrest, two secret reports on the NSW Police Integrity Commission are leaked to the press, revealing it is far from ready to oversee the beleaguered NSW Crime Commission, after mishandling two unrelated cases of alleged police misconduct dating back to 2003.

The NSW government continues to block the Australian Crime Commission absorbing its NSW counterpart—the state is in too much debt to want to share the spoils of its crime-fighting agency with the national group.

The following week, senior lawyer Ian McClintock SC reveals on the ABC's *Four Corners* program, that the home of a client suspected of importing drugs had allegedly been broken into three times by NSW Crime Commission investigators, contrary to all laws.

'How does one resolve the issue of being bound by secrecy with wanting to complain about acts that they [the commission] have undertaken or processes that may be regarded rightly or wrongly as dubious?' he asks.

It is a question that gains momentum as the full extent of the NSW Crime Commission's capabilities and full details of the Standen–Jalalaty plot are revealed.

6 June 2008

Five nights after Standen's arrest, the *Daily Telegraph*'s court reporter, Lisa Davies, is sitting at the bar in the city's Sheraton Hotel some time after 11pm, when she is approached by someone with an envelope, containing a 27-page document outlining the police cases against Standen and Jalalaty, as prepared for the Director of Public Prosecutions.

Davies has, until then, had limited involvement with the story, but has many contacts in the legal fraternity and is surprised by the document in her hand: they don't come along like this very often.

She is told to photocopy the document, then destroy the original, so its origin can never be traced.

As the anonymous document-carrier walks away, Davies flicks through the pages, lets out an expletive, then buys another round of champagne to celebrate with colleagues.

This story was never going to disappear in a hurry, but the leak of the detailed document sparks a new round of reports on the biggest scandal of its kind to ever hit law enforcement in Australia.

Two days later, over three news pages, the *Daily Telegraph* details the Hotmail coded messages, the secret meetings, Standen's desperation for money, and Jalalaty's wife's alleged knowledge of the plot.

Standen's damning 10 January phrase is also highlighted— 'the reality is someone else would be doing it and rolling in the money, so we might as well get a benefit'.

The newspaper's circulation department is forced to print extra copies, with the story's prominence on the front page every day attracting an extra 5000 sales a day for the week.

Pleased with its coverage, the newspaper's editor, David Penberthy, writes an editorial titled 'A difficult job deserves praise'.

'This week Michael Joseph Keelty has shown why he is precisely the right man to lead this country's federal police force,' he writes, in a veiled attack on the newspaper's broadsheet stablemate *The Australian*, which had for weeks been calling for Keelty's sacking over the AFP's perceived mishandling of a recent terror case.

While the AFP continues to compile a comprehensive brief of evidence for the case, the following week the worst fears of NSW

Police and the NSW Crime Commission head, Phillip Bradley, begin to materialise: lawyers begin to request adjournments for clients in unrelated cases being heard in courts across Sydney, which may or may not have been compromised by Standen's involvement—no matter how small or indirect.

Most critical of these is Standen's infamous case against a Sydney cocaine ring. Several convicted drug traffickers—including hotelier Bradley James Evans, former rugby league player Ricky James Montgomery and Maroubra surfer Hayden Rodgers—now apply through the NSW District Court for access to transcripts of intercepted Standen telephone conversations which may have related to them.

Standen led the massive surveillance operation against the men, for what police claimed was a plot to import 30 kilograms of cocaine from Panama to Sydney. The surveillance involved intercepted telephone calls between conspirators in Spain, Canada and the Clovelly Surf Life Saving Club in Sydney's east.

Lawyer Paul Hardin confirms he has issued a subpoena to both the AFP and NSW Crime Commission to release the taped conversations in the hope of finding some anomaly that could help his clients, who were convicted the previous November and are awaiting sentencing.

Bradley James Evans' barrister, Graham Turnbull SC, would sometime later tell the courts there was clear evidence Standen had a close relationship with a key rollover Crown witness, Steven James, who was now in jail—including twenty-eight telephone calls between the pair.

'The frequency belies the nature of the relationship [between Standen and James] portrayed at the time,' he says.

Two other men allegedly involved in a huge but unrelated cocaine import plot also apply for bail in the NSW Supreme

Court, on the grounds their cases may also have been tainted by Standen and the NSW Crime Commission's involvement. Their case had originally gained national profile after police raids uncovered a plot to import hundreds of kilograms of cocaine from America, but also found more than $20 million in cash, and a large stash of drugs and firearms, including a gold-plated .357 Magnum revolver.

The gang, known as the Golden Gun Gang, claim the Crown witness was a rollover gang member who gave a statement to the NSW Crime Commission at the same time as Standen had been allegedly involved in his own drug plot. The case has to be adjourned while the claim is probed.

Standen's previous involvement in having criminal charges against Hogan dropped are also publicly revealed—followed by revelations that Standen also appealed for the early release of another notorious criminal, Ian Hall Saxon.

Saxon was Australia's most wanted man in 1993 after he escaped from Sydney's Long Bay Jail, where he was serving a hefty sentence over a 10-tonne cannabis-resin haul. Saxon—a former multi-millionaire rock promoter to some of the world's biggest acts—was caught, and served thirteen years of an original 24-year sentence. He was released from jail early after Standen wrote to the parole board on his behalf. Saxon then left Australia, to initially live with family in New Zealand, and then with a fellow rock promoter in Thailand.

Federal Home Affairs Minister Bob Debus orders staff to determine how many other cases he may have unwittingly signed off, that may have also had Standen's involvement.

'I made the decision [to release Saxon] before I became aware of the serious allegations about Mark Standen,' he says, after being forced to front the media.

'If any criminal activity has taken place in relation to Standen's recommendation in this matter, the full force of the law will be applied. These matters need to be thoroughly investigated. It's unlikely the [parole] release can be revoked, but the government's looking at whether it is possible, if it's found corrupt information was provided.'

NSW Police detectives investigating the rape and murder thirty years ago of Sydney teenager Trudie Adams, as well as fourteen other rapes of young girls and women in Sydney's northern beaches, also move to question Standen, after it is revealed that a key suspect in the slaying—a career criminal—was a personal friend of sorts of the law enforcer.

The 68-year-old Central Coast criminal had been convicted a month earlier for smuggling cocaine from Panama into Australia, in watertight bags strapped to the hull of a freighter ship. He was sentenced to eighteen years for the $11 million haul.

At an inquest into Trudie Adams' death, Standen frustrated investigators by providing bland responses to questions, and claiming to have had only minor dealings with the murder suspect. It was then revealed, however, that he and Standen had spent weekends away together on scuba diving trips.

The Police Integrity Commission is called on to begin an investigation into this case as well.

In the NSW Court of Appeal, convicted drug importer Malcolm Gordon Field accuses Standen of fabricating a document used by the NSW Crime Commission to seize his assets, both in Australia and France, including a luxury villa.

Field, due for release in 2014, claims that two days after Standen's arrest, a NSW Crime Commission solicitor visited him in jail and offered to reduce his sentence if he gave evidence on Standen. He says he rejected the offer, but later makes claims in court against Standen.

There are also other cases that will need to be reviewed. In one such case, a woman who was charged with lying to the NSW Crime Commission is calling for her charge to now be dropped, since Standen had been involved and may have been lying himself.

Things will only get worse for NSW Crime Commissioner, Phillip Bradley, with the leaking of an internal video showing how his agency treated a key witness in the murder trial of former ALP councillor Phuong Ngo several years earlier.

It shows the witness being interrogated by Bradley himself, and being denied access to a lawyer more than a dozen times, an act that lawyers brand 'irregular'.

Meanwhile, Jalalaty languishes in a cell contemplating his fate. He is aware of all the media interest in his and Standen's arrests.

Some days after his arrest, Jalalaty telephones his wife.

'Hello?' Jalalaty says.

'Hello, darling.'

'Hi, sweetheart.'

'How are you?'

'Good. I've only got three minutes and I've been waiting for—I've been waiting for three days to get a time slot.'

'Okay.'

'Okay I'm sorry to put you through all what you are going through, but I'm paying the price, believe me. I'm in a little dog house with a two-inch plastic mattress on the cement floor, but I deserve it so I'm sorry.'

'Just listen, just remember . . .'

'Are you okay, sweetheart?'

'I'm okay, just remember we love you, I love you, the kids love you, your family are behind you . . . and we are going to get through this.'

The pair talk about their legal team. Jalalaty is confident he can get bail and get out of his 'hell hole'. He asks about the children, and Dianne tells him that she has told them he's been accused of doing something wrong. It breaks his heart.

'I'm just trying to keep everything as normal as possible, like, for the kids' sake—just to keep everything rolling along,' Dianne says, before warning him not to speak to any 'bush lawyers', or anyone at all.

'Yeah, well, I'll be in protective custody anyway,' Jalalaty responds.

'Will you?'

'Yeah, definitely, I'll be on my own. Don't worry about me—I'm just, uh, getting what I deserve, so don't worry, just as long as you keep things alright there.'

'Yeah, okay, just take it easy.'

'Alright.'

'And just remember we love you, okay?'

Dianne Jalalaty is desperate to see her husband, if only for the normal one-hour visit. However, because of the distance she lives from the jail, she is eligible to apply for a longer visit. The prison has a child-visits area, with slippery dips and a sandpit, so she thinks their children, aged eight and nine, should visit their dad as well, as they now know he is in jail. Because of their age they will be allowed to kiss and cuddle their father.

In a later conversation with his wife, Jalalaty again speaks about his isolation, and the cell in which he spends his whole day, with access only to a small portable TV.

'I . . . I can put up with anything, as long as I know you're okay,' he says, signing off the brief telephone call.

'We're fine, okay.'

'Just thank everyone for their support.'

'Okay darling, love you heaps.'

'Bye.'

His 21-year-old son from his first marriage also visits him.

On 13 June, Standen appears again in Sydney's Central Local Court—via video link from a secure room in jail—to formally apply for bail.

His two eldest children, Matthew and Simone, sit in the court—and through their father's lawyer, former AFP agent Paul King, pass Magistrate Allan Moore handwritten letters begging for their father to be given bail to help hold his family together.

Standen's brother Glenn, and 78-year-old father Kevin, also offer to put their houses up as security for bail.

'While it can be said that the circumstances leading up to the charging of the accused are suspicious—in fact gravely suspicious—they are yet to amount to proof beyond reasonable doubt,' King argues.

But Moore refuses bail; he believes the risks of Standen fleeing are too high.

'I can't ignore his position within the crime commission.

He has information about methodology that could assist his departure from the country,' he tells the court from his raised bench.

Moore, through a statement from police, had earlier been told Standen and Hogan had referred to a 'pension fund', which may have been a stash of cash the pair hoped to use to start new lives outside Australia.

About two weeks after his arrest, Standen is visited in jail by the AFP. He is handed a resignation letter, drafted by his crime commission colleagues.

Standen signs the document, effectively ending his thirty-year career as a crime fighter. An inglorious end to what had been a stellar career.

About this time, in a final humiliation, he is told that his wife wants nothing more to do with him, and has finally decided to leave him. Quite apart from the scandal, the revelations of mistresses and lovers and the lies over so many years are all too much to turn a blind eye to. She and the children move out of their home to live initially with family west of the Blue Mountains.

On 30 June, a very downtrodden Jalalaty also appears at Sydney's Central Local Court via video link to apply for bail.

His barrister, Greg Jones, argues that the AFP's own secretly recorded transcripts—referring to his client as the 'Mr Bean of the business world'—show Jalalaty was to have been cut out of the conspiracy, and therefore the charges do not hold.

He also says at least 50 per cent of the intercepted recordings are unintelligible, and therefore cannot be relied upon, and that his client is willing to surrender his passports and live with his large extended family.

'His whole life is here,' Jones argues.

With Jalalaty's wife Dianne watching from the back of the court, Moore again refuses the application due to the gravity of the charges.

No one is more surprised by Standen's arrest than actor Russell Crowe. Shortly after filming *American Gangster* and *3:10 to Yuma*, he was researching another potential film role and needed law-enforcement advice. Crowe had just finished touring the world promoting *3:10 to Yuma* and had time on his hands to research a film about large-scale international drug operations.

'He [Standen] was given to me as a [former] federal police contact that was, I think he was described as straight as a die, honest as the day is long, never steer you wrong, someone to talk to in terms of your ongoing research to a certain project, you know,' Crowe said of his meeting.

At the time he could not have imagined he was being monitored by an undercover AFP surveillance team, engaged in one of the most sensitive briefs in Australian law enforcement history.

'I had a very strange situation with him that came up. The day I was to meet him, I met him at Walsh Bay at those new apartments. I was actually doing something with the Sydney Theatre Company and they've got a little cafe there and so I met him out on the street, and we were walking down the alleyway between these buildings and there were these guys dressed as workmen, but there wasn't like a building site anywhere. And they sort of turned and came towards us, and if they wanted they could have very easily stopped us in that alleyway. There was quite a large group of them, and one of them looked at me and kind of nodded his head and said "Hey Crowey, how are ya mate?"

"'Ahh . . . yeah good mate," I said, you know.

'And then they stepped aside and allowed the two of us to pass. We walked a few steps—I had only just met the bloke, and I hadn't even spoken to him on the phone—I had literally met him thirty seconds before, and I said to him, "Fuck that felt like a hit", and he said "It did, didn't it." I just thought, what the fuck was all that about?'

Crowe still did not know what the incident was about, but described his moment—or perhaps Standen's predicament, or both—as 'not a good situation'.

'We go into these things, as you well know, with a certain level of inquisitive naivety, you know, and you can only take on the surface what you are told. I was very surprised, considering I had only ever heard of him in the context of him being a good guy.

'I rang the guy that put me onto him and said, "Geez, you are a fucking good judge of character, sunshine." He just brought a sort of strange, eclectic group of people towards me that I could have conversations with, that could have been negatively affected by certain things, or what-have-you, and he was sort of a principal contact.

'I never saw him again [after one meeting], it was only for about 20 minutes. I'm trying to think back when I had a block of free time. It was loosely associated with a completely separate documentary project I was working on, I had some footage to shoot . . .

'It did bring a thing on, of being a little more focused on research.'

*

By September 2008, the future ability of law enforcement to conduct 'controlled' undercover stings is undermined by a High Court decision, based on Standen's Operation Mocha back in 2005.

In yet another significant embarrassment to the embattled NSW Crime Commission, six High Court judges unanimously rule the commission was wrong to have allowed 7 kilograms of cocaine to have been sold on the streets of Sydney and Melbourne.

It finds the legal authority used by the commission for the undercover operation—led by Standen, and using an informant codenamed 'Tom' to sell the drugs in order to catch the drug-import masterminds—was invalid.

Counsel for the NSW Crime Commission try to argue, as Standen did years earlier, that the sale did not necessarily involve a health and safety risk to drug users, but the argument is rejected.

The 3.75 kilograms sold by Tom involved 100,000 dosage units of cocaine and, the High Court rules, had endangered the health of users. That risk rendered invalid the legitimacy of the NSW Law Enforcement (Controlled Operations) Act, because the risk was prohibited by another section of the same Act.

Deeming Operation Mocha invalid immediately throws in doubt at least three lengthy convictions for men arrested during Mocha.

Around the same time, another three men who Standen helped arrest for a cocaine-import conspiracy—namely Maroubra surfer Hayden Rodgers, hotelier Bradley James Evans and former South Sydney footballer Ricky James Montgomery—are found guilty and are sentenced to minimum jail terms of six, seven and eleven years respectively. They relist the matter, with plans to fight the charges on the basis of Standen's now alleged criminality.

*

Around this time, Dutch police chiefs and prosecutors decide to close down their anti-drugs bureau in Miami in the United States, and instead post a senior officer to the Dutch Embassy in Canberra to be better placed to liaise directly with senior AFP investigators.

The decision is made solely on the volume of work Dutch police are now doing jointly with the AFP to fight drugs coming into Australia, and specifically the Octans brief. Many believe the move should have been made years earlier.

'This is important to identify the problem at the source,' Dutch prosecutor Cees van Spierenburg says publicly of the move.

AFP Commissioner Mick Keelty resumes attending meetings at the NSW Crime Commission. These are cordial but strained.

The NSW Crime Commission annual report for the year ending 2008 states that about $30 million was netted from criminals for the state government's coffers, with about $11 million being in cash.

Meanwhile, the Police Integrity Commission begins investigating Standen's career in law enforcement, specifically his handling of cash and assets confiscated from criminals over the years.

It specifically looks at a boat worth more than $100,000, which Standen allegedly sold at half its market value, and is almost immediately struck by the NSW Crime Commission's poor reporting of its criminal seizures in general, let alone those made by Standen.

That probe is still continuing in 2012.

*

Octans police are still actively working on intelligence gathering, trying to determine who was to receive the drugs shipment, or were at least on the periphery of the import in some capacity.

They identify a Cypriot-born Briton as a key ally of Hogan—the man surveillance had photographed in a baseball cap pulled low over his eyes on the Sydney street with Jalalaty and Standen—and another man who was to have helped unpack the crates when they came in.

The man known only as 'Shaun', who had told Jalalaty he wanted to buy rice, could not be identified. Such was the jumbled import operation by Jalalaty that no one—from the criminals themselves to police—know whether he was actually a providore buyer, or a drug dealer using the cover product as code. They suspect he was innocent.

The team also continues following a money trail in the hope of finding the 'pension fund' Hogan and Standen had spoken about, and which they suspect is a pool of money set aside by the pair for future ventures. By January 2012 investigators will have found and seized $30,000 in Hogan-owned cash and assets in Australia and another $2 million worth in Portugal.

They discover Hogan has extensive contacts in the United States and Venezuela, and suspect other more substantial amounts of assets and monies are hidden around the world.

The continued scale of the probe, however, begins to take its toll. AFP agents are having to be pulled off active investigations and sent home because they have used up their maximum working hours of 520 hours per financial quarter, and there is no longer any money in the budget to pay for overtime.

The AFP's Sydney office—operationally the busiest in the country—has been particularly affected, and is now short of agents, especially in the organised crime and drug investigations field.

'That has the effect of putting more stress on the individuals, but it also means there has to be a limitation on what investigations are being conducted in those latter weeks of a quarter,' the AFP's union president Jon Hunt-Sharman tells the media.

A few weeks after his arrest, Jalalaty's lawyer approaches the NSW Crime Commission and says his client wants to make a deal.

For the commission it is a unique situation. While normally it is in a position to make such deals—or at least hear what is on the table—with its former top cop being a co-accused, such a move could contaminate a criminal case against all the alleged conspirators.

They refer Jalalaty to the Australian Crime Commission. It, too, is unsure what to do, and contacts the Australian Federal Police for advice.

It is told to have nothing to do with Jalalaty, or any deal he wants to make.

10

Behind Bars

Life in maximum security is tough.

It's tough for any man, but for an ex-copper it can be deadly. Fellow prison inmates call out threats to Standen who cowers at the back of his tiny cell in fear of someone showering him with boiling water or faeces if he gets too close to the walls that separate the cells.

When inmates do try to talk to him, he doesn't answer back. That's what he has been warned to do: don't engage, because it can only lead to trouble. Because of the risk of assault, Standen is placed in the jail's maximum-security isolation wing.

He's paranoid, anxious and can't sleep. He visits the prison doctor and is given benzodiazepine and temazepam to help his insomnia. The other inmates in the block—comprising eight self-contained units with bathrooms, and four-metre-square courtyards—know who he is. Everyone in jail now knows who he is. He has helped put away many criminals in his thirty years in the force, and some of them are now sitting in his jail, waiting for their chance at payback.

In September 2008, Standen is reading in his cell when he hears a door slam. There's a bit of talk, then suddenly someone in the next cell explodes.

'You're a fuckin' peasant, you fucking rat!' the inmate yells at him over the wall, after learning who he is sharing the cell block with.

The inmate then calls out to the others. 'He's a fucking dog, he's listening to us, cunt. I hope you die, you fucking cunt!'

The inmate then tells the others Standen had been responsible for jailing 'several friends' of another inmate. Standen listens, but can't make out the voice. It could be anyone. They all sound the same.

A few days later, all the inmates are chatting—but when they hear Standen stir, one calls out 'you know who is listening' and they all go quiet and agree to chat in the exercise yard. They are constantly chatting among themselves, either in the yard or through the cell bars, and every now and then 'Standen' comes up. Standen strains to hear what they are saying, but can't. It leaves him on edge; he suspects they are looking for ways to get at him.

Standen is not classified as a non-association prisoner, but effectively he is: alone in his cell, alone in the jail to fester in his own mental torment.

The next month, a new inmate arrives in the small unit. All the inmates call over the walls to establish who it is. He's 'solid', they agree, he's a recognised crim.

Then the new inmate says: 'I was hoping to get the cell next to Standen . . . so I could shit in a cup and throw it over the wall.' All the men laugh. Well almost all—Standen curls up tighter into a ball on his bunk.

The cells are separated with high walls, but the roof area is covered by bars. On hearing the latest threat, Standen knows he now must be quiet—shhhhhh—he doesn't like anyone to know now where he is at any time in his tiny cell, in case someone makes good on the threat. He pads across the cell floor in his socks. It's not exactly pacing, but he feels the need to keep moving.

Standen begins to keep a diary, mainly listing the times he is in lock-ins—that is, the times he is restricted to just his tiny inner cell. By 3 November, he completes fourteen pages of the basic log. His book records he had no visitors on Father's Day. He is, however, visited fairly regularly by his girlfriend. He suspects it won't last forever and he is right.

He spends most of his days alone, but on weekends he can receive a maximum three visits, for an hour and three quarters each. He has had visitors most weekends, but is not allowed presents or letters. He is only allowed visits from eight approved people, excluding children and lawyers, and they can't take anything with them. He can make phone calls to six approved numbers, excluding his lawyers.

Before his jailing, Standen had been studying for a Diploma in Law. He now has two subjects to complete—tax and succession—and there are final exams in March, but he struggles with the study. The jail has a library, but he says he can't use it.

After concerns are raised by Standen's legal team about his welfare, Commonwealth Director of Public Prosecutions solicitor Penelope Jane Grist visits the prison. There she speaks with the security manager, Jeff Schubert, six days before Christmas 2008.

At the meeting she is assured Standen has to be separated for his own security, and has been advised not to talk to other inmates. Standen may request access to a larger yard, which he has been doing; when other prisoners are not around he can use the gym for between one and three hours a day, which he has done.

He has access to a telephone, which she is told he uses several times a day, and is constantly visited by support staff such as psychologists and welfare and education officers.

Standen's solicitor Gordon Elliot—another former senior AFP agent—has visited him a number of times and views his situation very differently. According to Elliot, Standen is being held in virtual solitary confinement for up to twenty-three hours a day, in a place usually reserved for prisoners who have broken the jail's rules.

Standen tells his lawyer he is innocent and needs bail to properly prepare his case. He says he would particularly like to visit his daughter, who recently became engaged. She had recently visited him in jail, but rules prevented her bringing in her engagement ring to show him.

'He's very stressed,' Elliot notes in an affidavit he produces and signs on 19 December. 'He can't go to the library, has no computer access and can't join group sporting or educational activities. He's locked alone in the gym or larger exercise yard when he uses them. His activities in the yard are limited to throwing a basketball and chasing it, hitting a tennis ball against a wall and jogging around.'

Elliot concludes his paper, which he later tenders to the Magistrates Court, by addressing the central fear of the magistrates: 'The defendant does not know any criminal who would or could assist him to leave Australia,' he writes, adding Standen also no longer has operating bank accounts, building society accounts or any cash reserves.

A visit by forensic psychiatrist Dr Samson Roberts is arranged to evaluate Standen's mental health. Six months earlier Standen was a confident man with girlfriends he would shower with expensive gifts and take to the best restaurants. His only worry was how to pay and lay the next bet on all the big races. Now he is a shell of a man, caged in with some of the country's most notorious men—some of whom he worked hard to put behind bars. It's every policeman's greatest fear, but one few come to realise.

Standen tells the doctor of the verbal abuse, his sense of isolation, and his 'escalating frustration' at his predicament. He says apart from prison staff, doctors and nurses, he has almost no human contact.

Dr Roberts concludes Standen is frustrated, angry and worried. 'He's becoming increasingly despondent about his future . . . and he's at risk of developing a psychiatric condition,' Dr Roberts writes in his official report. When Standen was first arrested, he thought he'd only be in short-term custody. He had been psychiatrically assessed and no feelings of anxiety or distress were reported at that time. But it is clear he has changed, and not just mentally.

On 22 December, Standen appears at the Sydney Central Local Court, via video link, for a second bail application.

He appears thinner; he has told his legal team many times he has lost his appetite. He has also revealed to lawyers that his wife has left their home to live with relatives in NSW's west; they have sold their Bateau Bay home to pay off debts, and he can live with his father should he be given bail. His life has turned upside down since his arrest. Some members of his family no longer speak to him, his wife being one of them. She was deceived and betrayed on so many levels, and he knows it.

Barrister Greg Farmer tells the court that by the time his client faces a committal hearing on 11 February, he will have spent

225 days in custody, and needs his freedom now to prepare a proper defence. He says his client is at risk of developing a mental illness and will commit to reporting to police anywhere, any time, twice a day, if he is given bail.

He also challenges the strength of the Crown case. 'We still don't know the full story,' he tells the court.

Prosecutors stir in their seats: they still have not produced evidence to support which drug chemical—or how much of it Standen was allegedly trying to import. According to Farmer, police have simply used the worst interpretation of telephone calls made between his client and co-accused, Jalalaty.

Farmer adds that no equipment or other chemicals needed to convert a precursor into a drug had been found, in either Standen or Jalalaty's homes or the warehouse. (Both Jalalaty and Standen were relieved when the acetone and tap and bladder system were taken off their hands a year earlier.)

'There has still, as far as the defence is concerned, not been serviced a full brief of evidence,' Mr Farmer says. 'Not only is there an inability to serve a full brief of evidence, there is an inability to particularise the charges.'

AFP agent and Octans case officer Paul Watt is called to the stand. Farmer asks him, how is it that when police were requesting search warrants, the substance listed kept changing, from ephedrine to pseudoephedrine to pseudoephedrine hydrochloride?

Watt replies they were receiving changing information on the operation, and were awaiting police in the Netherlands to send them legally admissible documents on the case. These are expected before the end of February, he tells the court.

The Crown's barrister Hament Dhanji, says despite the lack of documentation, prosecutors are ready to proceed with a committal hearing, as they believe they can already prove what they are legally required to prove.

The long-standing, tough and respected Central Local Court Magistrate Allan Moore again hears the case. And again swiftly dismisses Farmer's appeal, saying he believes there exists a 'substantial case' against the former NSW Crime Commission assistant director who, if convicted, faces a lengthy sentence because of his position and standing in society. He also notes the former crime fighter's knowledge of police methodology makes him a flight risk.

Moore also dismisses concerns about Standen's mental welfare, and says tough prison conditions are 'a fact of life'.

'All persons on remand . . . are at risk of psychiatric issues,' he says.

Standen spends his first Christmas in jail alone.

Privately, Operation Octans agents worry Standen could be suicidal. He has nothing left to lose, after all.

But Standen believes in hope—hope the case collapses during the committal hearing, where it would then not proceed to court. Deep down, however, he knows that is unlikely: he has been given the brief and is experienced enough to know a strong case.

But anything can happen. Documents are still being prepared by the Dutch prosecutors, and they are taking their time. There is confusion there with ephedrine and/or pseudoephedrine, the substances not clearly understood or recognised by law enforcement in the Netherlands. As such their evidence is confused.

Some AFP agents fear the case is falling out of their grasp due to this confusion; lawyers close to the case warn them to get their act together—and fast—before the brief is thrown out of court.

*

Jalalaty is doing it equally tough. He too is in isolation, for his own protection, and is confined to his cell for twenty hours a day. He does have access to television and radio, and receives many visits from close family and friends, but it is a very trying time. He eats his prison food alone; the irony dawns on him that, as a successful small goods merchant, he once supplied meat to NSW prisons.

While no one except those close to him is supposed to know where he is doing his time, ahead of the expected trial, a card from Hogan, sent from his prison cell in Thailand, arrives at Jalalaty's cell door. It has an immediate impact. The postcard is amicable, but its sending has a clear message.

Jalalaty, who, since being jailed, has been writing thousands of words about the conspiracy and the effect of prison, had considered rolling over, but now is not so sure. He struggles to weigh up what may be more dangerous to his own wellbeing and circumstance against that of his family.

Standen, too, receives a postcard.

Everyone knows the stories about Bangkok's notorious Klong Prem prison, but Hogan is staggered by the squalor that surrounds him.

Chain gangs of men shuffle along the dirt prison yard, their wrists and ankles manacled together. There is little food, unless you have friends on the outside who will buy it for you; the only food they receive is a watery rice dish. Most prisoners spend their own money to exist, but Hogan's assets—including all bank accounts—are frozen. He has to rely on a few expat Brits and a few relatives who visit him to buy him food and basic goods such as soap.

Sanitary conditions are poor to say the least, and drugs are rife, with some men becoming addicts *after* they enter the jail.

Despite the hardship, Hogan tells fellow prisoners he'd sooner see out his days in Thailand than return to Australia, even though he is told that extradition cases can take anywhere between one and two years to conclude, one way or another. Later he is told it can take up to seven years.

Hogan initially gets few visitors. When a local Thai-based reporter visits, he makes his first public denial of any wrong-doing and claims he cannot return to Australia, where its judicial system and police force are out to get him.

'They spent two years bugging calls, offices, email,' he says.

'They had to justify it in the end. There's nothing there; nobody was doing anything. They couldn't back down, the AFP. It's all just their interpretation.'

He also denies having any sort of relationship with Standen or Jalalaty.

'What kind of lunatic would I be to trust the deputy of the crime commission, or Jalalaty, who I've described as a Mr Bean, a Walter Mitty character? It's one big farce. It's been one thing after another. I didn't even know what pseudoephedrine was until this. I am charged with him [Standen]. It's to put pressure on me, so that I would incriminate him, which I've refused to do.'

Hogan is confident the charge is unlikely to stick, since no drugs were found in the container. As for the 2003 charges being resurrected, he believes the case is well and truly over. He genuinely expects all seventeen charges against him to collapse.

'There is no new evidence—there's nothing,' he declares.

His belief could not be further from the truth. As Hogan publicly declares his innocence, AFP agents in Canberra are preparing to fly a team back to the Netherlands to re-interview a witness who, since the first case was prosecuted in 2003, has come forward with vital new information. It will prove critical to the case. There are also all the new phone traces and new reviews of old evidence, possibly converting the state charges into Commonwealth ones.

'The problem is, if I win this case, they'll appeal,' he says.

He then adds: 'That'll be another year. They had me for a year from 2003 to 2004. It's almost another year now. I'm a loser all the way around. I can never win. It would be easier to go to Australia, but it's the principle of the matter.

'If I was given a fair trial here, I'd win. But there's far too much interference from the Australian Embassy. They sent a representative from the embassy, from the AFP, but he wouldn't testify. They don't want to answer awkward questions. It's a farce.'

Hogan decides to fight his extradition from Klong Prem prison to Australia—the first person to ever do so.

By February 2009, a case against Standen has yet to be made. The prosecution simply does not have enough evidence to confidently surmount at least the first legal hurdle of the committal. Lose at this stage and two years of intensive work will be for nought.

AFP agent and Octans case officer Kate Fox admits in court the drugs are suspected to have been in one of two shipping containers of rice, but a search of both found no evidence that drugs, or even a trace of them, had at one time been in there.

Crown prosecutor Hament Dhanji then concedes in court the case is not strong enough to prove at least one of the three charges against Standen—specifically the plot to import a commercial quantity of pseudoephedrine—and he asks for more time, for evidence to arrive from Holland.

'The Crown's case is that that charge, without the additional material, will fail,' he says.

Standen's barrister, Gordon Elliot, seizes on the admission and calls for the case to be dropped, since the Crown has had enough time on it and eight months of solitary confinement of his client is enough.

'The courts have had a long recognition of the old adage that justice delayed is justice denied,' he urges.

'Even if there is some kind of communication breakdown between the Commonwealth Director of Public Prosecutions and other agencies—I'm not saying it's their fault—but Mr Standen should not be disadvantaged.'

Magistrate Julie Huber decides police have three weeks to obtain the extra material from the Netherlands or the charge will be dropped. Hurried phone calls are made to prosecutors in the Netherlands, pleading for more detailed and accurate documents.

After several weeks, these documents are prepared for delivery—but they are all in Dutch.

On 20 March, Standen gets a cell mate: disgraced former Federal Court judge Marcus Einfeld, who begins his spectacular fall from grace in a cell adjoining Standen's. The pair share a bathroom, a kitchenette and a small exercise yard.

Seventy-year-old Einfeld had pleaded guilty in the NSW Supreme Court to a charge of perjury and making a false statement with intent to pervert the course of justice, after blaming a $77 traffic fine on a long-dead professor. He was jailed for three years, to serve a minimum of two.

Einfeld's incarceration marks a turnaround for Standen's mental state. He finally has someone to talk to about his case, and his worries in general—a former member of the crime-fighting fraternity, no less. Einfeld has a television brought into his cell, has an appointed psychologist for the pair of them, and also a masseuse to combat the physical pain of being cooped up in jail.

Einfeld is his only jail friend, a fact he will later use in court in appealing again for bail. The two play Scrabble or do crosswords together most days, and keep each other company as they brave the insults and verbal abuse from fellow jailbirds whenever they walk through common areas. They even join an art appreciation course together. Standen is hopeless and can barely draw a stick figure, so they mainly talk about art history. And of course the law.

Although Standen has finally finished his law degree, he hopes to continue his legal readings. After months of being denied access to the prison library, he gets given a book. *Shantaram* tells the story of an Australian prisoner who escapes jail and flees to India; Standen can only dream of such an outcome for himself.

Hogan is also making some friends behind bars.

Hollywood had already turned Viktor Bout's life into a movie, with Nicolas Cage playing the real-life arms dealer in the 2005 blockbuster *Lord of War*.

But Viktor Bout, the big-talking mustachioed Russian—known around the world as the Merchant of Death—is now behind bars in Thailand (no doubt giving script writers material for a sequel), after allegedly attempting to sell 700 surface-to-air missiles and 5000 AK-47 assault rifles to the left-wing Revolutionary Armed

Forces of Colombia (FARC) rebels. There was also an order for unmanned aerial vehicles or drones, thousands of rounds of ammunition, C4 explosives and land mines.

The 42-year-old had been pursued around the world by various intelligence agencies, but was finally arrested in Bangkok, after being lured out of Moscow by undercover US Drug Enforcement Agency operatives. Now he is in Klong Prem, also awaiting extradition.

The burly former Soviet military hardman—has multiple Interpol arrest warrants and even UN sanctions against him, amid claims he is the biggest gun runner in the world, supplying weapons to forces in Liberia, Angola, the Congo and Sudan—and even the Taliban and American and Northern Alliance forces in Afghanistan. But Bout is confident he will beat any charges. After all, he tells Hogan, he is just a businessman who happens to be in Thailand to relax and sell the odd plane to a friendly nation.

Hogan smiles. He says he too is just a simple businessman, an 'investor and financial adviser'.

The pair become firm friends and Hogan is coached on how to beat the system. Thai justice, he is told, is malleable, with more flexibility than a Russian gymnast. Muddy the waters, cloud the judgement of lawyers and you will be free. And the longer a case goes, the better.

To Hogan it seems improbable his notorious high-profile friend, wearing the same faded orange prison outfit as himself, stands a chance of escaping justice and extradition to the United States. But he is buoyed, nonetheless, by the Russian's confidence, companionship and advice.

Hogan becomes even more keen on chess and plays with anyone he can find. It's all about strategy, forward thinking, outsmarting your opponent, second-guessing their move, juggling multiple plays in your head and being prepared to change tactics at a minute's notice.

This is how he has lived his whole life. And up to this point at least, he has always been one move in front of his opponents.

Standen is back in court on 3 April. The prosecutors make their case, then counter claims from Standen's defence team that since there were no drugs found, there had been no conspiracy to import.

'We can look at the fact it's a drug, it's illicit, it's coming from Pakistan, it looks like rice . . . we've got a whole lot of circumstances that build on that point,' prosecutor Tim Game SC says.

'Mr Standen is not an innocent abroad. He's in conversations with people in Customs, talking about what's coming in, what's coming out, what locations and the like, so it's not as though we're talking about a person who's blind to that which he is doing.'

Game explains that the fact that no drugs were found is immaterial if they can prove there was an intention for drugs to be present. Intention to participate in a drug run—whether successful or not—is all he has to prove, he tells the court.

'He was busy on the phone to people in Customs about what was coming in and from what locations,' Game says.

'We can raise an inference that's ultimately capable of proving beyond reasonable doubt his intention to participate in an agreement to import pseudoephedrine. He knew what he was doing. He was using his special knowledge as a senior officer of the Crime Commission to basically provide a source of information and advice that his co-conspirators could use to avoid attention.'

The case is adjourned while the new Dutch material is analysed by Magistrate Huber, with the file now pushing the Crown case beyond 8000 pages.

Finally, on 10 June, Standen is committed to stand trial in the NSW Supreme Court, with Magistrate Huber finding there is enough evidence for a jury to consider and possibly convict.

She says the evidence presented so far shows Standen had used his position to advise co-accused Bill Jalalaty about what authorities would look for in shipments.

'It is clear from conversations . . . that Mr Standen is using his position in order to either frustrate or deflect a prosecution of disciplinary proceeding,' Huber concludes.

A pale and gaunt Standen, after one year and eight days in solitary confinement, smiles and waves to one of his brothers and other supporters as he is led away.

He and Jalalaty are re-arraigned on reworded charges, and formally plead not guilty to plotting to supply 300 kilograms of pseudoephedrine used to make the drug ice.

It is a technicality, but for five seconds the charges against the pair are dropped—only to be reinstated, with different wording.

The months pass by. Each time Hogan's extradition hearing is listed, it is deferred, with one or the other side not ready. It's frustrating.

But in August he gets some good news: his prison mate, Viktor Bout, is being released. Inconceivable, but true.

There was a flaw in the extradition process; while most nations consider the FARC a terrorist group, Thailand did not, and therefore the US charges of gun running under Thai law were not applicable. The extradition is deemed 'a political case' and therefore not valid.

Viktor walks, saluting his fellow inmates with a V for victory, V for Viktor. Behind the scenes he suspects the Russian government has had a hand in freeing him. It is in their interests—after all they are the biggest benefactor from his offshore business deals.

Hogan thinks he can use a similar argument to place a firm question mark over the legality of his detention. With the AFP, he thinks, it is all political: they have spent a lot of time and money trying to catch Standen, and are now pursuing him because he has refused to roll over and give evidence against the NSW Crime Commission figure. He has proof the AFP has asked him more than a dozen times since his arrest to assist them and help convict Standen. A plan formulates in his mind and is later discussed with his lawyer.

'It's all a matter of interpretation,' Hogan says.

On 27 November, Hogan is brought to court from prison by bus wearing his faded orange prison shirt and shorts. His ankles are shackled, but he is as defiant as ever.

'There's no evidence, I spoke about nothing, it's farcical,' he calls out to media that have gathered outside his holding cell in the courthouse.

'The charges are based on statements by two anonymous witnesses. There's no evidence, it's manipulation, it's distortion. It's just lies and distortion of the facts and truth. The truth is there never is, and never was, any drugs.'

When asked how he is feeling, Hogan shakes his head. 'Same

as every day in prison in chains; how about this for this modern world?' he asks straining in his handcuffs to point to the iron shackles around his bare feet.

Lawyers argue over the legitimacy of the extradition request, given that Australia does not have a full extradition treaty with Thailand.

However, since 1911, Britain has had one with Thailand, and since Australia is 'a member of the Commonwealth organisation of former British territories' the request is legitimate, prosecutors counter.

There is initial confusion as Hogan's lawyer then claims the charges are political in nature, and a political charge is not covered by extradition laws. Bout's name is not cited, but his high-profile escape from Bangkok through a legal loophole is fresh in the minds of many.

But to Hogan's bitter disappointment, it seems the court may have considered this option already, and the argument is dismissed quickly.

'The court has agreed to send you back to Australia,' the court translator tells him, ending confusion and the hearing. Hogan drops his head and gently shakes it. On court orders, he is to leave within three months.

Hogan speaks a few Thai words and phrases, but needs the translator to confirm what he has heard. To that point, everything about his case has been in Thai, including the police papers he signed when he was first arrested.

Hogan's lawyer, Prachaya Vijitpokin, vows to launch an appeal, adding 'This could be a long time.'

Hogan is led back to the bus and this time does not say a word to the amassed media. Instead he places a surgical mask over his face, but nothing can cover his disappointment.

For the first time since his arrest, he considers what could happen to him in Australia.

About this time, the Police Integrity Commission passes its draft review of the NSW Crime Commission to the state government. Its 172-page report finds the state's top law enforcement agency in urgent need of oversight, with a lack of management systems potentially exposing its officers to manipulation by organised crime figures. The report challenges the 'deals' the commission would do with criminals, in exchange for forfeiture of criminal assets, and recommends an external review to rule on whether the commission needs to be broken up, or have its powers curtailed or overseen by a parliamentary committee.

Of particular concern, it says, is how the NSW Crime Commission pursued criminals and seized their assets and kept an audit of those assets, as well as how it maintained police intelligence. In essence the report questions the commission's core functions. It also questions why the commission had not seen fit to appoint a deputy.

The state Labor government does nothing with the report, but the Liberal Opposition, which will come to power in March 2011, promises an inquiry. The NSW Crime Commission, for its part, reacts to the threat of a public inquiry by taking action in the Supreme Court to stop it.

By December, Standen is contemplating another Christmas behind bars. His girlfriend, Louise Baker, has dropped him, and visits less. His only joy, if you can call it that, is his daily chat with the pompous Marcus Einfeld.

After more than six months in jail, Einfeld himself is still not quite settled in his surrounds and actually asks guards if they wouldn't mind leaving his cell door open at night 'as it gets a bit hot in here'.

Standen begs his lawyer to get him out of jail as he fears he is losing his mind. He is medically examined regularly, and is now deemed clinically depressed. 'I'm doing it tough,' he tells his lawyer on more than one occasion.

On 16 December, Crown prosecutor Tim Game SC puts Standen on the stand to testify as to his mental state, as the prisoner makes yet another bail application. Game uses Standen's friendship with Einfeld—identified in court only as 'Inmate A'—to challenge the validity of his bail application.

'Is Inmate A an antisocial person?' he asks.

'No,' Standen responds.

'Engaging?'

'Yes.'

'Intelligent?'

'Yes.'

'Interesting?'

[long pause] 'Yes.'

'It's not as if you're sharing time with a sociopath or psychopath?'

'I'm assuming not,' Standen replies with a smile.

He laments Einfeld is not interested in using the gym.

'We play Scrabble, do crosswords. I like to do both, but if I have a choice of going to the gym on my own or doing these other activities with him, I'd rather do the latter.'

Standen agrees he speaks with Inmate A most days, but not after 2.30pm or before 7am, when he is locked in his cell alone. Between those hours all he can do is stare through the tiny glass viewing window to see what Einfeld—who has a different prison classification and is given more freedom—is doing. He listens, too, to the fights and yelling between other inmates. Every now and then he hears his name, and sometimes Einfeld's, and his blood runs cold. He knows they would get him if they could.

'I'm aware that I am considerably more anxious. I don't like being locked up is the bottom line of it,' Standen tells the court.

Standen's brother Grant offers his Sydney home as surety and tells the court his brother could live there under virtual house arrest. If Mark tried to abscond, Grant says, he would dob his brother in rather than lose his home.

A day later, Justice Bruce James rejects the bail application, again on the grounds that Standen's extensive law enforcement history and the criminality he encountered as part of his job made him 'uniquely well placed' to escape the country and justice.

Standen prepares for another quiet Christmas and continues to study law, for one last throw of the dice for freedom in the new year.

He hears that some of the cases he genuinely had worked hard to crack were falling away. In that month, a court grants unspecified legal costs to the men involved in the Golden Gun case, the nation's biggest cocaine conspiracy trial he helped to bring to the courts, after finding the NSW Crime Commission and the Department of Public Prosecutions almost incompetent in their prosecution.

It's a low holiday season as Standen studies on in preparation for what he hopes will be a quick trial, ending in acquittal. He is still severely depressed about his situation and feels helpless to stop his family falling apart. With Standen's wife suffering a breakdown, his family is now scattered. A psychiatric report diagnoses Standen's mood as 'depressed and anxious but not suicidal'.

An interview Standen gives the doctors reveals he has grown accustomed to routine—7.30am breakfast, 10.30am lunch, 2.30pm dinner. He paces his own cell at five paces by three paces, and often stands in the kitchen where he can stretch out and touch both opposing walls with his hands. It is small, all small.

Sometimes they leave his cell door unlocked so he can walk about the kitchen area, but not often. He has had no visitors in months, and while Einfeld has been 'difficult, demanding and irritating' he feels a sense of loss when Einfeld is moved away.

In March 2010, Standen is given the job of sweeper in the wing, which gives him some movement away from his tiny cell; it helps but it is not enough. It just reminds him that even ordinary mundane chores are out of his reach.

He again fails in his bid for bail, again being deemed a flight risk.

On 17 May 2010, Standen is to finally get his day in court. Almost two years since his arrest, and finally he thinks he can argue the merits of the AFP case against him.

But on the morning he is to have his day, he is told Jalalaty had unexpectedly pleaded guilty the day before to the charges against him.

Jalalaty tells the NSW Supreme Court he is guilty of conspiring 'with Mark William Standen and diverse others to import a substance intending to use or believing that another person intended to use any of the substance to manufacture a controlled drug, the substance being pseudoephedrine and the quantity being a commercial quantity'.

It is a stunning development. The AFP had hoped someone would roll over early on in the case to gain concessions, but up until that day everyone had held out. Until that point, no one had spoken, although Jalalaty had always been considered the weak link.

For two years he had argued he knew nothing, but on the weight of evidence and advice from his lawyers, following a formal meeting with the Department of Public Prosecutions and AFP, he changed his mind.

After his plea change, Jalalaty still refuses to speak with the AFP, which he believes cannot be trusted. Ironically, he instead gives a written statement, hundreds of pages long, to Standen's former employer, the NSW Crime Commission. In it he details not only the import conspiracy, but divulges a whole host of other criminal gossip.

Indirectly, Octans investigators are able to piece more of the puzzle together and begin interviewing others in Sydney about their knowledge of the plot, and other drug and money movements.

After providing his written statement to the NSW Crime Commission, Jalalaty and his wife then become registered 'human sources', or informers, of the commission, and ironically are given codenames to be used on future intelligence reports. They also agree the information they have, including of alleged unrelated criminal conduct within the AFP, can be passed to the AFP.

Dianne is given immunity from potential prosecution for the information she provides, starting with Standen allegedly stealing money out of a work safe to help pay bills and buy groceries for his family, to more high-level corruption she knows of within the AFP.

The value of their information is deemed to be 'medium to high'. The security risk to Bill Jalalaty is formally classified as 'high', so the likelihood of him getting out of isolation and mixing with other prisoners is nil. Because of her cooperation, authorities also classify Dianne at 'risk'. She sells the family home and takes the family to live in an undisclosed location.

Privately, Jalalaty feels he has been used and played by Standen and Hogan, and was seduced by their conspiracy. After he lost Hogan's money, he then felt he had no choice but to get involved in the plot to pay it back, but he formally tells the court through his lawyer that this was not his primary driver in the plot. He thought he could make money, and lots of it—simple as that.

Unlike the intimidating Central Local Court on Liverpool Street where he first appeared behind a high-security screen, with guards standing by the doors, Jalalaty now sits in an open booth, in a small underground courtroom in the Queens Square courts, with his family sitting a few feet away.

He has lost weight since he was last seen in public, and anxiously sips glass after glass of water as his lawyers and prosecutors ask for a reduced sentence.

His wife had already given evidence to investigators to help her husband. It was a humbling experience, but a solid show to the court of Jalalaty's need to make amends now, prevailing on his wife to give evidence.

He and Dianne chat in the breaks, and wink and nod through the legal arguments. The public gallery is full to capacity. Among them sit NSW Crime Commission officials, AFP agents and even Hogan's Australian lawyer.

Jalalaty's lawyer, Clive Stern, reminds the court his client has no prior criminal record, has now given 'exceptional' assistance to authorities, and is entitled to a 50 per cent reduction in jail time. He has also spent more than two and a half years in jail, and Corrective Services has described him as a model prisoner.

Mr Stern describes the significance of Jalalaty's many hours of evidence to investigators as 'medium to high' on his own matter, and other material as 'potentially high'.

'He has given information of a significant kind in matters unrelated to the current matter; that material alone attracts the maximum discount,' he concludes.

He adds that rehabilitation is the subjective factor, and in his client's case 'he has learnt his lesson, learnt his lesson very well in the past two and a half years [in jail]'.

AFP agent Brett Thompson sits quietly in the back of the court gallery for Jalalaty's final appearance. 'One down, two to go,' he whispers to a colleague. For him it is a result of years of his working life coming to a close.

In his sentencing, Justice James notes Jalalaty was a minor player in the conspiracy, but as the legitimate food importer providing the 'cover' for the import, he was a crucial player—a 'principal'—of the plot.

'The Crown accepted, and I find, that Jalalaty was naive and inexperienced in the importation of illicit drugs, and that he was to some extent taken advantage of by the other conspirator,' Justice James concludes.

'However, the Crown disputed, and I do not find, that Jalalaty was regarded as "something of a joke" by [Hogan] and Standen.'

Justice James accepts the Crown argument that there is little to suggest Jalalaty's roll-over is an act of contrition, more pragmatism. He rules that he will not give Jalalaty the maximum sentence reduction available, since it is clear that Jalalaty has allowed the case to progress two years without genuinely taking the first available opportunity to plead to his guilt.

'Bakhos Jalalaty, I sentence you to imprisonment for ten years, to date from 2 June 2008,' Justice James declares to the teary prisoner.

'I fix a non-parole period of six years, to date from 2 June 2008. The earliest date on which you will be eligible for release on parole will be 2 June 2014.'

The judge adds that condition of his early release will be reliant upon the prisoner's 'promises of future assistance' to authorities.

Investigators agree Jalalaty's revelations are exceptional, and close many holes in their case against Standen and Hogan.

For Standen, it is a stunning blow. He suspected his friend may talk to authorities, but is shocked when he hears the news, briefed to him by his lawyers, as well as a member of the NSW Crime Commission, who visited him in jail to clarify his position.

If Standen had thought he was still in with a chance it was suddenly gone. An offer had been held out to him to cooperate with authorities and receive a reduced sentence, but he had maintained his innocence and refused to speak. Now, no matter what deal he may want to cut, it would be worthless.

The AFP decide nothing he says will now be accepted; his legal team has to rethink its defence preparation again. The trial date is unknown, but it is clear their client will be in prison for quite a while longer.

In Klong Prem, things are not much better for Hogan. He shares a cell with up to fifty other inmates, and another Christmas has come and gone, with no resolution.

He knows that if he goes back to Australia he will have to serve a long stretch. He will wait it out in Thailand—anything could happen. But it doesn't.

He tells those who visit that the only reason he is in prison is because the AFP wanted to arrest Standen.

'I have been guilty of many things, but the evidence will show I am not guilty of these trumped-up charges,' he writes in a diary.

He describes in notes to friends and supporters in the United Kingdom the horrendous conditions he is living in. He is evasive to all who ask about his imprisonment, but says that evasiveness comes from distrust of a system trying to lynch him.

He will speak when the time is right, he tells supporters, and that time he says will be when he is free. For the time being, his immediate concern is his own health and welfare.

'The food in the prison usually consists of rice and fish soup that is made up of fish bones and the occasional fish heads,' he records in his diary. 'Inmates can have food sent in from the prison shop bread etc and basic toiletries. The food from the prison is often contaminated and often makes prisoners ill, the prisoners can also suffer malnutrition, loosing [sic] teeth to name just one of the problems.'

There are other foreigners in the prison—some Australians and South Africans and a few South Americans—but Hogan finds solace in the company of a couple of local women, including the partner of a former fellow British inmate, who visit him regularly. Just twenty-minute visits via a glass screen, but they bring him sanity, a few bars of soap and some food.

By 2010, Hogan has a website created to bemoan his imprisonment. To a frustrated AFP, which now realises he plans to stay in Thailand as long as possible, the Hogan web page brings them some hint of how tough he is doing it—a small consolation to the team eager to bring him back to Australia and have him formally charged.

One page in particular even brings some of the agents a bit of amusement. It is a poem, full of literals and hatred for a perceived injustice.

Poem from within the walls of injustice

There once were some Feds from down-under, Who decide to charge me, why I wonder?

They were looking for Ice, but only found rice, Oh my what a blunder . . . Let's nick them and see said the feds to the DPP, But we tried that before and the results were poor, so I'm not so sure?

That does not deter us, the judge will hear us, We will say its worth millions and if cut billions . . . But there is no ice, its only rice . . . Maybe we need to seek some legal advice,!, No let's plan, plot and scheme so the facts there not seen . . . There is nothing better than a big smoke screen. The cupboards may be bare, the case going nowhere, But who will care? If it's legal or fair?

This prosecution it must not fail, We must make sure they stay in jail, There's 2 years surveillance of telephone and mail, All of this to no avail . . . ! We have a copper and an empty container, Surely we can say he's on a retainer?

I know we'll translate the papers to Thai . . . Then we can disguise this entire lie, Again I'm not sure, so let's plot some more.!

Written by [name deleted].
Bangkok Prison 2010

On another web page, Hogan claims he is being held illegally, with a lack of evidence, and abstractly adds that he himself 'has the greatest respect for the people of Thailand, the country and the Thai Royal Family'.

It is a line similar to one used by a fellow inmate Hogan is close to for a period—a Melbourne author arrested and detained for six months after allegedly insulting the Royal Family in a small book he had written. The offence of insulting or criticising the Thai monarchy carries a three- to fifteen-year jail sentence. The King gives pardons often, particularly to foreign prisoners, and Hogan's line may have some similar intent. The Aussie was certainly released soon after expressing contrition. But for Hogan it is not to be.

By the end of the year, even though the King of Thailand hasn't given Hogan his support, others have from around the world, with about thirty messages of support on Hogan's web wall—mostly from friends, but some from apparent strangers who read the news reports and feel an injustice is being done by Australian authorities.

Under another web page titled 'The Truth', Hogan supporters also question whether legal process has been followed, firstly in his arrest, and then in later attempts at extradition. They state that during his arrest, the charge documents were in Thai and Hogan had to sign what's called a CNR (Can Not Read). They describe the court hearings as a farce, and claim Australian prosecutors refuse to send any witnesses. This is what Hogan tells them has happened.

The unsigned attached commentary to the page claims:

The Australian Federal Police with the assistance of the Australian government have abused the trust of the court of the Kingdom of Thailand (Siam) and furnished the Thai authorities and judicial system deliberately with confusing and unreliable and worthless evidence.

The Australians have provided no admissible evidence but only false claims and have left the defendant to have the burden of proof to be placed on him to prove his innocence which is totally unfair and unjust . . . [The prisoner] believes he was lured to Thailand as it appears Thailand is Australia's preferred country to have him arrested in, as they are quite aware that in Europe they could not hope to detain him without grounds on the lack of substantial evidence and detain him without the possibility of bail.

In fact, the Octans team wish Hogan had indeed been arrested in Europe, as initially planned: there would not have been such a delay in delivering full justice. While Hogan was creating his website, most of his Dutch associates had been convicted and jailed.

It had been years since they were all first arrested, but Mr Brown, Mr Blue, Mr Suit (Loek), Foxtrot, Bravo, Jan and the others had enjoyed bail while they awaited trial.

But in July 2010, the five principals behind the conspiracy are sentenced to between four and eight years each. In all, eleven men and one woman are found guilty, sentenced to an average four years each. Two others are found not guilty. By Dutch standards, the sentences are high, but they barely make the news in the Netherlands. However, those allegedly involved with the group in the southern hemisphere are informed of the outcome.

Loek receives an eight-year sentence, the longest of the group, which he immediately appeals. While on bail, Dutch authorities reportedly give him approval to return to arms dealing, and he continues exporting armoured vehicle parts to the Middle East.

For Standen, the sentencings are another blow.

Hogan also hears of some discouraging legal developments. Almost a year after his Russian friend Viktor Bout beat US extradition moves from Klong Prem, a higher Thai court hears an appeal by the US government and grants extradition in November 2010.

The Russian government formally protests, but Bout is immediately sent to the United States, where he is eventually convicted on 2 November 2011 of arms and money-laundering offences.

In November 2010, charges against Standen are changed for a third time, due to the evidence Jalalaty had provided. The AFP had to rejig the wording of the three drug-related charges, but the essence of the alleged offences remained the same. A date for the trial, however, has finally been set—February 2011.

In the months leading up to the trial, Standen is visited several times by senior figures from the NSW Crime Commission. Those same figures also visited Jalalaty after he changed his plea: everyone just wants to know where they stand.

Despite the ban on contacting Standen, some friends and former commission colleagues send him mail. One senior law enforcement analyst, in particular, is convinced the whole affair is 'a set up and a big mistake', and she tells him she is not alone in that belief. He is buoyed by their support.

Come February 2011 and Standen is still not prepared to face the charges. He and his lawyers make a last-ditch effort to declare two of his three charges an abuse of process: the second charge of knowingly taking part in the supply of a prohibited drug, and the third charge of conspiring to pervert the course of justice—largely on the basis that the first charge, conspiring to import a prohibited substance, was sufficient.

The first charge has a maximum penalty of twenty-five years imprisonment; the second charge, life imprisonment; and the third, of perverting justice, five years. To the agents behind Octans, a 25-year sentence would be adequate, but the prosecutors need all three charges to stick, since at least two are dependent on each other.

In a 36-page judgment, Justice Bruce James dismisses Standen's application. Standen is not done, though, and his lawyers declare they are prepared to go to the Court of Criminal Appeal to have the charge of knowingly taking part in the supply of a drug—with its maximum sentence of life in jail—thrown out. The matter is heard quickly in the appeals court a few weeks later, and again it is dismissed.

11

Trial

Standen's trial finally begins on 15 March 2011, nearly three years after he was arrested.

Court 3 in the King Street Supreme Court complex in the heart of Sydney is one of Australia's oldest still used for criminal matters. First opened for business in 1827, the small sandstone courthouse was originally earmarked for demolition when a larger, more modern complex was being built next door, but it was saved in 1973, and fully restored, retaining grand oak-panelled rooms with stencilled and handpainted walls, and convict-carved sandstone facades.

Court 3 is a classic courtroom with a second-floor public gallery looking down on the tight court space.

Standen enters the court building wearing a bullet-proof vest for his own security, but enters the actual courtroom resplendent in a dark suit, blue shirt and tie. Someone in the gallery snaps a photograph of him on their mobile phone and court sheriffs move on them. His trial is highly anticipated and work experience students line up outside the court for a view of proceedings. Security is tight, with all entering the court having to pass through an airport-style alarmed archway, be scanned with a hand-held metal detector, and pass all their metal objects through an X-ray. Five sheriffs also sit in the courtroom in case of trouble.

The trial is expected to last fourteen weeks and call upon up to forty witnesses. The first day, however, is dull, and includes little more than legal discussion before the six-man and six-woman jury, one of whom chose to postpone an overseas trip to sit on the panel.

There is also the question of comfort in the remodelled but still outdated courtroom. 'This is not the most suitable room,' Justice Bruce James declares to a jury anxiously shifting in their seats. 'Among other things the air-conditioning is not very good, and the lighting is not particularly good,' he says.

Nor are the acoustics, given the room's high gilded ceilings, with the jury and packed public gallery all leaning forward to hear him and the softly spoken prosecutor, Tim Game SC, speak.

The courtroom is packed, and not just with people. Row upon row of lever arch folders, numbering more than a hundred, choke the back corner, as well as trolleys of exhibits, including photographs and transcripts. Each jury member is given a 'pack'—one folder in which to write notes and store transcript materials. By Day 2 they each have three folders, and the number will continue to grow to the point where they can only carry in to court the folders that are to specifically be relied upon on a given day.

*

On Day 2, perhaps sensing the occasion and not wishing to delay the hearing that has already taken almost three years to eventuate, Justice James makes a few observations, pauses, then nods towards prosecutor Tim Game and motions, 'Yes, Mr Crown.'

After explaining the nature of the charges and providing a basic outlay of the courtroom, including pointing out where the accused is sitting, Game decides to give the case context. He starts by talking about the intrusive powers of the NSW Crime Commission—powers that go way beyond the police force's and Standen's trusted position as the commission's deputy, with thirty years' experience in law enforcement.

It's a complex case, but Game narrows it down: Standen is the adviser, Hogan is the offshore coordinator, and Jalalaty is the on-hand Australian operator. But Standen is the pin that holds the three and the plot together.

He then briefs the jury on Hogan, his earlier 2003 arrest, and how he later rolled over and became a registered informant. Game also reveals Hogan forfeited more than $900,000 of ill-gotten gains to the state coffers before he left Australia to return to the United Kingdom.

It's all about context: be prepared to hear some big figures, he tells them.

'The Crown will allege that at some point in time, the relationship between the accused and [Hogan] changed from a mere handler/informer relationship to an improper one, and the Crown case is this happened by December 2005,' he says.

He then details Hogan's £20,000 ($47,500) payment to Standen, ostensibly for a laser eye operation; that is the start of the monies, and they go up.

Dianne Jalalaty is also singled out for mention, as a former detective who had worked closely with Standen in the AFP in the mid-1980s. Her position has to be stated, since she will later be a Crown witness who will confirm what she was told by her husband about the plot.

Game then introduces the motive.

> The Crown case is that the accused's motive in committing these offences ... was financial. Throughout the relevant period the accused was facing serious financial difficulties mainly due, on the Crown case, to over commitment and excessive spending but whatever the cause of them throughout—and you will hear again and again and again in the conversation about as it were his desperate need for money.
>
> The sums are very significant. They go well beyond the tens of thousands of dollars and go into the six figures ... the prosecution will allege that the accused was spending beyond his means and there is a chicken and egg aspect to that because in a sense he was spending beyond his means in an expectation that at some time in the future he would receive a windfall of cash from the importation.

Standen's lover, Louise Baker, is also mentioned, including her trip with him to Dubai, again since she was later to be a Crown witness.

Standen is furiously scribbling his own notes and shakes his head. Two of his brothers sit near the accused's dock; they too shake their heads and roll their eyes. They smile as the evidence is read of the nicknames and codes. It's all child's play. Standen leans over to them at one point and says, 'they're just joining dots', shrugs, then shakes his head. Surely the jury will see it is all a game of double Dutch.

For much of the day, Game outlines the case against Standen, giving the public gallery—which again includes members of the NSW Crime Commission, media and some AFP agents—a sneak peak of things to come. He reads some emails from 'Maurice' and 'Myrtle' that outline the advice 'Maurice' (Standen) was giving the others, showing his 'deeply inside position' in the plot.

Recognising the likely line of attack from Standen's barrister, Mark Ierace SC, Game wraps up his opening remarks by highlighting why Standen was charged specifically with those three charges.

Turning to his right to address the jury directly, he says:

The Crown says Mr Standen, the accused, did a number of things. Some of them involve not doing things, like not reporting, but they include the following sorts of things: not performing his duty as a law enforcement officer assisting [Hogan] in monitoring Mr Jalalaty in his communications with [Loek] and [Hogan], assisting Mr Jalalaty retrieving the money provided by [Hogan] and lost by Mr Jalalaty . . .

After a lunch break, defence counsel Mark Ierace begins his opening address. He doesn't waste time with a preamble, but rather goes to the heart of Standen's defence.

'The accused did have a business relationship with Mr Jalalaty and [Hogan]—but he denies that, so far as he was concerned, these relationships had an ulterior criminal purpose,' Ierace tells the court.

The accused intended eventually to cease employment in investigations and join Mr Jalalaty in legitimate business ventures, and was already providing some assistance to Mr Jalalaty in that regard. This was the plan he was working towards, and the context in which he received payments from time to time. Regardless of whatever Mr Jalalaty or Mr [Hogan] expected to be in the second container, the accused expected it to contain only rice.

Much of the evidence that the prosecution intends to call is basically not disputed by the defence. Accordingly we do not require many witnesses for cross-examination, and you will hear the effect of their evidence given by others reading out their statements or referring to the content of their statements.

The overall tone of Ierace's case is that Standen didn't play by the book in recording certain friendships or financial transactions, but he was no criminal.

For Octans investigators, the claim that Standen was going to resign from his high-paying job to become a basmati rice importer is laughable. They were anticipating a more convoluted explanation as to why Standen was associating with Hogan and Jalalaty, and ultimately conspiring to import drugs.

Specifically, investigators were anticipating the defence to argue that Standen was actually luring Hogan and others into a conspiracy, to then expose the entire criminal syndicate. That seemed a reasonable prospect, given the murky world the NSW Crime Commission operated in, and of course the fact that Standen—rightly or wrongly in the eyes of the law—had done this before in 2005, in allowing 'Tom' to sell cocaine across Sydney in the hope of gleaning criminal intelligence.

But AFP investigators such as Thompson, receiving updates of the case in Bangkok, where he is working on another case, are still only cautiously optimistic of putting Standen behind bars. The case is still highly complex and sensitive, and a jury will still need to be convinced. And as other cases have shown, juries can do anything.

Ierace says he does not intend to dispute much of what will be read from transcripts or played to the court, including conversations between his client and Hogan and Jalalaty: in such conversations, he tells the court, Standen is simply humouring his friends.

He continues:

The Crown has referred to what's been described as draft emails between the accused and Mr Hogan.

You will hear evidence that one of the reasons the accused partook in this form of communication with Mr [Hogan] was that it was a type of game or distraction between them, but also you will hear from the accused that he agreed to use that system because Mr [Hogan] expressed concern that his safety might be compromised if past criminal associates discovered he was communicating with a law enforcement officer. As noted by the Crown in his opening to you, the draft email system was not used between the accused and Mr Jalalaty.

Although there are other disputes between the prosecution and defence case, this is the essential difference between the two cases. Thankyou.

And with that sign-off, Ierace concludes his short but punchy opening address.

The first witness is Paul Watt, the AFP agent who first dealt with Dutch police and was working with them to unravel how the bogus MDL Food and Services worked and who it was dealing with, before his team stumbled onto the wider plot.

Watt details at length the system of getting warrants to tap into Jalalaty's home and work phones and faxes—and specifically Standen's computers and the ability to take screen grabs every ten seconds to see what Standen is reading and writing.

Watt also reveals that since Hogan, Standen and Jalalaty would write over each other's draft emails, he had to develop a sense of who was who from their styles. Hogan, particularly, often double- or triple-punctuated his sentences for effect and was also a bad speller.

Sometimes Watt could see who was writing because of references such as the sign-offs 'Maurice' and 'Myrtle', or he simply knew because of screen grabs.

Then the court hears the first of hours upon hours of telephone conversations. Without context these sound like little more than banter between mates Standen and Jalalaty. But there are specific references to tracking down the 'psychic investor Bruce Way, and then recordings with Jalalaty arranging to meet Roger Rogerson to discuss ways of finding that lost Hogan money.

After every recording is played, the jury members are given a written transcript to add to their fast-filling folders. The media too are given copies of the recordings at the end of each day.

At the end of the week, Justice James calls for proceedings to end after lunch, with the Court 3 air-conditioner not working to capacity, and autumn temperatures still warm. The relief on the faces of the jury, which has been asked to absorb in just a few days the complexities of the law, and their role and responsibilities, is clear.

By the third week Paul Watt is still on the stand, leading the court through the AFP's listening-device recordings and transcripts at a painstakingly slow pace. At times the recordings are inaudible or undecipherable, with interferences and other noises being picked up.

'Might I place on the record that the defence does not

necessarily accept the accuracy of the transcript as to what's being said on the tapes,' Mr Ierace says, after prosecutors conceded one particular recording was in parts totally inaudible.

At this point Justice James reminds the jury:

> Yes ladies and gentlemen, I have said this before and I will be saying it again: the transcript that you have got in front of you is an attempt by somebody to set down what that person apparently believes can be heard when the recording is played.
>
> But the transcript has no authority. It's for you to determine what you consider that you hear when the recording is played. You may conclude that the transcript is generally right, or you may conclude that it's right in parts or wrong in parts, or you may conclude that it's generally wrong. It's entirely up to you. As you have heard counsel say, counsel for the accused does not accept that this transcript is an accurate or a fully accurate transcript of what's to be heard when this recording is played.

'That goes for the other transcripts as well,' Ierace interrupts.

'Yes that's completely correct, I have concentrated on this transcript, but what I have said applies to all the transcripts.'

'Thank you your Honour,' Ierace says.

Justice James concludes: 'It's for you to determine what you consider that you hear when you listen to the recording. The transcripts are offered to you as possibly affording some assistance, but you may conclude that the transcripts are not of any assistance at all.'

Some intercepted overseas telephone calls, made between July and September 2007, are then played to the jury. These record conversations between Loek in the Netherlands and Rene Asbeek Brusse, who was at the time in Pakistan.

The jury is then told that one of several exercise books seized from Standen's work area included a brief reference to 0–9 and the word 'pass'. The prosecution tells the court that 0–9 is a code for the change of Hotmail account to the Switzerland account, where '0' to '9' equals 'S' through to 'D', and the word 'pass' meant that the Hotmail password was 'passport'.

This causes confusion, because there are eleven letters in the word 'Switzerland', thereby meaning the code is one numeral short. (Standen himself will later explain that there are a few words or phrases in English where letters are not repeated, and you simply use as many letters as required to fit a telephone number into it.)

By the end of the first few weeks, the demeanour of the jury has changed. They appear more slumped in their chairs, and when directed to certain parts of evidence by prosecutors, their perusing of their personal lever arch folders appears more lethargic.

The case was originally supposed to end in fourteen weeks, but at this pace it appears unlikely. The prosecution asks Justice James whether he will make it clear to the jury that both sides of the bench are trying to expedite the matter as best as possible.

As prosecutors outline the first shipment of rice in painstaking detail, Justice James points out the obvious to try to keep things moving.

'Mr Crown, there is sort of almost chaos about this first shipment. One could feel some sympathy for Mr Jalalaty attempting to deal with these people. In the Crown case is it relevant to the charges?' his Honour asks the court, after one particular lengthy piece of evidence involving exchanges between the Pakistanis and Jalalaty.

'Your Honour, it is not directly relevant other than the unfolding of the process. We will move from here to the process in relation to the second container. It might have some significance because ultimately your Honour will appreciate that there was in fact no pseudoephedrine in the second container, although it was expected to be there. It may have some significance,' prosecutor Hament Dhanji, assisting Game, replies.

'I am not suggesting that we don't need to go into it,' his Honour clarifies.

'I appreciate there is a lot of detail and a lot of chaos,' Dhanji concludes, before a short adjournment is called.

While the jury are waiting to come in, the counsels and the Bench light-heartedly revisit the case's complexity and confusion.

'Mr Crown,' says Justice James, 'it might subsequently be suggested by the Crown that there was no pseudoephedrine in the shipment in April 2008 or thereabouts, but that might well be attributable to these people in Pakistan who—there is some evidence of their conduct in what we are looking at now.'

'I should be frank,' replies Dhanji, 'and say that is not something that is clearly formulated by the Crown—but I think the way your Honour put it is correct.'

'It might be subliminally, if not expressly suggested by the Crown,' confirms Justice James. 'One has to really sympathise with Mr Jalalaty, the number of times he is promised something and it doesn't happen.'

'I was sympathising more with the Pakistanis having to deal with Mr Jalalaty,' Ierace adds jokingly.

'There seems to be a complete breakdown of communication. Perhaps we shouldn't attribute fault to either party,' Justice James says.

'This will emerge in due course,' the defence responds. 'It is interesting how many times—because there are so many, many times—that Mr Jalalaty is recorded as saying one thing to one person, and within minutes or a few hours says something entirely different to someone else.'

'Yes,' says Justice James. 'I have the understanding that the Crown says that Mr Jalalaty was not aware that the person he was speaking to as Mr Rashid was [Loek].'

'Certainly not by name, although there were—in terms of being the contact person—there are previous emails, emails previous to the point we're at, where Mr [Hogan] is instructing Mr Jalalaty to deal with only Rashid, so whilst he might not know the name, he seems to know—' Dhanji explains.

'I was rather getting the impression that he thought Mr Rashid was a Pakistani.'

'He seems not to have noticed the difference in accent, I think it is true to say.'

Ierace again steps in. 'If I could make this observation: of course, there is theoretically the possibility of Rashid being someone with such a name living in Europe, and your Honour might recall from the last telephone intercept there was reference to Mr Rashid being in Europe and meeting up with someone else, unnamed, who one might think was clearly [Hogan].'

'Yes I noticed that.'

For the court, the brief exchange highlights the tiring minutiae of the case, that on some days are difficult to follow. Another troubling factor is that someone could inadvertently stall the trial. The media are reporting on the case, and on more than one occasion a photo is published alongside court reports, showing Standen clearly in handcuffs and heading to jail. Such images may subtly prejudice the jury's mind.

Prosecutor Dhanji also inadvertently oversteps the mark, literally.

'There is one matter I should raise,' he tells the court in the absence of the jury. He explains:

> During the luncheon break I was taking a walk and found myself walking along the path near the coffee shop there, and I was intently looking at the direction towards the church, and when I looked up I realised I had effectively walked into the jurors, assembled as a group in front of the coffee shop area. I got, I must say, something of a surprise when I looked up and realised I was in proximity to the jury, and continued walking along and there was no exchange. I am concerned it may have seemed a trifle odd.

'Would you like me to say something to the jury?' Justice James asks.

'Perhaps if your Honour . . .'

'I could go back to some remarks I made near the beginning of the trial.'

'If you could do that, they will well understand that is what it is a reference to, and I would be comforted.'

In front of the court Justice James later says:

> Ladies and gentlemen, there's some brief remarks I would like to make to you. Near the beginning of the trial I told you that you might by chance see some legal representative of the parties, or some other person associated with the case, outside the courtroom, but in the vicinity of this complex. Any legal representative or any person associated with the trial will try to avoid having any contact with you. It is obviously important that there be no contact between you and persons associated with

the trial outside the courtroom. If somebody seems to you to be avoiding you, it is done so as to avoid any contact. It is not done out of impoliteness.

Louise Baker then takes the stand, but her evidence is brief. She confirms Standen's lavish lifestyle, provides a catalogue of expensive gifts she accepted and talks through a diary she kept of her life with her former lover.

Dutch builder Rene Asbeek Brusse also gives evidence, via video link from his lawyers' office in the Netherlands. He was earlier charged with conspiring with the Dutch cartel, but his case is yet to be finalised after he agreed to help authorities. He is the only Reservoir Dog to offer to help police.

The only addition he can make simply confuses the court further. His written statement had quoted him as saying: 'I have to know, we have to plan the rice.' But on questioning, through an interpreter, it appears the word 'rice', as translated, should actually have been 'travel'—with the Dutch word for 'rice' (*rijst*) being similar to 'travel' (*reizen*).

Midway through the trial, in a highly anticipated moment, Mark William Standen takes the stand.

He makes eye contact with the jury and nods in their direction—standard legal advice for defendants to engage. He wastes no time, immediately going into some detail as to what it means to be a law enforcement handler of an informer, and how to control the informant to ensure a continued relationship.

Yes he may have been friends with Hogan, but this was natural, normal. Indeed, it was best practice, and any money he received from Hogan was from one friend to another.

He then elaborates further.

My starting position is that, with only a few exceptions—I have met a few people who I classify as bad people—but with few exceptions informers are people who commit offences first, so by treating them humanely, pleasantly, in a friendly manner, they tend to respond.

A lot of people have a perception that, when they deal with police, police will always be—or investigators will be—officious, domineering, dominating, standoverish, fierce, or any number of adjectives could be applied, and people are frequently surprised when someone takes time to talk to them normally, sensibly, show interest in them, their families, their own circumstances—and people respond well to that, and they always have done so in my experience.

'When you say they respond well, what do you mean?' Ierace asks.

'It makes them comfortable, establishes an element of trust and comfort. If someone doesn't trust you, they're hardly likely to place their life in your hands, and that's the way it is in relation to some informers.'

Standen is on a roll now and continues to detail his modus operandi. It is about convincing the court that his friendship with Hogan is part of the work plan. Working with Hogan was worth all the time and effort, he says.

He describes Hogan as lonely—someone who would ring at night just for a chat as he prepared himself dinner for one.

He says Hogan felt his criminal associates were 'lunatics', and therefore jumped at the chance to assist Australian authorities—and in particular Standen—in unravelling not only his own criminal network, but those operating in other parts of the world, including Australia, the United Kingdom, the United States and the Netherlands. Hogan, it seemed, had a wide network of contacts, and knew all the comings and goings of the European criminal milieu, the buyers and sellers, the front companies and the smuggling routes.

Standen continues:

> It was a positive and promising sign that he divested himself of what appeared to be substantial information, if not all the information that he had, in relation to not only the matters that we knew of from our investigation, but matters about which we were previously unaware—matters where he did not need to tell us about his involvement in other serious offences, but he did.
>
> And the information that he provided generally, which was: 'Here is who I work with, here is what they do. Here is what I do for them. Here is what I have done for them. Here is what they have done. Here is where the money was made. Here is where the money was sent. These are the people involved in that process. And here is what I know about the other groups that are doing similar activities, where they operate and who they operate with.'
>
> So to that extent—and it also included people in Australia with whom he had criminal dealings; in other words, apart from speaking about—sorry, am I going too fast? Apart from speaking about the overseas groups, he also spoke about the persons who he was dealing with in Australia.
>
> And, in my experience and just being reasonable, it is hard to expect anyone to do any more than that.

Finally Standen tells the court of the curious draft email system that for three years had baffled and entertained authorities trying to piece together who was 'Myrtle' and 'Maurice', and more than two dozen other cyberspace personalities.

It was Hogan's idea, Standen says—one he came up with shortly before leaving Australia in 2003.

'Well, two reasons that he conveyed,' Standen tells the hushed court of how it came about.

One, that he was concerned about any—especially inquiries that might be made by his criminal associates that like drop in, and I am aware of similar things happening in Australia where, when people were trying to find sources of information, they pay surprise visits, check your phone, computer, whatever it might be, and he also had concerns about the authorities downloading his computer as he passed in and out of airports, and similarly finding communications with the crime commission . . .

I am happy to accommodate those needs as far as is possible and legal—and of course there's nothing illegal about using a draft email, and that was the method he preferred to use. We first discussed my Yahoo account and again that necessitated my name being sent—and my name was known among the criminals that he was concerned about, so he wanted to use the draft emails, and I was more than happy to do that—as I said, more than happy to accommodate his concerns.

And ultimately in these situations it's the other person's concerns that have to be addressed as well as mine.

Standen goes on to describe Hogan's desire for anonymity and his own desire to accommodate his source, so he could continue to receive top criminal intelligence from his informant. Nothing more sinister than that.

And what of their curious codename selection?

Standen explains:

When I started writing to him I used to address—like as you write a letter, you write 'Dear John'—in the addressing of him I used every name that I could think of that started with the letter J, other than [real name deleted]. So it would be addressed to John, Jeff, Jacob and so on. When I ran out of male J names, I used female J names. I signed off on the emails using every name that I could think of beginning with the letter M, other than Mark. So I was—a range of names.

Over time, through persistent or frequent use he favoured—or I noticed that he favoured—I think Julie and Jo Jo. I saw he responded with that more often than not, and Maurice was used more often than not with respect to me. So whilst they weren't set in concrete as being the necessary names, they were used more frequently than others. But it was just a progression of names starting with J and M . . .

I think it was 2005—I may be mistaken on that—but he told me that one of his daughters gave him a birthday present which was, as best I recall is—the detail may not be a hundred per cent—was a novelty gift of a Certificate of Title for a piece of land in the UK, and this is the part I'm not sure about, but it may have been a foot square—as in one square foot of land—and the novelty gifts available and you get a full certificate of title and other documents that go with it, of a novelty nature.

When he received that he joked to me that he might have to apply for a driver's licence and adopt a title of Lord to go with his new land ownership. So I commenced addressing the emails 'your lordship', 'your Royal Highness' and so forth, and signed off, you know, 'your humble servant Maurice, your humble servants Mary and Joan, your loyal subjects Joan John and Uncle Jeff', and over time the members of the Royal family grew in number, and the number of loyal servants grew in number, and over the time the names took on a life of their own, and developed from that point in a similar fashion to the way the subject matter and the name—sorry the subject matter in the emails we saw—develop through the case, with attempts at humour developing on a word or a theme.

The humour seemed to have dissipated by the time I saw them in court, but at the time they were attempts to play on words and they grew a life their own.

Standen tells the court Hogan had, since 2004, been trying to live a criminal-free life. Hogan had been dabbling in property development and real estate with a man in the Philippines, and another from the United Arab Emirates, gold trading as well as exploiting an apparent loophole in the Valued Added Tax (VAT) scheme attached to exports in the United Kingdom. An associate of Hogan also had a commercial cleaning company, a branch of which Hogan hoped to establish in Sydney.

Standen details how he then came to meet Jalalaty, and despite having a good job as a law enforcer, was attracted to doing business with the affable grocer.

'I had a good job, and despite what may have—or was written in—one or two emails, I actually liked the job that I did. But I wasn't so sure that it was something I could do for a further ten or fifteen years at the pace that was required to do the job I did,' he tells the court.

'Because perhaps the best description of my job was that it was hectic in the extreme—long and hectic.'

'Did you find it demanding?' Ierace asks.

'Very.'

'Physically or mentally or emotionally or a combination? In what way did you find it demanding?'

'All of the above.'

'And are you saying that for those reasons, the prospect of continuing to do that job for many years was not entirely appealing?'

'That's fair to say. As I said, it was a very good job, but I'd had, by that stage, some 32 or 33 years in law enforcement, and it was only getting busier.'

Standen's defence team use his first three days in the witness box to offer solid explanations for every aspect of the connection between Hogan, Standen and Jalalaty. Not just how they all met, but why they all continued to remain in contact. There were business ideas and a desire to succeed in enterprise that Standen believed they all shared, but they all also wanted to buy each other gifts, Standen tells the court.

The start of the significant money transfers between the three began, Standen says on the eve of Christmas 2005.

'In December 2005, when I was speaking with [Hogan] and I had ongoing discussions with him throughout the year, he had said that he wanted to give me something for Christmas,' Standen tells the court earnestly. 'I did the usual "oh no, that's fine, don't worry about it".'

He says Hogan then insisted:

'No, I would like to do something for you for Christmas'—we had spoken about my intention at some point to have laser treatment on my eyes; at the time I wore glasses—and he said 'how about I pay for your eyes to be done, I'd like to do that'.

Again the usual polite, 'no, no that's fine, thanks anyway'; 'no, no, I'd like to do that'. 'Okay matter for you, that'd be really nice', and he said 'I will send it to you'. I said 'Well, how about you send it to Bill.'

By that stage he and I had spoken many times about Bill because I kept him apprised of developments with Bill, if I could call them that, and he said, I said, 'Be better if you sent it to Bill'; he said, 'Okay, send me the details', and I did.

'Why did you tell him that it was better that it be sent to Bill?' Ierace asks Standen.

'So that—as I said—a thin disguise really. You know, a transfer from the name [Hogan] into my account would ring alarm bells at the crime commission if for whatever reason they saw that transaction, and such a transaction may or may not have been triggered on AUSTRAC—I don't really know.'

Standen tells the court he had told Hogan that such an eye operation cost $5000 and Hogan agreed to pay—but then sent him, via Jalalaty's bank account, £20,000 ($47,500). He said he knew it would transgress the NSW Crime Commission rules to receive any gift from a criminal informant, but a gift was a gift.

He continues:

Having the benefit of close to two years of ongoing discussions with [Hogan] as to his activities and the source of funds, given my own financial situation, I was not unattracted to the idea of him paying for my laser surgery on the eyes as a Christmas gift.

I also in my mind—as opposed to the commission's view, as I said earlier—compartmentalised things, and I operated on the basis that provided the work compartment remained intact, and that I did all the things that would be required and expected of me in relation to any information coming from [Hogan], that the business prospect or prospective business compartment could operate independently of that.

Standen later tells the court he never thought for a moment the money could have been unlawfully gained.

'No, nothing sinister,' Standen says, when asked whether the size of the gift was unusual.

'I mean, he is a very affable chap, and by that stage, by all accounts—certainly on *his* account—he was doing particularly well.'

Despite apparently being on the verge of success with a number of import deals, including the non-alcoholic Bavaria beer and the B-52 energy drink, Jalalaty was going to stop those contracts to concentrate on his meat export business.

Standen says Jalalaty told him he had cash flow problems, so he wanted to put all the other deals on hold.

Standen adds that when he told Hogan this, Hogan was mad, and then offered to buy into the business to share in what he saw as potential profits. And thus the money began to flow between the three.

Standen then describes how Jalalaty and Hogan met in Thailand to discuss distribution of the Bavaria beer and B-52 energy drink. Even though he has forgotten some aspects and details of the past few years, Standen vividly recalls the time Jalalaty received $1 million, shortly after meeting Hogan and returning to Australia in January 2006.

'I was at home on a weekend—I think a Saturday—when I got a phone call from Bill, and that was the next occasion,' he tells the court.

He said 'I just met'—he said, 'I just met my new best mate.' I said, 'Yeah, pray tell.'

'Yeah, I've—I'm ready to'—I can't remember—'ready to rock and roll. I'm in business. I've got a very good investment. Your mate's invested a million dollars.'

And I said, 'Are you sure?' And he said, 'No,' he said, 'I've just met a bloke at Coogee.' I think he said, Bondi or Coogee.

I said, 'Who?' And he said, 'Oh, your mate's mate, a Portuguese guy.' And I said, 'What? What Portuguese guy?' And he said, 'Oh, he's my best mate in the world now. Bald guy. Married. Got two kids. Owns a car dealership.'

And I said, 'And he gave you what?' And he said, 'Gave me a million dollars in a bag.'

And at the time of the call it was quite noisy in the background. There was sporting-type noise, and I can't remember the detail, but it was quite noisy, and I said, 'Oh, yeah, and where are you?' and he named a place, which I can't recall because it was a sporting venue—I don't remember whether it was tennis, swimming, soccer, football, whatever, but he was at a sporting venue—and I said, 'Oh, yeah where is this money?'

And he said, 'Oh, in the boot.' And I remember rolling my eyes thinking, 'Oh, yeah another Bill story.'

I said, 'Well, we should catch up and discuss where we go from here,' and we then arranged to meet and I saw him about two or three days later in the city.

Standen tells the court that Jalalaty had told him some of the Hogan money was to be used to lease a forklift and a new warehouse in Blacktown. Instead, says Standen, he had been duped by his friend, who, during a cafe catch-up, admitted the money he was expecting to reap dividends from was the same money Hogan had given him.

He recalls Jalalaty as saying, 'I know I told you it was my money but I invested B-52's money.'

'When he told you that, how did you feel?' Ierace asked.

Perhaps as you might expect, something of a sinking feeling, because it was inconsistent with all the things that he had told me that he had been doing with that money over the previous year, ever since February/March 2006.

I said, 'Have you told him that?' He said, 'No, I thought it might be better coming from you.' I said, 'Not much chance of that happening.'

I said, 'First of all you really need to make sure you have done everything you can to get the money back.' He talked about some enormous amount of money he was expecting—like 6, 7, 9 million dollars, or something ridiculous.

I said, 'Perhaps you should just focus on getting the investment back—the amount you put in, the principal; you should just get that back.' He said, 'I'm not sure I am going to get anything back.' He said, 'Is there anything you could do through the Crime Commission?' I said, 'No.'

I said that there is a private investigator who is a debt collector who may be able to assist. I said, 'Let me check with him first that it's okay with him to give you his number. His name is Frank Wheeler.'

I said, 'How much have you invested?' And he said, '$1 million.' And I think you can work out the rest. I rang Frank Wheeler, told him that, gave him Bill's number—or gave Bill his number, I can't remember which—and they obviously met and discussed the matter from there.

For police listening to the evidence, Standen's story is laughable and bears little resemblance to the truth. Standen never misses a beat in his responses to questions. His recollections of some things are delivered word-perfect, heavy on detail but light on truth.

At other times he is argumentative, pleading his innocence in rather convincing fashion. When he can't answer, he dismisses it as irrelevant at the time, and thus a memory lapse. No one could be so silly as to have done what he was alleged to have done with the simple Jalalaty, he says.

Standen also tells the court of 'Bill-isms'—random thoughts that Jalalaty would often share which made no sense. Lear jet trips he made with prominent Australian businessmen, catering on multi-millionaires' yachts, his belief he would work undercover for law enforcement. When Standen would ask for money, Jalalaty would come out with rubbish why he couldn't pay him at that particular moment.

'Just double Dutch as to an explanation as to why it took him so long to make a payment,' Standen says, missing the irony of the reference to the Dutch.

As for Hogan, Standen straight-faced says his friend is a legitimate smart businessman:

> A clever—although not perhaps well-educated—witty person who had turned the corner, as it were, and had abandoned his previously illegal activities, assisted the Crime Commission and other authorities in that process, including the AFP and Dutch police, and who was using his natural talents and wit and everything else to engage in legitimate business enterprises . . .

Midway through Standen's evidence, as more and more listening-device recordings are played and transcripts of intercepts are read, a new term is introduced into his defence: the 'unlawful scenario'.

This brilliant tactical move initially catches police and the prosecution off-guard. No mention was ever made of the 'unlawful scenario' in his record of interview, but now suddenly Standen has an alibi for why it was, apparently, he was talking about a shipment of illicit goods.

Jalalaty, Standen explains to the court, had in one of his many strange conversations introduced the fact that he could import drug-making chemicals, or drugs themselves. Standen tells the court he pitied his fool-fantasist of a friend, and thought he would humour him and his unlawful scenario. Jalalaty often fantasised about being a criminal, and making money was part of his strange fantasy that the pair spoke long and in detail about. It was a game the two middle-aged men would play to amuse themselves. (Indeed, police have fifteen secret recordings about the illicit shipment over a nine-month period.)

Standen then tells the court:

I was uncomfortable with it, because it offends my natural instincts. But given the somewhat unusual history of my dealings with Bill, particularly what had transpired through 2005 and 2006 and his uniquely unusual character, I reflected on his conversations and basically told or said whatever it was he wanted—I thought he wanted—to hear at any particular time. But in so doing, took every opportunity I could to shut the door on the subject, or to bring him back to what I hoped and wanted him to do—that is, normal business pursuits.

As for why the 'unlawful scenario' never came up during his formal interrogation, Standen says he'd had a 'brain snap' at the time of his arrest, triggered by the unrecorded conversation he had had in the car with Venchiarutti, when he heard about the

'600' apparent kilograms of ephedrine. It so shocked him that it temporarily slipped his mind.

'Mr Standen, the situation is this: you gave those answers in the record of interview, since that time you have realised that the listening devices bear a meaning which is not consistent and not capable of being made consistent with what appears in the record of interview,' Game declares.

'I disagree with that.'

'So you have had to come up with another story—another story which inculpates Mr Jalalaty, but exculpates Mr [Hogan]. That's what you have done, isn't it?'

'No.'

'You have just told an entire fresh set of lies in your evidence over many many days?'

'No.'

'And the "unlawful scenario" is just shorthand for the fact that you can't answer the clearly incriminating conversations that took place over a nine-month period between you and Mr Jalalaty?'

'The "unlawful scenario" is, in fact, what happened.'

It is all fantastic theatre for a recharged jury and public gallery.

Standen also declares he did not provide any 'insider' law enforcement information to anyone. 'Absolutely not,' he says, adding that anything he may have said to Jalalaty could have come from TV shows like *Border Security*, or *Customs UK* and the New Zealand *Border Patrol*.

He replies to questions from his defence counsel to reinforce the point.

'Did you ever tell Bill Jalalaty anything in relation to investigative procedures that you believed to not be in the public domain?' Ierace asks.

'No, I deliberately did not.'

'Did you ever make inquiries of Customs officers or the staff of any other investigative agency on behalf of Mr Jalalaty?'

'Definitely not.'

'Did you ever make such inquiries with a view to assisting him—that is, Mr Jalalaty—with the importation of either of the two containers?'

'No.'

'In relation to intelligence—or the fruits of intelligence, if I can use that phrase—that you passed on to [Hogan] that we have heard evidence of, did you ever, in passing on that information, contravene the requirements of the Crime Commission in relation to the handling and dealing with informers?'

'No.'

And as for speaking in code, no says Standen—it was all just double speak. It was double Dutch.

'Why do you have to speak code? In an email that destroys itself instantly, why do you have to speak code?' Game asks.

'I have already said it's not code, it's just double talk, and no one's needed that to be explained to them.' Standen will refer numerous times to 'double speak'; he thinks it sounds less criminal than 'code'.

Hogan's criminal background is brought up at length during the trial. Despite objections from a lawyer who said he would be representing the Briton if and when he came to Australia, the evidence is accepted, since it forms a crucial part of the prosecution case against Standen.

Standen spends twenty-five days in the witness box. His brothers have attended so many days of the trial that they become 'frequent club card' members of the small coffee-cart operation outside the courthouse.

Many in court are weary of the cat and mouse question-and-answer game. At times, Standen has to be reminded that he is there to *answer* questions, not ask them, and often needs to be asked questions several different ways before agreeing with the proposition.

It is tiresome for the jury, particularly. At one point they hand the judge a note which causes him great concern. In part it states the trial is having a serious detrimental effect on their physical, emotional and financial health.

Many of us are forced to work nights and weekends to maintain roles that could not be replaced with one day's notice. We understand our rights when it comes to employment however we're sure you can appreciate the reality is another matter. Pressure from employers when we have no end in sight is increasing.

The note explains how one juror was unable to maintain the rent on the allowance the court paid to be a juror, others had been denied work bonuses and promotions in their absence, and two others, who had been out of work prior to the trial, had been unable out of court hours to adequately find work. One self-employed juror with three children had to turn down four months' work because of the trial, and another with children had to pay fees for before and after school care because of the hours of the jury sittings.

'We do not deny the accused has a right to a fair trial but ask that our rights to earn a living, seek employment, look after our families, go on vacation and plan our lives are taken into equal consideration,' the jury note stated.

Standen's defence counsel ask Justice James to consider discharging the jury on the grounds that their low morale and other expressed disadvantages they are enduring will adversely impact the case.

James describes the jury's performance as heroic, and says he will see what ex-gratia payments the state government could make to certain jurors on the grounds of hardship, but refuses the application to discharge the jury. He does, however, instruct both counsels to expedite their arguments where they can.

Before the end of the trial, one juror will depart, leaving it to eleven others to decide the case, which will continue for another three weeks.

Finally the case begins to wrap up, with the Crown summarising the months of hearings to a word: liar.

'It is not a nice thing to say, but the Crown case is that he lied without cause for the 25 days, and transparently so, and with a kind of level of conviction, or an apparency of conviction—but many, many demonstrable lies, over many, many days, involving quite complicated ins and outs of evidence, which we would submit to you was ultimately—it may have been clear on itself without even any cross-examination—but it was untruthful,' Game says.

Many others surely concur with Game's summation: after all, Standen's explanations defy belief. A law enforcer with thirty years' experience, aged in his fifties, playing games of codes—or 'ducks and drakes' and 'double Dutch'—with a friend he considered 'off his dial'? And taking lots of money from a seemingly generous career-criminal-turned-informer-turned-legitimate-international-businessman? It was all just too ridiculous.

As the judge is summing up the exhaustive 98-day trial, which had produced more than 5300 pages of transcript, ten very large men enter the public gallery of the court. They glare first at the bench, then the jury. The ten men too are eyed with fear and suspicion by the jury and the legal bench.

They stay for only a moment, then file slowly out. When the court takes a break, and in the absence of the jury, Ierace tells the court that, for the record, he is concerned about what impact the unidentified men may have had on the jury.

AFP agent Paul Watt, still sitting in court, had followed them out and questioned who they were. He was relieved to hear they were transit security guards on a training day out. Nothing sinister intended.

The jury then retire to reach a verdict. Standen's family are confident he has done enough to prove his innocence. Standen packs up his modest prison belongings in anticipation of being released. He has planned a holiday to get away from it all, and can't wait. He had looked at the jury and believed they believed him. He will be acquitted, he thinks.

On 11 August 2011, after two days of deliberations following the five-month-long trial, the jury returns to the court and finds Mark William Standen guilty on all three charges.

There is little fanfare or emotion. An ashen-faced Standen remains seated for the verdict, which is unusual, given he has stood as a mark of respect every time the jury entered or left the courtroom each day.

He is swiftly led away to an isolated cell in an unnamed high-security prison to await sentencing, facing the prospect of life in jail.

The relief is written all over the jury members' faces as they leave. The next day their decision is vindicated, as they now learn of public revelations about a host of details about Standen and Hogan and their plot that the court couldn't be told about, and how Jalalaty had earlier pleaded guilty to the charges, and how on his death bed, career criminal Mick Hurley (arrested in Operation Mocha) declared he had proof Standen was dealing in drugs and money. The *Sydney Morning Herald* reveals the NSW Crime Commission had information Standen had in 2006 asked Jalalaty to hide $90 million in cash inside one of his meat exports. The money was apparently Hogan's and was to be shipped from Western Australia to Dubai with Jalalaty offered a percentage of the monies for his efforts. The export did not eventuate and the whereabouts of the money remains unknown.

In November, counsels for the prosecution and defence submit sentencing reports. The written reports from both parties are lengthy and detailed.

In their signed submission, Tim Game, Hament Dhanji, as well as solicitor Simon Buchen, state Standen had been motivated by greed, pure and simple. They summarise Standen's offences in lengthy dot points and conclude Standen had: agreed with Hogan and Jalalaty to import, introduced the pair, overseen Jalalaty's import business growth as a front for drug imports, extensively communicated with Jalalaty about business to add credibility to their cover, helped Jalalaty and Hogan to recover the lost invested monies, supervised Jalalaty, acted as intermediary between Hogan and Jalalaty, advised and educated Jalalaty of quarantine, Customs and law enforcement practices and what to say if caught, and abused his position by contacting Customs to ascertain whether his venture had been detected. Their submission concludes:

> The offender was a principal in the offence. He co-managed the importation with [Hogan] and maintained a supervisory role in relation to Jalalaty. He used his special position as a very senior law enforcement officer to further the objectives of the conspiracy and to maximise its chances of success. Considering that the offender's position and duties were focused on combating serious drug crime, it is difficult to conceive of a more grave breach of trust than that involved in the importation offence.

They argue the toughest sentence possible is warranted for all three charges, not least of all because of Standen's one time seniority in law enforcement.

In their response, Mark Ierace and Greg Farmer challenge the technical legal aspects of the charges and the conclusions drawn by the prosecution. But perhaps anticipating a lengthy sentence, they conclude Standen's prospects for rehabilitation were good.

'He has suffered the humiliation, shame and notoriety of these convictions, constituting a public fall from grace of extraordinary proportions, which will continue to have a salutary impact and enhance his prospects for rehabilitation,' they conclude in their written summary.

A submitted psychiatrist's report notes while there had been no connection between Standen's marriage breakdown and his offences, it had placed him in a desperate situation and therefore may have contributed to his actions.

Defence counsel's sentence summary states Standen's attempts to physically keep his family together came at a considerable emotional cost to himself, and his adult children continue to

hold him in esteem for having done so. Any lengthy prison term
in virtual solitary confinement, as determined by his protected
prisoner status, will be detrimental to his wellbeing, they say.

'It is submitted that the court would find that, consistent with
the nature of his previous employment, the prisoner is a tertiary-
educated, intelligent, inquisitive and socially focused individual
who is likely to be more disadvantaged than most by existing for
perhaps two decades in such an environment, as opposed to in
the mainstream prisons,' they state.

In mid-November, Phillip Bradley retires from the crime
commission ending 22 years of service. Within days of the
retirement, the NSW Auditor-General Peter Achterstraat
tenders to the NSW Parliament a report he has produced which
concludes the commission's public reporting in how it deals with
confiscated assets needs improvement and it needs to spend more
time auditing its own law enforcement operations.

Two weeks later, on 30 November, a Special Commission of
Inquiry report on the NSW Crime Commission, ordered by the
State Government in August, reports the commission had been
operating without adequate oversight for almost two decades. The
258-page report, by retired NSW Supreme Court judge David
Patten, recommended sweeping reforms to the commission
including governance, structure and management of informants.
Critically it questions the commission's power to cut deals with
criminals and 'inadequate accountability'.

'There are suggestions that criminals have bought freedom
to continue their criminal activities,' Mr Patten reports. 'Other
perceptions include that criminals are given a green light to
commit other crimes and that any money or property they
ultimately retain, whatever its source, has become effectively
laundered with the authority of the commission.'

A chapter is dedicated to Standen but largely in the context of the managerial process in the years from 2003 that allowed him to engage in 'dishonest behaviour' and his direct initial appointment to the crime commission based on a recommendation by Mr Bradley rather than a selection process.

12

Twenty-two Years

On 8 December, the fall of Mark William Standen is complete, with Justice James sentencing him to 22 years in jail with a non-parole period of 16 years. Dressed in his prison greens, Standen just hangs his head before turning to his two brothers in the public gallery and giving them a wink and a thumbs up. He had been expecting a hefty sentence. In his 42-page sentencing, Justice James tells the court he found the relationship between Standen and Hogan went far beyond just a relationship between an informer and a law enforcer as highlighted by the 2005 Christmas 'gift'.

'I find that by his acceptance of this substantial sum of money Mr Standen was irretrievably corruptly compromised so far as [Hogan] was concerned,' he states. He said that after 25 days in the witness box the jury had an extended opportunity to assess Standen's general credibility but clearly made an adverse finding and rejected 'as not even reasonably possibly being true' the many explanations he gave to apparently incriminating evidence. This included his claim that despite his being a veteran law enforcer, he had no suspicion that the $1 million in cash Jalalaty received in the sports bag was anything other than a business transaction. Critically, James labels Standen a principal in the plot.

'In July when a deeply worried Jalalaty was contemplating withdrawing from the venture, Mr Standen in coded language applied pressure to Jalalaty to remain in the venture, not to "pull out of the course" and not to "pull out of the tennis match". Jalalaty submitted to this pressure. I find that Mr Standen was a principal in the group on the same level as [Hogan] and superior to Jalalaty.'

Three years after his arrest and a five-month criminal trial, Standen's public profile ends in a two-hour sentencing chronicling his rise and fall.

Within days of the verdict, the Police Integrity Commission visit Standen amid media reports he has allegedly told other prison visitors he was not the only 'bad egg' at the commission and the AFP and he was now willing to name names and criminal incidents by former colleagues. He now has nothing to lose and his legal team warn him he faces a lengthy jail term.

A lengthy secret statement by Dianne Jalalaty about corruption of certain individuals within the AFP ranks is passed to the Australian Commission for Law Enforcement Integrity, which oversees the AFP, and is still currently being probed.

The Liberal state government vows to never again allow the NSW Crime Commission such unchecked powers, and announces an independent inquiry into its operations to ensure public confidence in it can be restored. Within weeks it receives evidence of other questionable practices within the secretive body.

A brief of the Standen matter is lodged with the FBI in the United States as a precedent case-file example of how things can go bad.

Assistant Commissioner Tim Morris makes the Australia Day Honours List, for outstanding service to the community as an astute investigator and manager of police. It is his second gong, having already received an Order of Australia for exemplary leadership in the investigation of the 2002 Bali bombings.

Tony Newton, Standen's loyal friend and colleague who loaned him $210,000, never gets his money back. He is forced to sell his home and lives in rented accommodation on the Central Coast, pulling in a small salary as a solicitor. Standen never apologised for what he did to him, a fact not lost on a shattered Newton.

Louise Baker left the Independent Commission Against Crime and now works in the financial sector. Standen still has feelings for her and asks the media to ensure she is left alone to get on with life.

Many trials and cases appealed after Standen's arrest are still before the courts.

AFP investigators Glen McEwen and Brett Thompson continue undercover work overseas, including collaborating with the same Dutch counterparts on another drug conspiracy involving the two countries. They are again joined by Boersma, Aurik and Cees van Spierenburg, who delays retirement to work on another Dutch–Australian brief, which in mid-2011 involves a secretive trip to Sydney.

Dutch media report that the armoured-vehicle parts Loek supplied to the Egyptian government, while he was on bail over the conspiracy, were used in the tanks that were deployed to crush anti-government demonstrators on Cairo's Tahrir Square in the last days of Hosni Mubarak's reign in February 2011.

At the time of writing, Hogan continues to fight his extradition to Australia to face charges, and continues to maintain his innocence. Since being jailed, he has become fluent in Thai, both speaking and writing, and continues to look for loopholes in local law. After the Standen hearings, it is clear he has been named as an informant and a valuable one against cartels across Europe. The AFP warn Thai authorities he could be a target for execution since the details of his rollover had been given in open court and covered widely by the media. Despite telling some close to him he was considering returning, by early 2012 he was still actively fighting extradition.

The giant haul of precursor chemicals and drugs once hidden in warehouses in the Congo still remain unaccounted for. Law enforcement agencies are continuing the worldwide search, but classified intelligence points to it having been broken up for storage deep in a Congolese forest and a known fortified compound in Kinshasa.

It's 2012 and Standen starts the new year of his prison sentence knowing the dimensions of his prison cell well—4.3 metres by 3.1 metres. He is branded a 'limited association prisoner' and has contact with only two other prisoners. Usually it's just him sitting alone on his small bed with a radio, TV, shower, sink and toilet in close proximity. He writes in the small amount of natural light available when the door between his cell and private, very small exercise yard is open. He has since 2008 been keeping a diary of sorts, more a log of his own limited movements from cell to kitchenette to courtyard and back. His prison file shows he is a prisoner unlikely to cause trouble but trouble could find him. His corrective services file states: 'Mark Standen is potentially at risk of violence from other inmates because of his law enforcement background and he is therefore being held in a "special purpose prison'"—'A' classification—the highest for at-risk prisoners. Even if he is of good behaviour, he knows he will be held in these conditions until the last three years of his sentence, when he may be housed in a prison farm. He thinks there is a book in this, like that book about Howard Marks he once liked—*Hunting Marco Polo*.

Standen will be 67 when he is released from prison but authorities suspect he will still have a spectacular story to tell.

Acknowledgements

For me, this story began from little more than gossip back in 2007 but five years, four countries and thousands of pages of telephone intercepts later, a plot for a book emerged.

In the early days, my investigation (which I envisaged would make nothing more than a short syndicated newspaper series) was akin to trying to put together one of those complex 3D jigsaw puzzles without the aid of the picture on the front of the box. But a structure eventually emerged through the words, trust and goodwill of the numerous people I met from both sides of the criminal game. For that I thank them. Their recollections provided the basis for the recreation of some scenes in the book where telephone or listening device intercept transcripts, eyewitnesses or official confirmation were not available. I thank those AFP agents who agreed to speak with me but also particularly the Dutch officers, who found discussing their work with a journalist—Australian or otherwise—an unnatural act. They also indirectly prompted me to experience their wonderful country during numerous trips chasing leads, and for that I'm grateful.

Recognition is also due to News Ltd who had faith that it was worth me pursuing the story, and later my wonderful editors at Allen & Unwin, who no doubt were driven nuts by my newspaperman's style of short and sharp prose. Lastly, I thank my family for putting up with my many late-night phone calls and frequent absences from home as I chased this story and other assignments across Europe and elsewhere for a couple of years.